Yale Studies in English

Benjamin Christie Nangle, Editor

Volume 163

THE PILGRIM'S PROGRESS

AND TRADITIONS IN PURITAN MEDITATION

U. MILO KAUFMANN

NEW HAVEN AND LONDON, YALE UNIVERSITY PRESS, 1966

Copyright © 1966 by Yale University.
Designed by Arthur G. Beckenstein,
set in Janson type,
and printed in the United States of America by
The Colonial Press Inc., Clinton, Massachusetts.
Distributed in Canada by McGill University Press.
All rights reserved. This book may not be
reproduced, in whole or in part, in any form
(except by reviewers for the public press),
without written permission from the publishers.

Library of Congress catalog card number: 66-12504

Published with assistance from the Kingsley Trust Association
Publication Fund established by the
Scroll and Key Society of Yale College.

PREFACE

Will *The Pilgrim's Progress* endure? A few generations ago, the question would have seemed frivolous. On the shelf above the red velvet cushions of the Victorian window seat, *The Pilgrim's Progress* stood in serene estate, flanked by such ageless companions as the Bible, the works of Shakespeare, and the *Home Doctor Book*. But time would show that these companions were not all equally hardy. The *Home Doctor Book*, for one, with its lore of plasters and broths, deployed a traditional wisdom of the hearth that came to be threatened by a more cosmopolitan wisdom.

The Pilgrim's Progress, a book of traditional spiritual remedies, was likewise threatened. A more cosmopolitan physic for souls was taking the field, one which dared to isolate and give alien names to spiritual diseases and to prescribe novel cures too sophisticated for the sick man to administer to himself. More threatening still, it dared to call some of the domestic cures downright dangerous, insisting that they fostered lingering infections of the soul.

True enough, new diagnoses and cures for man's spiritual disorders have not, even now, wholly supplanted the old, but in the present neglect of *The Pilgrim's Progress*, we may see evidence of a precarious relationship of work to audience which Bunyan's masterpiece shares with other central works of the Christian tradition. We are ill at ease with religious affirmations we only half-believe. The incontrovertible truth and the plain fancy both have a good chance for a hearing, but not so the half-believed catechism. Today's college teacher is, I venture to say, quite prepared to find his students blindly ignorant of the Judaeo-Christian roots of Western culture. For the materials of this tradition are not true enough (apparently) to be taught and learned effectively in home and church, and not false enough (apparently) to be handled in school with the untroubled attention the academic concedes to Greek and Roman faiths. Not surprisingly, we are unsure what distance to preserve between us and Bunyan's Christian. Do we empathize with him in his assurance, or sympathize with him in his delusion?

Several lines of affirmation are open to those who believe that *The Pilgrim's Progress* is not fated for oblivion. One might on the one hand predict that a widespread spiritual awakening will reacquaint the general reader with the language and assumptions of Bunyan's allegory. This I think to be ill-advised because ill-reasoned. No religious awakening is likely to be an awakening of a seventeenth-century Puritan sensitivity and a recovery of its categories. Too much has happened in the meantime. A more rewarding course, it seems to me, is to affirm that *The Pilgrim's Progress* offers us the handsomely-articulated structure of literature's basic plot: the career of a human life. We might in fact suppose that this has always been the central appeal of the work.

The reader who shies away from *The Pilgrim's Progress* undoubtedly has a few fundamental reservations about the work in mind. He is persuaded that, apropos of matter, it is the simple narrative of a Christian pilgrimage and, apropos of manner, it is a simple allegory. What a discomfiting combination! Who

PREFACE   vii

now, for example, feels at home with the ancient and well-worn type of *pilgrimage?* The figure implies world-renunciation and utter assurance of direction, neither of which is in special currency in our day. Yet it takes no special talent to see in Christian's pilgrimage another type indigenous to all ages. A *life* is a made thing, not a happenstance. And the spectacle of a man taking his fate or givens (what some moderns might call his *Dasein*), and hammering out a certain shape of life has enough of the patent and imitable, as well as the deep and inscrutable, in it to hold a diversity of spectators. Furthermore, Bunyan's Christian, by ascetic pursuit of objectives that encourage a funding of vital force, on more than one occasion is startled by intense joy, representing, if we like, the ecstatic expense of energy when certain long-awaited fulfillments are attained. We may be out of sympathy with the notion of a Celestial City, but we must concede that Bunyan makes plausible Christian's state of mind when he reaches that bright place. Walter Kerr reminds us, somewhat ironically, of the decline of pleasure in our day. There may be a pattern in *The Pilgrim's Progress* well worth scrutiny. It is suggestive that F. R. Leavis chooses to refute a Marxist critic of Bunyan by quoting at great length the lofty conclusion to Part Two of the allegory, in which Christiana and her companions are admitted to the divine presence. His immediate point is that Bunyan was more than a proletarian pamphleteer, being an artist as well. A latent point is that Bunyan was as capable as a Marxist of painting a consummation devoutly to be wished and was perhaps a bit more capable of showing the consummation organic to a pattern of life.

As narrative, then, *The Pilgrim's Progress* deserves to be read as something more than Christian pilgrimage. But what of the charge that in manner Bunyan's masterwork is simple allegory? In our convoluted age, to brand the relation of surface to depth in a work as allegorical is to damn it outright.

Our passion is for complexity, antinomy, or, at the least, symbolic openendedness. We will have many meanings, or a diffuse titillating meaningfulness. This state of affairs, embodied in the work, we are prone to call realism. Let the artist hold his mirror up to the confusions of nature and society, we say. Allegory is too close to discursive statement to serve such a purpose.

Against this complaint, one is obliged to range the evidences for *The Pilgrim's Progress* as being so intricate in form as to make the descriptive term *allegory*, by itself, a misnomer. The work is both complex and verisimilar as the following chapters will show in a diversity of ways. Suffice it here to say that *The Pilgrim's Progress* partakes of the complexity of its age. Bunyan's century anticipated our own in its confident empiricism and exploration of new worlds, in its political distemper and ordeals of faith. It wed the old order to the new, looking behind to authoritarian faith, revealed texts, the cultus of magisterial personalities, and looking ahead to the methodological doubt of science, with text as program and hypothesis rather than fixed truth. In a number of ways it cultivated that parliamentarian spirit which is a signature of the modern era and the historical accessory to the rise of realism. Because solitary man had access to truth in his solitude, his voice deserved to be heard in public matters of faith, knowledge, and governance. His taste, making itself felt in the world of letters, was a powerful impetus toward a new fixing of the real world in imagination. Bunyan reflects his time. In his masterwork he displays not only a proficiency in allegory which is rooted in the old order, but also an imaginative realism, deepening and qualifying the allegory, which signals the new. In his use of Christian Scripture, which provided him pattern and rationale for his allegorization, we find a conception of revealed authority which harks back to earlier centuries. In his sure grasp of particularity, in his employment of the imagination which dwells fondly upon the immediacies of private experience. he anticipates later courses in literature. Indeed, in his imaginative use of Scripture—with provenance to be explained—lay the seeds of historical criticism, evident also in the work of Richard Baxter, that came to bloom only after the lapse of a century.

To return to the opening question: Will *The Pilgrim's Progress* endure? one must parry with another question: Are action which deals in the constants of the human condition, and form which accurately evokes the variousness of the perceived world, marks of durability? If so, for a surety we must defy the dark prophecies of those who extrapolate too hastily from the work's present lack of readers. Whether the future sees a recrudescence of the particular tradition Bunyan honored, or its final decay, it is certain that Bunyan's profound statement about the crafting of a life will come once more to just appreciation and a broad readership.

On such a conviction, at least, this study proceeds.

ACKNOWLEDGMENTS

Parts of Chapters 1, 2, 6, 7, 8 and 9 of this volume constituted elements in my Yale doctoral thesis, written under the acutely perceptive and warmly humane guidance of Louis L. Martz. The research for the remainder was undertaken at the Yale Sterling Library in the summer of 1963, on a faculty fellowship made available through the good offices of the University of Illinois Research Board.

Arthur Barker of the Illinois English faculty read the manuscript in its penultimate draft, and provided such substantial help that I am embarrassed even to mention now that I had imagined the draft he was reading might be the final one.

My wife Helen has sustained me with a variety of encouragements, chief among which was her unfaltering confidence that sooner or later one of the orderings of the material would prove permanent.

CONTENTS

Preface	v
Acknowledgments	xi
1. A Tension in Bunyan's Aesthetic	3
The Pilgrim's Progress: Some Problems of Origin and Form	3
Bunyan's Apology as Aesthetic Brief	8
The Episode of the Burning Mountain	15
The Relevance of Puritan Hermeneutics and Devotion	21
2. Puritan Hermeneutics	25
The One Sense of Scripture	27
The Case Against *Mythos:* The Issue of Authority	41
The Word as *Logos:* Implications for Poetry and Parable	49
Revelatory Word: A Note on Puritan Semantics	55
3. The House of Interpreter	61
Faith, the Word, and the Holy Spirit	61
Example and Precept, Promise and Threatening: The Seven Scenes	67

4. Exemplary History: Parabolic Drama and Character-as-Example in *The Pilgrim's Progress*	80
The Idea of Exemplary History	80
Parabolic Drama in *The Pilgrim's Progress*	83
Character-as-Example in *The Pilgrim's Progress*	89
5. The Analogy of Faith and the Unity of *The Pilgrim's Progress*	106
6. Two Divergent Traditions in Puritan Meditation	118
The Line of Joseph Hall	120
Heavenly Meditation	133
7. Meditation and Bunyan's Imaginative Realism	151
Bunyan and the Imagination	151
Biblical Metaphor in Two Episodes of *The Pilgrim's Progress*	156
Imagery and Realism in *The Pilgrim's Progress*	165
8. Occasional Meditation and *The Pilgrim's Progress*	175
Occasional Meditation in Puritan Practice	175
Occasional Meditation in *The Pilgrim's Progress*	187
9. Meditation on Experience and *The Pilgrim's Progress*	196
The Rationale of Meditation on Experience	196
The Methodology of Meditation on Experience	205
Meditation on Experience in *The Pilgrim's Progress*	216
10. The Interior Voice in Meditation and Aural Features of *The Pilgrim's Progress*	232
Bibliography	253
Index	259

THE PILGRIM'S PROGRESS

and Traditions in Puritan Meditation

1

A TENSION IN BUNYAN'S AESTHETIC

The Pilgrim's Progress
Some Problems of Origin and Form

The origins of *The Pilgrim's Progress* are problematic. The person who knows little else about Bunyan's masterpiece knows that it was written by a Puritan mender of pots; but Puritans did not ordinarily write imaginative romances, anymore than traveling tinkers did.

The mysteries surrounding the inception of the work are commented upon by the author himself in the Apology prefacing the First Part of the narrative. The fact that his comments are made in 108 rhyming couplets contributes to the reader's total impression that the Apology, while frank, is not artless, and that Bunyan's observations about the fortuity of his work are in some way part of the problem as well as of the solution. Yet when all this is admitted, there is good reason remaining to consult the man closest to the origins of the narrative. Bunyan opens his Apology with these words:

> When at the first I took my Pen in hand,
> Thus for to write; I did not understand
> That I at all should make a little Book

> In such a mode; Nay, I had undertook
> To make another, which when almost done,
> Before I was aware, I this begun.
>
>   And thus it was: I writing of the Way
> And Race of Saints in this our Gospel-Day,
> Fell suddenly into an Allegory
> About their Journey, and the way to Glory,
> In more than twenty things, which I set down;
> This done, I twenty more had in my Crown,
> And they again began to multiply,
> Like sparks that from the coals of Fire do flie.
> Nay then, thought I, if that you breed so fast,
> I'll put you by your selves, lest you at last
> Should prove *ad infinitum*, and eat out
> The Book that I already am about.
>
>   Well, so I did; but yet I did not think
> To shew to all the World my Pen and Ink
> In such a mode; I only thought to make
> I knew not what: nor did I undertake
> Thereby to please my Neighbour; no not I,
> I did it mine own self to gratifie.[1]

Bunyan's vehemence about the fortuity of his work has a plain thrust, the reader shortly discovers. He is not to be held wholly responsible for the deviation of his work from Puritan norms for literature, for he implies that the budding work had a will of its own. He was present at the time and watched things happen.

However valuable a point in his defense against Puritan accusers this confession of intention may be, it is also the inadvertent witness to a radical irresolution on Bunyan's part,

---

[1]. For all quotations from *The Pilgrim's Progress*, I have used James Blanton Wharey's edition, as revised by Roger Sharrock (Oxford, Clarendon Press, 1960). This quotation from p. 1 represents the first 24 lines of the Apology.

SOME PROBLEMS OF ORIGIN AND FORM

and diverse puzzling features of *The Pilgrim's Progress* which the present study offers to explain may be traced back to it. The complexity of attitudes Bunyan entertained while making his narrative was embodied in his work as a continuing dialectic among diverse modes of narration and exposition. There is a conspicuous tension in Bunyan's practice between the didactic and literalist methods widespread in Puritanism and the imaginative methods native to the grand tradition in literature.

Anticipating later arguments, we may say here that *The Pilgrim's Progress* is moral allegory and much more As allegory, it bespeaks an author steeped in the special materials of Puritan hermeneutics, with its encouragement of an allegorical temper and the didactic straitening of narrative. As something more than allegory, or as "myth," it implies a writer roused by significant developments in Puritan devotion, particularly meditation, to the possibilities of imaginative apprehension of circumstance. Our immediate concern here, however, is the fact of the formal variousness, or "impurity," of the work traceable to the tension existing in Bunyan's aesthetic *ab origine*, and we shall list the diverse modes of narration and exposition in *The Pilgrim's Progress* as the mythic, the allegorical, and the literal-didactic.

Bunyan, perhaps more than he realized, was calling attention to the enduring strength of his work when he asked in the Apology, "Would'st thou see / A man i' th Clouds, and hear him speak to thee?" The "clouds" are the "dark and cloudy" figures which he takes great pains to defend in an earlier portion of the Apology as one of the principal attractions of his work. He seems aware, however, that behind these tropes looms the figure of a man whose mythical biography constitutes the real attraction of the book, and it is certainly true that many readers since Bunyan's day have preferred the "man" to those clouds of allegorical equivalences that surround him. Coleridge was among the first critics to call attention to the mythic side of the work. He declared that Bunyan's "piety was baffled by his genius, and the Bunyan of Parnassus had the better of Bunyan of the conventicle; and with the same illusion as we read any tale known to be fictitious, as a novel, we go on with his characters as real persons, who had been nicknamed by their neighbors." [2] More recently the biographical aspect of *The Pilgrim's Progress* has been approached obliquely by Gordon Rupp, who suggests that "the greatness of *Pilgrim's Progress* is that it is not an allegory but a parable, or rather a series of parables. It lives just as it escapes being allegorical." [3] By "parables" he means, of course, episodes which can be taken as illustrative of truth without being construed as systematic *double entendre*. So understood "parable" might be used to describe a great part of realistic fiction, but only enthusiasm would lead one to say that such "parable" completely supplants the allegorical mode of exposition in *The Pilgrim's Progress*. Yet Rupp assuredly speaks for many when he asserts that the deepest appeal of the work must be traced to that dimension in which it transcends the allegorical.

Bunyan's mythic mode of exposition is only one among several, however, and it coexists with the others in a state of tension. That the more straightforwardly edifying modes —the allegorical and the literal-didactic—are not to be overlooked is a fact eloquently testified to by the ease with which some readers of Bunyan have been able to emphasize them, and thereby to discredit the mythic mode. Roger Sharrock, noting that *The Pilgrim's Progress* is "now liable to be admired for its qualities of style and merits as a piece of character fiction," suggests that "all modern readers of *The Pilgrim's Progress*

---

2. S. T. Coleridge, *Coleridge's Miscellaneous Criticism*, ed. T. M. Raysor (London, Constable and Co., 1936), p. 31.

3. Gordon Rupp, *Six Makers of English Religion, 1500–1700* (London, Hodder and Stoughton, 1957), p. 97.

meet on the same footing; they are in danger of reading a book which was not there for Bunyan or his original readers. Donne and Milton recognize an aesthetic category. Bunyan does not: he accepts only the category of edification."[4] We shall later have appropriate occasion for considering the evidence Sharrock draws from the Apology in his determination of what *The Pilgrim's Progress* is. Here we can simply note that Sharrock would deny that one should look for a mythic mode of exposition in *The Pilgrim's Progress* as a published work and would suggest that only those modes which directly implement the category of edification can be isolated. Perhaps his position is a needed corrective for the expansive statements of critics as diverse as Coleridge and Gordon Rupp, but it is not free from error.

The third mode, the literal-didactic, needs only to be mentioned to be accepted as characteristic of *The Pilgrim's Progress*. The aura of discovery which surrounds a relevant statement of Herbert Greene's made before the turn of the century is not out of place, for his observation is one infrequently made: "The clearness of BUNYAN's allegory may be due in part to a cause that is not generally suspected,—namely, that much of it is not allegory at all. Whenever there is any danger of obscurity, BUNYAN lays aside the allegorical disguise and speaks openly and directly."[5] Greene's choice of words regarding the "danger of obscurity" is apt; he points deserved attention to the fact that, regardless of his brilliant achievement in the "mythic" and allegorical modes, Bunyan was never free from the fear that he might betray his first obligation, that of communicating truth.

Now this tension in Bunyan's aesthetic is witnessed to by

---

4. Roger Sharrock, "Personal Vision and Puritan Tradition in Bunyan," *Hibbert Journal*, 56 (1957–58), p. 48.
5. Herbert Greene, "The Allegory as employed by Spenser, Bunyan, and Swift," *PMLA*, 4 (1888–89), p. 161.

a variety of evidences. One can hint at them by reminding the reader of his characteristic development of an episode: an action is described, often with striking realism, while Bunyan watches it solicitously either from the fringes of the plane of action or from his perch in the margin; its simple meanings are then carefully expounded by discussion between agents in the action or by a mentor such as Evangelist who appears on the scene for the sole purpose of giving comment; sometimes Bunyan himself steps to the center of the stage to ask for a point of clarification. Despite these precautions, the actions do not wholly yield to doctrinal reduction, a fact amply supported by the defensive tone of the poetic Apology and of the postscript which follows Part One. Certainly Bunyan's myths are not to be dismissed as constructions of the modern reader's unrestrained fancy, but should rather be accepted as the product of the writer's conscious intent, even though that intent existed in tension with another.

Bunyan's Apology as Aesthetic Brief

The central objection Bunyan attempts to meet in his Apology is that his work is "dark," and a careful study of the objection and his reply reveals much about his ambiguous attitudes toward Puritan literalism. The imagined objector explains that "metaphors make us blind," but his plain sense becomes apparent when one inquires, "blind to what?" The answer, of course, is, blind to that simple edifying truth which, on the objector's presupposition, the metaphor is apt to conceal. The objector conforms closely to the stereotype of the "Puritan stylist" whom Perry Miller describes, apropos of another context, as one who "studiously held his fancy in check" and remorselessly extracted the last ounce of meaning from rhetorical figures "by a direct translation of the trope into moral so that nothing would be left to the imagination of the reader."[6] Metaphor, by juxtaposing quantities in order to transfer attributes from one to the other, appealed to the imagination, which might insist upon seeing a variety of likenesses. The situation was *in posse* highly ambiguous. The demand that metaphor yield up a single clear edifying meaning was, quite naturally, conceived to be one sort of thing when scriptural metaphor was confronted, since God could be expected to manage clear communication even through dark media, but another when the Puritan writer attempted to steer plain doctrine through such tortuous passages.

Two terms—*mythos* and *logos*—are of great usefulness in clarifying the issues of the Apology (and will prove highly relevant to later discussions of Puritan hermeneutics and devotion, for the Puritan, reflecting the attitudes of the spiritual progenitor of Puritanism, John Calvin, was oriented toward *logos* rather than *mythos* as the fit vessel of truth). In suggesting brief working definitions of these terms, it is convenient to turn to Aristotle's *Poetics*, where he discerns six elements that go to make up tragedy: fable (or *mythos*), character, diction, thought, melody, and spectacle. The first named is by far the most important; "it is the action in it, i.e., its Fable or Plot, that is the end and purpose of the tragedy; and the end is everywhere the chief thing."[7] In contrast to the action, thought "is what, in the speeches in tragedy, falls under the arts of Politics and Rhetoric; for the older poets make their personages discourse like statesmen, and the modern like rhetoricians." Thought is "shown in all they [the characters] say when proving or disproving some particular point,

---

6. Perry Miller, in the Introduction to his edition of Jonathan Edward's *Images or Shadows of Divine Things* (New Haven, Yale University Press, 1948), p. 5.

7. Aristotle, *Poetics*, ed. Richard McKeon, in *The Basic Works of Aristotle* (New York, Random House, 1941), p. 1,461.

or enunciating some universal proposition." The relevance of these remarks reaches far beyond Greek tragedy, for in them Aristotle divorces the category of action from the category of discourse. It is the action which embodies purpose, and if the tragedy has a theme, it must be a motif in action. Philosophical generalization, whose province it is to translate the manifold of action into suitable verbal statement, belongs, according to Aristotle, to the category of thought. Since he neglects to devise a seventh category for that kind of theme which might offer itself to the reflective spectator as a verbal generalization bringing together the implications of the other six elements, we may believe that for the critic-spectator, in Aristotle's view, thought cannot truly digest action. Characters think and speak, and they act, but neither they nor the spectator can reduce action to discourse. The viewer of action discerns meanings in the action on which the accompanying "thought" and his own abstract reflections are a kind of feeble descant.

René Wellek and Austin Warren have expanded upon this obvious antithesis in their explanation of the meaning of *mythos*, or simply myth, as it is to be distinguished from image, metaphor, and symbol:

> [Myth appears] in Aristotle's *Poetics* as the word for plot, narrative structure, "fable." Its antonym and counterpoint is *logos*. The "myth" is narrative, story, as against dialectical discourse, exposition; it is also the irrational or intuitive as against the systematically philosophical: it is the tragedy of Aeschylus against the dialectic of Socrates.[8]

For our purposes, the words "irrational" and "intuitive" should be underlined, since it was those aspects of the human response to action, presented or represented, that were generally repu-

8. René Wellek and Austin Warren, *Theory of Literature* (Harvest Book ed. New York, Harcourt, Brace and Co., 1956), pp. 179–80.

diated by the Puritan in his approach to word and experience. In the case of *logos*, words were supposed to be the vessels of meaning, independent of the imaginative appreciation of referents.

Now, curiously, Bunyan's first line of defense against the objection that his work is dark is to insist that his metaphors *are* unambiguous, are *logos*. He says, for example, "My dark and cloudy words they do but hold / The Truth, as Cabinets inclose the Gold" (p. 4, ll. 25-26). This conception of the relationship between truth and words is conventionally Puritan: truth was "contained" in words, ready to be emptied into the mind in the simple process of reading, and little allowance was made for the possibility that it might be incommensurate with its containers, that the event might perhaps be a slightly more commodious vessel than the word. This statement suggests that Bunyan's conscious allegiance was given to a literalistic understanding of language, and yet we would be surprised if the Apology prepared us in no way for the quite different way in which he regards event and metaphor in the body of *The Pilgrim's Progress*. There is indeed ample evidence in the Apology for an ambivalence in Bunyan's attitudes toward *logos* and myth.

The first item to be noted in this connection is a curious contradiction in Bunyan's announced intentions in writing *The Pilgrim's Progress*. It was, of course, tacitly assumed by Puritanism that edification must be the end of all art, and Bunyan himself would lead us to believe that this was his end. His defense of the easy accessibility of the meanings in his metaphors stems from the need to show that his work could function as the edifying discourse his Puritan audience expected it to be, that his meaning could be so readily discerned that even the humblest reader would not be disappointed. He says, for example, "May I not write in such a stile as this? / In such a method too, and yet not miss / Mine end, thy good?"

(p. 2, ll. 31–33) The questions are significant, for they show that Bunyan sensed the need of showing that his metaphors were unambiguous if edification were indeed his chief intent. Some lines before he witnesses to such a connection between unambiguousness and edification, however, he makes the avowal, quoted above, that edification was in point of fact *not* his intention when he was in the actual process of writing *The Pilgrim's Progress*. Indeed, he claims that he was not sure during the heat of creation what his purpose was, but that, if he had any, it was personal gratification. It is after he introduces his imagined objectors and is locking horns with them that he introduces the matter of edifying intent, in such statements as, "Yea, that I might them better palliate, / I did too with them thus Expostulate. / May I not write in such a stile as this?" (p. 2, ll 29–31). The end of edification certainly entered into the inspiration and elaboration of *The Pilgrim's Progress*, as we shall see in some detail later, but it was not the only purpose of the author. What Bunyan is in fact pleading is that the work will prove edifying if it is given the chance.

When Roger Sharrock, cited earlier, denies the reader the right to admire *The Pilgrim's Progress* "for its qualities of style and merits as a piece of character fiction," he disputes the presence of the mythic mode of exposition in the work. Modern readers, he affirms, meet on the same footing; "they are in danger of reading a book which was not there for Bunyan or his original readers." When his argument is traced out, however, he is seen to be contending that Bunyan did not wish the book *as published* to be regarded as anything but edifying discourse. He concedes that the work as it took shape under its author's hand was an aesthetic achievement:

> Though *The Pilgrim's Progress* clearly sprang from the depths of the creative imagination, when Bunyan saw what his genius had employed him at he preferred to send

the book forth as a sugared pill. In the revealing prefatory verses to the First Part he gives an honest account of a purely artistic process in which the material is theological but no theological purpose is imposed upon it; . . . . But once Bunyan begins to think of his toy of the mind as a tract among other tracts to be sold to the public he becomes the censor of his own aesthetic impulses; in the rest of the verses he carefully defends what might have seemed too daring use of similitudes against the anticipated charge of frivolity.[9]

Even though one must agree wholeheartedly with these observations, which reflect a fair reading of the Apology, one is entitled to protest the conclusion that reading the book as a "piece of character fiction" is to read it for features that were not present for either Bunyan, or his first readers. The evidence surely warrants nothing stronger than the statement that those features that have constituted the work's enduring appeal were publicly renounced by the author when he came to court his audience but are nevertheless present in the work, legitimately to be discovered by the reader for the good reason that the author put them there. The only dictates of the author that are coercive in interpretation are those which in some way find their embodiment in the work itself.

Bunyan's endorsement of the imagination, his appreciation of metaphor *qua* metaphor and of myth as a legitimate vehicle of meaning, is also evidenced at other points in the Apology. When, for example, in an especially vigorous jousting with an objector, he says, "Come, let my Carper, to his Life now look, / And find There darker Lines, then in my Book / He findeth any" (p. 5, ll. 1–3), his signification is complex. The term "darker" here means "more ambiguous," and the statement seems to be nothing more than a particularly explicit

9. Sharrock, "Personal Vision," p. 47.

evidence of that invidious distinction the Puritan was wont to make between the univocal word and the ambiguous event or experience. His book, Bunyan suggests, is quite free from the equivocations which every human life presents in its tangle of motives and subrational whims and passions. But the passage says even more, for in confessing his awareness that life may have sides which defy rational explication, Bunyan ironically authorizes certain inferences about his work seen as the biography of a man in the clouds which, early and late in the Apology, it claims to be.

How fully conscious Bunyan is that his book, at least in part, constitutes life addressing life is shown in the closing lines of his preface:

> Would'st thou be in a Dream, and yet not sleep?
> Or would'st thou in a moment Laugh and Weep?
> Wouldest thou loose thy self, and catch no harm?
> And find thy self again without a charm?
> Would'st read thy self, and read thou know'st not what
> And yet know whether thou art blest or not,
> By reading the same lines? O then come hither,
> And lay my Book, thy Head and Heart together.
>
> (p. 7, ll. 18–25)

Here he calls attention to a depth of meaning in his work quite incommensurate with his earlier remarks about his words' holding the truth "as Cabinets inclose the Gold." In his query, "Would'st read thy self, and read thou know'st not what?" Bunyan implies a conception of his narrative as one which speaks on the intuitive levels of communication, the fictive life evoking those subtle responses in the reader which enable him to discern that the narrative is faithful to the mysteries of the heart. He reads himself, though he reads he knows not what. Bunyon's prior question, "Wouldest thou loose thy self, and catch no harm?" has already implied a conception of his narrative as one of vicarious experience and so prepared the way for the succeeding query: a reader coerced into the vicarious life of a narrative as a participant is susceptible to the meanings which the narrative communicates on levels other than the rational.

The Apology, then, bears witness to a tension in Bunyan's aesthetic. Some passages speak clearly his sympathy with the traditional Puritan orientation toward an understanding of truth as *logos*, while others speak with equal force his appreciation of his narrative as myth. The apparent contradiction, however, does not obscure one's understanding of the narrative which follows; it rather illuminates it, for the tension which appears in the Apology as apparent antinomy appears in the body of *The Pilgrim's Progress* as a continuing dialectic among modes of exposition and narration. This point can be illustrated by considering a notable episode from the story.

The Episode of the Burning Mountain

Christian's experience at Mt. Sinai is one of several adventures in his pilgrimage that leave the reader with a persisting image. When he returns to the text to examine the passage, the reader may well be surprised to discover that Bunyan has visualized the memorable scene in only one brief paragraph. The paragraph is then followed by four pages of interpretative commentary which somehow avoids destroying its effect. I quote the paragraph, and the first words of the paragraph which follows:

> So *Christian* turned out of his way to go to Mr. *Legality's* house for help: but behold, when he was got now hard by the *Hill*, it seemed so high, and also that side of it that was next the way side, did hang so much over, that Christian was afraid to venture further, lest the *Hill* should fall on his head: wherefore there he stood still, and wotted not what to do. Also his burden, *now* seemed heavier to

him than while he was in his way. There came also flashes of fire out of the Hill, that made *Christian* afraid that he should be burned: here therefore, he swet, and did quake for fear. And now he began to be sorry that he had taken Mr. *Worldly Wisemans* counsel; and with that he saw *Evangelist* coming to meet him; at the sight also of whom he began to blush for shame. So *Evangelist* drew nearer, and nearer; and coming up to him, he looked upon him with a severe and dreadful countenance: and thus began to reason with *Christian*.

Evan. "What doest thou here?" said he: at which word *Christian* knew not what to answer: wherefore, at present he stood speechless before him. (p. 20)

This provides a glimpse not so much of a dialectic between abstractions as of a man confronting brutal circumstance. To put it more precisely, we ourselves confront the brutal circumstance as the man Christian. It is noteworthy how carefully Bunyan constructs the scene working from the inside. The very appearance of Evangelist seems, by some sympathetic magic, to be connected with Christian's change of heart: "And now he began to be sorry that he had taken Mr. *Worldly Wisemans* counsel; and with that he saw *Evangelist* coming to meet him." The repetition of the word "nearer" in the phrase "So Evangelist drew nearer, and nearer" suggests that Christian waits in the immobility of conviction and that his state of mind protracts Evangelist's approach. The action eddies about a node of perfect quiet.

If Bunyan's interest in the inner workings of his character is one significant feature of this episode, another is his handling of scriptural allusion. Bunyan's Sinai is anything but the historical Sinai. (Most of his mountains, indeed, seem to be visualized as having the altitude of several-story buildings. One of his ill-fated pilgrims, it will be remembered, lost his way in a "wide field, full of dark Mountains, where he stumbled and fell, and rose no more.") But if he is not interested in reproducing the historical Sinai, he is interested, we may assume, in re-creating the atmosphere of numinous dread that surrounded the historical mount, and his skill in employing a minimum of scriptural detail to produce the desired effect is suggested by the fact that he limits himself to only two such details. His statements about the "flashes of fire" that issued from the hill, and his description of Christian's sweating and quaking represent a deft excision of evocative details from the description of Sinai given in Exodus and again in Hebrews. He must have been deeply stirred by the rhetoric of the latter description:

> 18 For ye are not come unto the mount that might be touched, and that burned with fire, nor unto blackness, and darkness, and tempest,
> 19 And the sound of a trumpet, and the voice of words; which voice that they heard intreated that the word should not be spoken to them any more:
>
> . . .
>
> 21 And so terrible was the sight, that Moses said, I exceedingly fear and quake. (Hebrews 12)

His selection of detail gives evidence of Bunyan's drawing upon the Word for what at many points it is, a reservoir of imagery amenable to use in the fashioning of myth.

The points developed above illuminate Bunyan's elaboration of his meanings in realistic action which can justly be described as myth. But there is much more to the episode than the paragraph cited. The myth is set like a gem in a context of simple allegory and straightforward homily that illuminates the tension in Bunyan's loyalties. Evangelist is the Gospel or revealed truth peripatetic, and Bunyan uses him to counterbalance that allegorical figure with whom the episode of the mount begins, Mr. Worldly Wiseman, the *soi-disant* advisor who is natural knowledge. The allegorical structure fashioned out of the flaming mount and these two polar opposites is a relatively simple one, and its content is eminently Puritan in emphasis. A movement prepared to agree with Isaac Barrow's declaration that "the proper work of man, the grand drift of human life, is to follow reason, (that noble spark kindled in us from heaven)" [1] was, we may suppose, peculiarly vulnerable to the preachments of the Worldly Wiseman who was a separable element in every Puritan's inner self. For a movement tinged with rationalism, the appeal of a rational religion of works was insidious and unrelenting. Bunyan himself confessed at the close of *Grace Abounding* that one of his besetting sins was "a leaning to the Works of the Law." [2] The plight of the Puritan was a difficult one: at the same time that his understanding of depravity and grace completely undercut the value of works, his high regard for reason meant that a religion of works must be appealing. Did not reason, even when rectified, discern virtue in benefactions? In his manipulation of Worldly Wiseman and Evangelist, with Mt. Sinai as an imposing backdrop, Bunyan elaborates the predicament on a simple level, revealing the clash between unaided reason and the Word on the issue of works. The Word, or revealed truth, triumphs.

As allegorist, of course, Bunyan had to look within upon his apprehension of a complex relationship with an analytic eye, for allegory is discursive. The unitary truth of the artist's intuition undergoes a fragmentation by reason in the course of expounding that truth as a dramatic interplay between sep-

---

1. Isaac Barrow, *Against foolish Talking and Jesting*, in *The Theological Works* ed. Alexander Napier. (9 vols. London, Cambridge University Press, 1859), *2*, 30.
2. John Bunyan, *Grace Abounding*, ed. Roger Sharrock (London, Oxford University Press, 1962), p. 103.

arable elements. Thus, though Worldly Wiseman, Evangelist, and Mt. Sinai all represent significant elements in Bunyan's understanding of the problematic issue of works, the unitary apprehension is communicated more effectively in the glimpse of Christian at the foot of the mount. Here Bunyan drops the allegorical mode and incarnates his state of mind, not as a dialectic between dramatized abstractions in a broad field of action, but as the state of mind in one of his characters. With his concentration upon Christian's irresolution and anxiety, shame and conviction, coupled with an affective expansion upon the allegorical props such as Mt. Sinai by means of imagery seen through the aperture of Christian's eye, he fashions a vehicle of meaning that conveys much of the Puritan's complex state of mind regarding a religion of works.

Bunyan is not content with elaborating his message in myth and allegory, however. Evangelist's appearance on the scene marks the beginning of a lengthy discourse in yet another mode, the literal-didactic. Evangelist, in fact, takes pains to unravel in his homily all the allegorical significations of Christian's false counselor, as well as those of Legality and Civility. If one were defending *The Pilgrim's Progress* as simple allegory, he would have difficulty indeed explaining this hiatus, where one of the characters is tutored in the covert meanings of those characters with whom he is sharing the arena of the action. The fact is that Evangelist and Christian are both momentarily out of the allegory while Christian learns the plain sense of the allegorical action in which he was a moment before participating. This is a clue to Bunyan's unstinting use of the literal-didactic mode throughout the book. He is concerned that Christian learn from his experiences, but in the last analysis he does not trust the adequacy of event as a vehicle of edifying meaning. It is not enough that Christian pass through learning experiences: he must have them interpreted for his understanding as *logos*. In this connection it is of interest to note how Evangelist confirms his exposition for Christian:

> After this *Evangelist* called aloud to the Heavens for confirmation of what he had said; and with that there came words and fire out of the Mountain under which poor Christian stood, that made the hair of his flesh stand up. The words were thus pronounced, *As many as are of the works of the Law are under the curse; for it is written, Cursed is everyone that continueth not in all things which are written in the Book of the Law to do them.* (p. 24)

The capsheaf has been put upon Bunyan's explication of the meanings of the episode, for here a voice from heaven gives a normative comment upon all that has occurred: "As many as are of the works of the Law are under the curse." Works are not enough. The myth of the overhanging hill may have conveyed the same meaning in other more subtle and convincing ways, but Bunyan must make sure that sign is accompanied by word. One is reminded of Calvin's declaration that "whenever God offered any sign to the holy Patriarchs, it was inseparably attached to the doctrine, without which our senses would gaze bewildered on an unmeaning object."[3] Bunyan has not fully broken with an orientation toward *logos*, and the voice of revelation must attend his myth.

Both Bunyan's Apology and the experience of Christian at the foot of Sinai indicate that Bunyan's aesthetic is characterized by division. His genius finds its congenial vessel in realistic narrative which at many points deepens into powerful myth, and he candidly reveals the joy that was his in the process of creating. But his creative process was not uncom-

---

3. John Calvin, *Institutes of the Christian Religion*, trans. Henry Beveridge (2 vols. London, James Clarke and Co., 1949), 2, 494 (4.14.4 in Calvin's book, chapter, and paragraph numeration; for subsequent quotations this numeration will be given in addition to the volume and page listing).

plicated by ends other than aesthetic. He wrote for an audience that demanded edification and expected it to be readily available in the written word, and in large measure he felt the imperative felt by that audience.

The Relevance of Puritan Hermeneutics and Devotion

Admittedly, the imaginative realism of Bunyan's narrative is in a puzzling tension with the seventeenth-century Puritan aesthetic, and it has frequently been asserted that by a freak of genius this one Puritan produced a work of imaginative realism which remained faithful to the conservative Puritan ethos at the same time that it employed the imagination in a way wholly foreign to that ethos. But the problems latent in this view are as troublesome as the original. Genius has never been discontinuous with its historical setting, and perhaps determinative influences ought to be sought within Puritanism, on the assumption that every genius will turn out to be a *genius loci*, strongly attached to a local habitation which disciplines his peculiar energies.

Some have explained Bunyan's qualification of the Puritan aesthetic within the framework of his rigorous acceptance of Puritan theology by pointing to his reading in romance when he was an unregenerate young roisterer. This view is surely to be given due weight, but to judge from the enormous popularity of such romances, they found many furtive readers among unregenerate Puritan youth, for most of whom a religious conversion in mature years meant a total repudiation of the romance, with its gaudy secular supernaturalism and pagan morality. The fact that such a total repudiation is not found in Bunyan suggests the presence of other variables which influenced his achievement. The picture is further complicated by the fact that Bunyan's early reading in romance, however much weight we attach to it, cannot explain the extraordinary freedom he exercised in his imaginative approach to the Bible. Any reader of *The Pilgrim's Progress* is aware that the allegory shows an intimate relationship with the English Bible, but he may not realize that Bunyan's imaginative approach to his texts is one violently repudiated in the main line of Puritan hermeneutics. Whence did Bunyan take such license? Was his act one of madcap daring, or did it have precedents?

At this juncture, a *tour de force* of the sort which William York Tindall, in his *John Bunyan, Mechanick Preacher*, comes close to staging may argue that *The Pilgrim's Progress* does not present the kind of problem we have been describing, that Bunyan was merely doing something a bit better than the many others who were doing the same thing. This emphasizes the polemic and didactic sides of the work to the exclusion of the more strictly aesthetic; but the last is an area in which Bunyan wholly transcends the hosts of pamphleteering tinkers and typologizing Benjamin Keaches who were his contemporaries. Who would deny that they have only survived in the half-light on the periphery of the circle of his enduring popularity?

In dealing with these questions of form and provenance, the present study takes for its special historical materials the substance of Puritan hermeneutics and meditation. This procedure is based on the belief that, while Bunyan's acquaintance with secular literature (other than the popular romances) is apt to remain a matter of conjecture, there is no doubt whatsoever that he used the Bible with typical Puritan diligence and Puritan methods. Within Puritan hermeneutics and devotion themselves may be found not only adequate precedents for the revelatory dream and the allegory (precedents which Bunyan himself in fact cites) but also signal illuminations of these issues we have been considering.

The crucial difference that obtained between Puritan and Catholic hermeneutics will be discussed in the next chapter, but here we may observe that, while medieval Catholic hermeneutics had wedded exegesis and devotion, with the consequent proliferation of secondary spiritual meanings not implicit in the letter, Puritan hermeneutics, by and large, divorced exegesis from devotion and instead wed it to homiletics. The implications of this change were far-reaching. The union of exegesis and devotion, while constituting an imperfect science, at least gave marked scope to the imagination in the confrontation with the Word. In contrast, the Puritan union of exegesis and homilectics meant that approaches to Scripture were eminently rational and practical. The Word was consulted for clear authoritative instruction, and the imagination was irrelevant. This prejudice was of course hostile to the imaginative appropriation of the Scripture found in Bunyan. True, the need to press all Scripture into the mold of doctrine encouraged allegorical reading (and this fact must be properly explored for its relevance to Bunyan as allegorist), but to understand Bunyan the imaginative realist, we must turn to Puritan devotion, in particular Puritan meditation.

While the exercise of the imagination was discouraged in Puritan hermeneutics, it was always at least latent in Puritan meditation. Within a particular line of development in Puritan meditation, involving Richard Sibbes and Richard Baxter among others, this predisposition finds an overt and programmatic exploitation. Indeed, ten years before Bunyan betook himself to dreaming of Christian's pilgrimage, Richard Baxter in his *Saint's Everlasting Rest* gave a resounding defense of the devotional use of the imagination. His work draws together the significant notions in the mature and popular tradition of "heavenly" meditation and also witnesses to the movement of Puritan approaches to the Word toward at least a slight degree of rapport with Catholic approaches. But, curiously, while the particular tradition of heavenly meditation moved toward a massive qualification of the estimate of

Scripture as *logos,* or unambiguous doctrine, other popular traditions in Puritan meditation, important because they too help to shape the substance of *The Pilgrim's Progress,* preserved an attitude toward the specific matter of their individual disciplines that clearly displays the continuing reduction of myth to *logos,* event to doctrine. In occasional meditation every creature and every immediate event was subject to such reduction, while in formal meditation upon the individual's past experience autobiography became assimilable as *logos;* and both types influenced Bunyan's work. Meditation as inner debate or oratory, though not an independent tradition but, rather, a methodology of use to all the other traditions we have mentioned, is worth considering by itself in a final chapter, since it helps to gloss Bunyan's remarkable aural orientation in *The Pilgrim's Progress.*

If the arguments advanced here seem to imply that works like *The Pilgrim's Progress* should have been more common in Puritanism, we need only remark that it is striking how fully *The Pilgrim's Progress* illustrates the cliché that events occur in the fulness of time. The first part appeared in 1678, 18 years after the Restoration, the second part in 1684, and if, as the evidence suggests, internal developments in Puritanism marked a gradual liberalizing of attitudes toward the imagination by the time of the Restoration, the fact of the Restoration marked an equally significant influence in the direction of transforming Puritanism into Whiggery. The work appeared at a moment when the Puritan mind was opening to the imaginative apprehension of scriptural truth. No longer regnant, Puritanism was assuming those diverse and sublimated forms which it has kept ever since as a constituent of the English and American mind. Imaginative realism in Whig literature, such as Defoe's *Robinson Crusoe,* presents quite a different problem from the one we are here discussing.

2

PURITAN HERMENEUTICS

Bunyan's references to his scriptural sources sprinkled in the margins of the pages of *The Pilgrim's Progress* have undoubtedly served to blunt the interest, whether casual or scholarly, of many modern readers. For the seventeenth-century reader, of course, such references were intended more to permit the tracing of edification back to its wellspring than to gloss indebtedness, but the modern casual reader is troubled by suspicions about the originality and wholeness of a work that so persistently points beyond itself, while the scholarly sleuth after sources is tempted to believe that Bunyan has done most of his work for him. Neither view is quite justified: the casual reader may go on to find that Bunyan bends his borrowings to his own ends, just as the scholar discovers that the interesting questions remain even after the last stray allusion has been tracked down. No elaborate exploration of sources is necessary to indicate that Bunyan was doing a variety of things with Scripture that were actively discouraged in the received Puritan hermeneutics.

As the science of interpretation (especially of Scripture), hermeneutics is concerned with the critical exposition of a text, but in Puritanism such exposition, or exegesis, was undertaken with a homiletic concern and was therefore expressed ordinarily in homiletical categories. Exegesis was homiletical simply because preaching was thoroughly exegetical. The Puritan sermon itself was usually referred to as the Word: Richard Rogers declared that one must receive ministers "as the Lord himselfe, and the word which they preach, *not as the word of man, but* (*as it is indeed*) *the word of God*";[1] and Thomas Case added, "*Scripture-Inference,* is *Scripture;* that is to say, *That which may be inferr'd from Scripture, by natural and necessary consequence, is to be received as the Scripture it self.* The word of God *rightly interpreted,* is the word of God."[2] Needless to say, this lofty estimate of interpretation dignified the role of the minister and rendered awesome the exegetical task, which, like the original inditement of Scripture, had to be inspired. Nicholas Byfield entitled his exposition of Colossians in this manner:

> An Exposition upon the Epistle to the Colossians. Wherein, not onely the text is Methodically Analysed, and the sence of the words, by the help of Writers, both ancient and moderne is explayned: But also, By Doctrine and Use, the intent of the holy Ghost is in every place more fully unfolded and urged.[3]

Doctrine and use are, of course, two rubrics of the Puritan sermon, and Byfield's, like many commentaries of the period, was first presented from the pulpit. But, significantly, it did not flinch at spelling out the intentions of the Spirit. If one were rigorously to apply the point made by Case, then commentary as well as homily was the divine Word. There are

1. Richard Rogers, *A Commentary upon the Whole Booke of Judges* (London, 1615), p. 82.
2. Thomas Case, *Mount Pisgah: or, a Prospect of Heaven* (London, 1670), p. 67.
3. Nicholas Byfield, *An Exposition upon the Epistle to the Colossians* (London, 1615), title page.

two important implications of the homiletical cast of Puritan hermeneutics: one, the Word was conceived to be doctrine rather than image and event (A hermeneutics funneled through the pulpit might be expected to have an explicit doctrinal orientation.) and two, the historical materials bearing upon Puritan exegesis must be sought in treatises on homiletical procedure, or in actual homiletical practice.

The One Sense of Scripture

The modern reader, superficially acquainted with the fact that medieval exegesis sought after three or more "spiritual" meanings in the text as well as the literal or historical, and aware that Puritanism argued for one sense of Scripture, might be excused for supposing that the Puritan achieved this economy by discarding the spiritual meanings and preserving only the literal or historical. In fact, however, the Puritan, like the Anglican, retained the spiritual senses, but he regarded them, not as independent meanings collateral with the literal, but as ancillary and derivative. Insofar as they were present at all, they were treated as implications of the radical meaning of the text and, taken in conjunction with that radical meaning, comprised the single entire literal sense. Furthermore, if and when the radical meaning most immediately present in the letter contradicted the accepted "analogy" or "proportion" of faith, or made nonsense (as in the case of certain scriptural tropes), that meaning was promptly spiritualized in the interests of sense and consistency and then denominated the literal.

When the exegetical positions of Catholic, Anglican, and Puritan are placed side by side, it becomes evident that both of the latter show a concern for meaning rooted in the words of the text which can readily be related to the issue of religious authority. Both, to put it differently, take pains to define the office of exegesis apart from the concerns of devotion. But

Puritanism, more beset with the question of religious authority than was the Establishment, more distrustful of the imaginative approach to truth, and more concerned that the Scriptures should constitute a guidebook offering accessible and comprehensible instructions in every exigency in life, moved far in the direction of a repudiation of the Word as anything but *logos*. And Puritan hermeneutics took upon itself the problems intrinsic to sealing a union between exegesis and homiletics.

A most convenient way to clarify the contrast of Puritan literalism with Catholic hermeneutics is to consider the Anglican position on the one meaning of Scripture, since this stands as a model of the Puritan objections against ambiguity, combined with a sensitivity to biblical event, by which Puritan hermeneutics may be judged. While Anglicanism, like Puritanism, separated exegesis from devotion, it never divorced them so irrefrangibly, and neither in its homiletics nor its devotion did it evidence those prejudices against an imaginative approach to Scripture that were typical of Puritanism. The estimate of exegesis as a science not to be adulterated with the arbitrary meanings of value to devotion did not mean, as it did in Puritanism, that devotional use of Scripture was governed by conservative and rational ends. For certain ends, the Word was *mythos*, and a conservative exegesis was companion to a homiletics that could nurture a Jeremy Taylor and a devotion that could sustain the imagination of a George Herbert.

William Whitaker (1547–95) is perhaps the outstanding figure in the Anglican controversy with the Roman Catholics over the interpretation of Scripture. Made Regius Professor of Divinity at Cambridge in 1579, and master of St. John's College in 1586, he was a man widely appreciated for his learning, his personal charm, and humble spirit. It is reported that one of his chief opponents, the Jesuit Bellarmine, kept a picture of Whitaker in his room and explained to those who twitted him upon the subject that, though the man was a heretic and an adversary, yet he was a learned adversary. Whitaker's *Disputation on Holy Scripture,* published in quarto at Cambridge in 1588, undertook to dispute with the Catholics, especially Robert Bellarmine and Thomas Stapleton, the issues of canon, translations, authority, perspicuity, and interpretation of the Bible, and the perfection of Scripture apart from tradition. His case for the senses of the scriptural text is of particular interest here. Mentioning the four senses—literal, tropological, allegorical, and anagogic—he makes a distinction between that which words express and that which "things" express, a distinction that is absolutely basic to the dispute:

> The Jesuit [Bellarmine] divides all these senses into two species; the historic or literal, and the mystic or spiritual. He defines the historic or literal, as that which the words present immediately; and the mystic or spiritual, that which is referred to something besides what the words express; [sic] and this he says is either tropological, or anagogic, or allegorical. Thomas Aquinas, in the first part of his Sum. Quaest. 1. Art. 10, says out of Gregory, Moral. Lib. XX. c. 1, that it is the peculiar property of scripture, and of no other authors, that not only the words, but the things also, have a signification; and this he says is denoted by that book mentioned Ezek. ii. 10, and Revel. v. 1, which was "written within and without." [4]

Radically different exegetical approaches are demanded by the two vessels of meaning, and, in what at first flush seems a

---

4. William Whitaker, *Disputation on Holy Scripture against the Papists, especially Bellarmine and Stapleton,* trans. and ed. for the Parker Society by Rev. William Fitzgerald (London, Cambridge University Press, 1849), pp. 403–04.

rejection of the second category of meaningful terms, Whitaker insists upon the priority of the word:

> We concede such things as allegory, anagoge, and tropology in scripture; but meanwhile we deny that there are many and various senses. We affirm that there is but one true, proper and genuine sense of scripture, arising from the words rightly understood, which we call the literal: and we contend that allegories, tropologies, and anagoges are not various senses, but various collections from one sense, or various applications and accommodations of that one meaning. (p. 404)

Since a person who knows what the words of the text mean should be able to come by all its spiritual meanings, the public conventions of reference which words embody are not to be bypassed and supplemented by private conventions in which objects function as signs. A book in which words set forth such significant objects and circumstances would be dark indeed to the uninitiated.

But while Whitaker argues in this way for spiritual meanings as determinate in the words of the text, he is nonetheless able to accept at least one category of significant object and circumstance in Scripture, the typological. Catholic, Anglican, and Puritan alike, of course, accepted the presence of typological correspondences in Scripture (Manna, for example, was believed to typify Christ the bread of life; Israel typified the Christian Church; and the crossing of the Red Sea typified Christian baptism), but neither the Anglican nor the Puritan felt that the typological interpretation qualified a literal exegesis, presumably because the correspondences represented part of the public and conventional reference of the words of Scripture. Given general agreement that the meaning of the word "manna" included a typification of Christ, a literalist approach to the term could without misgivings draw out the typological significances as part of the determinate content.

But the strong sacramental note in Anglican typology gave a distinctive stress to the belief shared with the Puritan that, for the believers of the old dispensation, the types were ordinarily sacraments. Whitaker demonstrates that when one takes with full seriousness the idea that biblical typology is a system of correspondences not merely read but *experienced*, he must reckon with sacramental event as a vessel of meaning apart from the word. Whitaker notes:

> As the water flowing from the rock refreshed the weary people, and the manna fed them, so Christ cheers and preserves us. As they were enveloped in the cloud, and set in the midst of the waves of the great deep, so all the godly are washed by the blood of Christ. These were all sacraments to them, and so the pious understood them. (p. 408)

The crucial point about the experienced type as a sacramental event is made in greater detail by John Jewel, Bishop of Salisbury, whose position will serve as a foil for the sharply divergent statements of Calvin and derivative English Puritanism. Jewel supposes that sometimes God "expressed his holy will, not in words" but in "some deed which the people saw done before their eyes." The Hebrew fathers were capable of reading events. Anticipating Whitaker in his choice of specific illustration, he says:

> God opened his mind sometimes . . . by some notable kind of deed; and the people heard God speak unto them, not with their ears, but with their eyes. The people of Israel, as they were passing through the wilderness, lacked water to drink, and were like to perish: there stood a mighty great rock of hard stone, which Moses smote

with his rod: it opened and yielded out a great stream of water: the whole people drank of it, and was refreshed. The same people, being likewise in the same wilderness utterly void of bread and all other sustenance, was like to famish: God sent them manna from heaven above . . . . This was an allegory, that is to say, a secret and mysticall kind of utterance. For by this manna and by this rock the people was led to understand and think on that bread and that water that should come from heaven.[5]

Bishop Jewel does not take pains to explain how this "mysticall" and prophetic meaning of the event happened to suggest itself to the Israelite, but it is clear that he believes the description of sacramental events which could speak without words to be part of the literal statement of Scripture. In general, the Anglican's confidence in the powers of the descriptive language of Scripture was a continuing spur toward the devotional appropriation of Scripture as *mythos* even if the private meanings found were confessedly provisional. The literalist orientation of Anglican hermeneutics (which, like Puritan hermeneutics, had dissolved the union of exegesis and devotion) was not compromised.

Apt illustration of the hermeneutics wedding exegesis and devotion, which both Anglican and Puritan rejected, can be found in the work of St. Bernard. In writing on the *Song of Songs*, St. Bernard exhorts:

> Let us seek . . . if you please, these three words in the Holy Scriptures: the storehouse, the garden, and the chamber. For a soul that is athirst for God willingly occupies itself with, and lingers in, these, knowing that in them it will assuredly find Him whom it thirsts for. Let, then, the *garden* represent the plain and simple historical sense

---

5. John Jewel, *The Works*, ed. for the Parker Society by Rev. John Ayre (London, Cambridge University Press, 1847), pp. 968–69.

of the Scripture; the *storehouse* the moral sense of it; and the *chamber* the secret and mystical truth, reached by Divine contemplation.[6]

John P. McCall observes[7] that, "like many medieval writers," St. Bernard "belittles the literal text." Quoting two passages from the saint, he remarks that the writer 'shows little concern for the intention of the author or for the meaning of the letter; he is intent on discovering a multiplicity of edifying spiritual meanings." The "chamber" referred to in the passage above is reached, we may note, by *contemplation* rather than by the procedures of rational explication, and the passageway which connects it with the "garden" may be most tortuous, if it exists at all. Bernard argues, as Robert Bellarmine does later, that it is quite possible for the same passage to have two distinct meanings, but secondary meanings are in no wise determinate in the primary, as Whitaker insists they must be.

If this is the freedom which, undoubtedly felt to be not unnatural when Scripture is securely couched in ecclesiastical tradition, was expressly abjured by the Reformation as perilous libertarianism, it certainly did not provoke identical disclaimers. John Calvin, whose views in the matter constituted the disclaimer that informed English Puritanism, denounced imaginative or contemplative approaches to the Word, glorifying *logos* and decrying *mythos*. In a passage cited above, Calvin observes that signs must be attended by doctrine, "without which our senses would gaze bewildered on an unmeaning

---

6. St. Bernard, *Cantica Canticorum: Eighty-six Sermons on the Song of Solomon*, trans. and ed. by Samuel Eales (London: Elliot Stock, 1895), p. 132.

7. On p. 237 in his most useful collection of statements on medieval exegesis prepared as a supplement (pp. 216–54) to William F. Lynch's *Christ and Apollo* (Mentor-Omega ed. New York, New American Library, 1960), where he cites passages from *Life and Works of Saint Bernard*, ed. Dom Mabillon and trans. Samuel J. Eales (London, 1896).

object."[8] Revelation was verbal, not visual, and contemplation of dumb objects availed nothing, or very little. In a passage in his commentary expanding upon Exodus 33:19, he says:

> Although a vision was exhibited to his [Moses'] eyes the main point was in the voice; because true acquaintance with God is made more by the ears than by the eyes. A promise indeed is given that he shall behold God; but the latter blessing is more excellent, that God will proclaim His name so that Moses may know Him more by His voice than by His face, for speechless visions would be cold and altogether evanescent did they not borrow efficacy from words . . . . The soul of a vision is in the doctrine itself from which faith takes rise.[9]

The orientation toward the verbal and rational, as opposed to the sensual and imaginative, is noteworthy. The *Word* of God is exactly that. One can guess Calvin's assessment of any approach to the Scriptures as revelatory event rather than word, and imagine his reaction to the assumption among diverse modern historians of religion that sacred acts or ritual always antedate and determine the statement of doctrine. Ronald S. Wallace, who by careful perusal of the body of Calvin's writings has collected his views upon the Word, provides a useful summary statement:

> Revelation, according to Calvin, never takes place without a word. There is never a genuine sign given without a voice which at some stage in the event comes from God to man. The word may be spoken in various ways. It may be put in the mouth of some figure in a dream. It may be

---

8. Calvin, *Institutes*, 2, 494; 4.14.4.
9. Cited by Ronald S. Wallace in his *Calvin's Doctrine of the Word and Sacrament* (London, Oliver and Boyd, 1953), p. 72.

spoken by an angel. It may come as in the New Covenant, from the lips of one who preaches. However it comes, the voice must be there or it would not be revelation according to the true Biblical pattern. Revelation in the Bible is never a dumb event.[1]

Since events cannot speak, the host of wordless meanings which an action intrudes upon the attentive spectator are spurious, dangerous, not worthy of acceptance. Revelation does not come as *mythos*.

The remarks on exegetical method by William Perkins (1558–1602), a Congregationalist teacher at Cambridge who was important to New England Puritanism for his early statement of the federal theology and to English Puritanism for, among other things, his work on homiletical method, *The Arte of Prophecying* (1592), were echoed and followed throughout seventeenth-century Puritanism. Whether they represent a determinative influence or merely a convenient resumé of what the Puritan preacher was in fact doing, they are worthy of attention in this context. Counseling the pastor on the interpretation of texts, Perkins declares that "*There is one only sense, and the same is the literall. An allegorie is onely a certaine manner of uttering the same sense. The Anagoge and Tropologie are waies, whereby the sense may be applied.*"[2] Later in his treatise he gives an illuminating example of how metaphor should be approached by the pastor-exegete. The discovery of doctrine is of first importance;

1. Ibid.
2. William Perkins, *The Workes* (3 vols. London, 1612), 3, 737. *The Arte of Prophecying*, which closes out the third volume, bears a separate title page dated 1609, with a note that the work was translated from the Latin by Thomas Tuke. The translator declares that the work concerns the true understanding and using of Scriptures, an observation in keeping with the intimate relationship between exegesis and homiletics commented upon in the text.

edification may be found even in the fact of the metaphoric substitution but the image which the trope suggests is by no means to be lingered over:

> All tropes are emphaticall, and besides delight and ornament they doe also affoard matter for the nourishment of faith: as when *Christ* is put for a *Christian* man, or for the *Church* of God. Mat. 25.35. 1. Cor. 12. *As the bodie is one, and hath many members: and al the members of one bodie, though they be many, are yet but one bodie: so also Christ,* that is, *The Church.* Act. 9.4. This trope doth comfort a faithfull soule, and nourish faith. (p. 745)

Perkins nicely sidesteps any comment on the metaphor of the body, which viewed with a modicum of imagination suggests a host of meanings apropos of organicity, solidarity, harmony, and, with eminent conservatism, singles out for comment the overt identification of Christ and Church that is authorized by the word of the text.

The consequences for *mythos* latent in such hermeneutical procedure are hinted at in the basic idiom of the three basic terms of classification used in Perkins' resumé of the processes of finding doctrine:

> *Resolution* is that, whereby the place propounded is, as a weavers web, resolved (or untwisted and unloosed) into sundrie doctrines . . . . Resolution is either Notation, or Collection.
>
> *Notation* is, when as the doctrine is expressed in the place propounded . . . . *Collection* is, when the doctrine not expressed is soundly gathered out of the text. This is done by the helpe of the nine arguments, that is, of the causes, effects, subjects, adiuncts, dissentanies, comparatives, names, distribution and definition. (p. 750)

THE ONE SENSE OF SCRIPTURE

The rational procedure implicit in the use of the heads of logical argument requires no comment, but the image of "Resolution" may. The usage implies that determination of the doctrines present in a text exhausts its substance, for to separate the "weavers web" into warp and woof is to leave nothing of the original fabric. Resolution, then, might well be the dissolution of narrative or trope as imaginative fabrication.

John Owen (1616–83) makes the same point about the comprehensiveness of the single literal meaning of a text and also touches on the issue of *determinateness* as basic to acceptable meaning:

> There are things that fell out of old which are meet to illustrate present things, from a proportion or similitude between them. And thus where a place of Scripture directly treats of one thing, it may, in the interpretation of it, be applied to illustrate another which hath some likeness to it . . . . We call them allegories; so doth our apostle expressly, Gal. iv. 21–26. Having declared how the two covenants, the legal and evangelical, were represented by the two wives of Abraham, Hagar and Sarah; and the two sorts of people, even those that sought for righteousness by the law and believers, by their children, Ishmael and Isaac; he adds that these things are an allegory . . . . But the truth is, he [Paul] doth not call the things themselves an allegory, for they had a reality, the story of them was true; but the exposition and application which he makes of the Scripture in that place is allegorical,—that is, what was spoken of one thing he expounds of another, because of their proportion one to another, or the similitude between them. Now this doth not arise hence, that the same place of Scripture, or the same words in any place, have a diverse sense, a *literal* sense and that

which is *mystical* or allegorical; for the words which have not one determinate sense have no sense at all: but the things mentioned in any place holding a proportion unto other things, there being a likeness between them, the words whereby the ones are expressed are applied unto the other.[3]

Though the literal meaning may include likenesses and connections intended and stated, or implied, by the author, they are as such determinate, accessible to anyone who can digest the words of the text. Furthermore, in cases of typological correspondence less explicit than that of Galations iv. 21-26 one must still speak of a single meaning determinate in the single passage. The single descriptive passage, it is true, asks to be juxtaposed with other passages, and when this is done, a new meaning, that of the configuration, appears. So, presumably, when two such passages as the description of manna in Exodus 16 and the description of Christ in John 6 are juxtaposed, the likeness that emerges is so striking that we are driven to see the total configuration of words as affirming an identity which no contributing passage sets forth in itself. The single passage does not have one literal and another, separate typological meaning, rather, sundry configurations of passages offer sundry typological meanings as their plain and literal import.[4]

3. John Owen, *An Exposition of the Epistle to the Hebrews, The Works*, ed. Rev. William H. Goold and Rev. Charles W. Quick (17 vols. Philadelphia, Leighton Publications, 1869), *13*, 34-35.

4. A blind spot in literal interpretation throughout the period prevented the *Song of Songs* from being seen as anything but the romance between Christ and the Church. There must be some moral in the fact that, in the context of the general agreement that allegorizing was the correct approach to the literal truth of this book, in contradistinction to other books of the canon, the Puritan commentators utterly exhausted themselves in the prying of spiritual meanings from unpromising corners. Faithful Teate in his exposition of the book (*A Scripture-Map of*

Later in his *Exposition of the Epistle to the Hebrews,* Owen again takes up the matter of the single determinate sense of Scripture, and here he makes explicit another element of Puritan hermeneutics: its enlistment of the procedures of dialectic.

> This is the genuine and proper way of the interpretation of the Scripture, when from the words themselves, considered with relation unto the persons speaking them, and all their circumstances, we declare what is their determinate mind and sense.—Hereunto, on the due apprehension of the literal sense of the words themselves, the studious exercise of reason, in all proper ways of arguing is required.[5]

Perry Miller in *The New England Mind* calls deserved attention to the significant influence of Petrus Ramus upon Puritan thought, with the divorce between argument and rhetoric that it encouraged, and the downgrading of figurative language to mere ornamentation. It must be noted, however, that the ground had been prepared for the seed of Ramist thought by those predispositions of the Puritan mind, deriving from other sources, that are hinted at in this passage. The Puritan was interested in truth to which any rational man could lay claim, truth that was self-validating to reason, not marred by the whimsicality or eccentricity of imagination. That redundancy of meanings which event offers to imagination was felt

---

the *Wildernesse of Sin, and Way to Canaan* [London, 1655]) says, "I can say in simplicity, so farre as I have known my wretched heart, that I have *feared* to *strain,* but *hated* to *pervert* the *holy Scriptures,* whereof I reckon the CANTICLES a *portion so transcendently spiritual,* that I accord with those that judge it to be understood *most rightly* (if the sense be faire and scriptural) when *most spiritually.*" After these prefatory remarks, he pushes into a wonderfully ingenious hunt for Christian doctrine. One thinks of a gamekeeper licensed for one day of the year to shoot anything he finds on the lord's estate.

5. Owen, *The Works, 16,* 91.

to vitiate truth: if one meaning, like Aaron's rod, did not immediately declare its preeminence by assimilating all contenders, how could any contender be declared the claimant to belief? This recurrent strain is struck in William Ames' observation, "Hence also there is only one sence of one place of Scripture: because otherwise the sence of the Scripture should be not onely not cleere and certaine, but none at all: for that which doth not signifie one thing, signifieth certainly nothing." [6]

The basic hermeneutical issue between the Catholic, on the one hand, and the Anglican and Puritan, on the other, was the relevance of imagination to exegesis. Anglican and Puritan agreed that exegesis should concern itself with words and their logical implications rather than with images and their evocations and associations. The Puritan parted company with the Anglican on the question of whether this exegetical practice for discerning the true literal sense of a passage meant in fact that the Scripture was never to be approached as *mythos*. Whitaker's and Jewel's readiness to admit that dumb events may eloquently speak would seem to license a certain freedom on the part of the reader of Scripture who, sure of the true literal sense, sought inspiration and edification in an imaginative response to the revealed events. In fact, an imaginative devotional use of Scripture was a conspicuous element in the practice of the Anglican preachers and poets of the era.[7] A conservative hermeneutics, interested in a sound *explication de texte*, might live in harmony with a variety of homiletical and devotional uses of the Scripture which gave legitimate scope to the imagination, but the Puritan literalism that

---

6. William Ames, *The Marrow of Sacred Divinity* (London, 1642), p. 151.

7. See W. Fraser Mitchell's helpful discussion of this aspect of Anglican preaching of the time in his *English Pulpit Oratory* (London, SPCK, 1932), esp. pp. 162 f.

repudiated imagination in the primary procedures of exegesis also repudiated it in the secondary procedures of homiletical and devotional exploration. It could in no way countenance an approach to the Word which, having conceded an inclusive literal meaning to a text, went on to glory in the evocativeness of a poetic image, the richness of a sacramental event, or the sensuousness of a trope. Although, as we shall see later, within a specific line of Puritan meditation, this orientation came to be qualified, it was powerful enough to leave its plain impress on *The Pilgrim's Progress* in a variety of ways.

The Case Against *Mythos:* The Issue of Authority

For the Protestant reformers the problem of authoritative interpretation of Scripture was primary. If the divine counsels were "dark," subject to a diversity of interpretations which needed to be judged by a secondary authority, the situation was perilous, since the Protestant had no acceptable secondary authority to invoke. Varieties of private illumination might be cited, and in practice were conceded a certain respect, but public endorsement of them as suitable surrogates for corporate traditions was avoided. One reason for this attitude, undoubtedly, was that the strengths of such illumination were not of the sort to recommend them to polemic defense. If their refutation on the grounds of eccentricity and privacy was shallow, it was good forensics, since any position which by nature questions the value of the *consensus gentium* affronts the public before which it pleads its case. The course taken by the Reformers, to review the familiar, was to defend the Scripture as perspicuous, self-validating authority.

A Bernard or a Jerome might feel free to defend several independent meanings for a passage of Scripture. Bernard says, "A prudent person will not, I think, condemn the giving of two senses to the same passage, provided that each appear to be grounded in truth, and that charity, which is the rule in interpreting Scripture, shall edify the more persons." Such multiplicity of meanings is commendable if one is hedged from serious error by an independent arbiter. One can even go to subjective extremes: "But I will, as far as I have received from the Lord, seek out the spirit and the life in the deep and mysterious meaning of the sacred text; this is the portion which belongs to me, as a believer in Jesus Christ," confides Bernard.[8] If edification rather than unimpeachable authority is required, such a procedure is wholly legitimate, for fidelity to author's intention and the literal truth is not indispensable to the ends of spiritual nourishment.

For the ends of religious authority, however, such fidelity is indispensable. "[I]f the trumpet give an uncertain sound," Paul the Apostle asks, "who shall prepare himself to the battle?" Bunyan's Christian trod his way in armor. The Christian battle was a grim reality, and the soldier had to be able to read his fighting orders unambiguously in the revealed Word. When the Puritan Christian went to the Scriptures, he was looking for a transparent rather than translucent revelation. He wanted no half-silvered surfaces that let his gaze only partially penetrate to spiritual truths while they reflected the fancies of his own mind, but authoritative words of counsel and promise. John Owen declares: "But as for those who have forsaken the only true guide herein, endeavouring to be wise above what is written, and to raise their contemplations by fancy and imagination above Scripture revelation (as many have done), they have darkened counsel without knowledge, uttering things which they understood not, which have no substance or spiritual food of faith in them."[9] Such practice was, in the words of Richard Greenham, to mingle the word

8. Cited by John. P. McCall, p. 237.
9. *Meditations and Discourses on the Glory of Christ*, in Owen, *Works*, *1*, 275. *Meditations* was first published in 1684.

with 'mens devises." [1] To find such, one did not need to consult the Scriptures.

Aquinas, following Gregory, had suggested that not only the words of Scripture, but also the *things* described, had meaning. Objects and events had mystical truths to offer the assiduous contemplative. It was exactly this sort of approach to Scripture as *mythos* which the Protestant, by reason of his position on religious authority, was obliged to qualify. He feared the consequences for a movement of dissent from ecclesiastical authority if, while finding its sole authority in a corpus of written documents, it allowed these documents to be construed as *mythos*, rather than *logos*. As the history of the Reformation will readily show, the Reformers tried to avoid the consequences by assuming that Scripture was, from an exegetical point of view, wholly reducible to revelatory words.

The problem of authority was especially acute in the mainstream of English Puritanism, since, to its right, the Anglican Establishment put under judgment religious dissent that did not in some way make scope for corporate tradition and, to its left, a host of schismatics and "inner light" groups claimed that Puritans had not followed out to the end the implications of their position. Puritanism repudiated Protestantism to its left with enormous fervor, certainly in the recognition that in the radical's fierce libertarianism the centrifugality which threatened the whole movement of reform was realized. Curiously, in radical Protestantism could be found that same confidence in intuition which Puritanism rejected in Catholic imaginative approaches to the Word, though in its Protestant versions there was a glorying in the lack of supporting secondary authority rather than a tacit assumption of such authority as license and safeguard. The typical Puritan reaction

1. Richard Greenham, *The Workes* (London, 1599–1600), p. 40.

was voiced by John Owen in his comment upon Quaker exegesis:

> It is the known way of the Quakers amongst ourselves [sic], if they can get any one single text of Scripture which, in the sound of the words, or on any other account, seems to favour some fancy they have a mind to, instantly they take it up, not once considering whether it do not dissolve the whole proportion of faith, and overthrow the most fundamental articles of Christianity: so from the outward sound of that one text, John i. 9, "That was the true Light, which lighteth every man that cometh into the world," they fear not to take up a pretended sense of them, destructive to what is taught about the nature of Christ, the work of the Holy Spirit, of faith, grace, conversion to God, plainly and evidently in a thousand other places.[2]

While Owen does not call special attention to it, there is in his protest an implied assumption which ironically witnesses to the role of intuition in Puritanism. The belief that particular readings, as that of John 1:9, must be made in the light of a received unitary body of doctrine—the proportion of faith—in the last reckoning rests either on intuition or delusion, depending upon how one assesses the proportion of faith. Only too often it meant little more than a résumé of what the arbiter chose to believe was vital to the Christian message, and its invocation in argument was ironic in the sense that the context clearly indicated that the inability of Christians to agree on what was vital cleaved the touchstone itself.

The Case Against *Mythos:* The Issue of Guidance

Another substantial motivation for regarding Scripture as *logos* was the need for specific instruction. This requirement

---

2. *An Exposition of . . . Hebrews*, in Owen, *Works, 13,* 316.

and the need for clear authority are complementary, of course: it was authoritative teaching, nothing less, which the Puritan required of the sacred text. Readers of E. M. Forster's portentous parable, "The Machine Stops," may recall the place occupied in his dystopia by the Book of the Machine, in which could be found apposite answers to all the questions which man, seduced away from nature and firsthand experience, was likely to ask. The cosmos occupied by the seventeenth-century Puritan had little in common with that of Forster's story, but securely planted at its axis was a book conceived to have an uncanny and sure relevance such as Forster attributes to the Book of the Machine. If the point of Forster's parable was that man might by his abulia and insouciance allow his bondage to technology to make his life utterly predictable, and so amenable to the instructions of one master guidebook, the point of the Puritan's belief was that divine omniscience and benevolence collaborated to bring predictable human need and inerrant divine wisdom together. In both worlds human predictability could be served by a single enduring text.

The specificity of direction which the Puritan expected from the Scriptures is not startling in view of the implications of his conviction that the Scripture was a self-validating authority intelligible even to the unlearned. If authority had to be unmediated by interpreters who can take the general rule and translate it into specific directions, it had to speak in specifics. Juxtaposed with the moral earnestness of the typical Puritan Christian, this necessity produced a situation calculated to produce a certain estimate of the Word as transparent teaching. Such teaching—verbal, specific, unequivocal—was of course *logos* rather than *mythos*, and, even with due appreciation of the rationale, the position is apt to prove puzzling to the modern in its luxurious confidence. Thomas Gouge, more restrained than some, says that "there is not a condition into which a Child of God can fall, but there is a Direction and

Rule in the Word, in some measure suitable thereunto." [3] Richard Sibbes observes, "There is not anything or any condition that befalls a Christian in this life but there is a general rule in the Scripture for it, and this rule is quickened by example, because it is a practical knowledge." [4] And in John Owen's assurance we have holy optimism which gives no quarter to reservation:

> Another end of God [in inditing the Scriptures] was, that we might have a *safe rule* and *infallible guide* for the due performance of all the duties, towards himself and one another, which he requires of us in the whole course of our obedience, 2 Tim. iii. 15–17. God hath, in infinite wisdom, treasured up in this book every thing that, either for the matter or manner of its performance, is any way necessary for us to know or do, that we may be wise unto salvation, and thoroughly furnished for every duty that he requireth at our hands. And here lies our next end. We come to the Scripture to learn these things; and nowhere else can we so learn them as to attain either assurance and peace in our souls, or so perform them as that they should be acceptable unto God. This mind, therefore, ought to be in us, in all wherein we have to do with the Scriptures. We go to them, or ought so to do, to learn our own duty, to be instructed in the whole course of our obedience, in what God requires of us in particular.[5]

Plainly, when the Puritan approached the Scriptures, he was expecting to be addressed with words of personal counsel.

---

3. Thomas Gouge, *Christian Directions*, *The Works*, with a preface by Timothy Rogers (London, 1706), p. 201. *Christian Directions* was first published in 1660.

4. *Divine Meditations and Holy Contemplations*, in *The Works*, ed. Rev. Alexander Grosart (7 vols. Edinburgh, James Nichol, 1862), 7, 209. *Divine Meditations* first appeared in 1658.

5. *An Exposition of . . . Hebrews*, 4, 313–14.

Calvin says, "And although oracles are not now brought down from heaven, let us know that continual meditation on the word is not ineffectual . . . . Our duty, indeed, is attentively to hear God speaking to us." [6] The divine address, oracle rather than vision, used words to communicate with the human reason rather than images which courted the senses and the refractory (and refracting) medium of the imagination.

Not surprisingly, theory was not perfectly corroborated by practice. There were always anomalous instances when the believer faced conflicting commands and had to choose to break one or the other, or when he had to choose only one of two novel goods and could not discern the greater. Canon law or common law might settle cases of this sort by judgment on precedents, but Scripture did not clearly address itself to them. The so-called Puritan Scholasticism, which sprang to prominence early in the movement and left as its memorial a host of volumes on cases of conscience, is the readily explicable corollary. Still, the chastened optimism of an Arthur Hildersham expresses the conviction that the Bible *must* be regarded as clear instruction directed to the individual:

> There is no good worke any man can doe . . . but he may have cleere direction for it in the Word of God. I grant that this cleere direction in every thing is not easily found in the Word, (much diligence in reading and studying of the Word, in attending upon Gods ordinance in the Ministry of his servants, and in humble and fervent prayer is required hereunto) yet may we certainly (if the fault be not in our selves) find cleere, and certaine direction in the Word for all these things.[7]

6. John Calvin, *Commentaries on the First Book of Moses Called Genesis*, trans. Rev. John King (2 vols. Edinburgh, Calvin Translation Society, 1847), *1*, 265. The Commentaries on Genesis constitute the first 2 vols. of the Works, published in 52 vols.

7. Arthur Hildersham, *CLII Lectures Upon Psalme LI* (London, 1635), p. 381.

The fascinating dialectic between the direct assertions and the parenthetic qualifiers witnesses to an ironic ambivalence. The instructions are and are not "cleere," for Hildersham refuses to make the concession implied in the rejection of the adjective.

The picture is interestingly complicated by the blossoming of science, which well before Bunyan's time had suggested to the religious that God had disclosed his mind in nature in a language of remarkable simplicity, order, and clarity. If Kepler's formulas were divine statements bodied in the hieroglyphs of the creatures, perhaps God spoke more clearly in nature than in His Scriptures. William Ames (1576–1633), a student of Perkins at Cambridge and a theologian and casuist of great influence in both old and New England, raised the question in his *Marrow of Sacred Divinity*, which testifies to his concern, shared with other Puritan thinkers, to prepare a systematic theology which arranged architectonically what was not so ordered in the Bible. Speaking of instruction in the Word, he concedes what he must but is quick to offer an explanation.

> As touching the manner of delivery the Scripture doth not explaine the will of God by universall, and scientificall rules, but by narrations, examples, precepts, exhortations, admonitions, and promises: because that manner doth make most for the common use of all kinde of men . . . . Also the will of God is revealed in that manner in the Scriptures, that although, the things themselves are for the most part hard to be conceived, yet the manner of delivering and explaining them, especially in those things which are necessary, is cleere and perspicuous.[8]

The search for instruction encouraged a peculiar handling of the genres in the Bible. In practice, every kind of exposition

---

8. *The Marrow of Sacred Divinity*, p. 151.

and representation was reduced to a species of straightforward didactic preachment. Poetry, parable, history, anecdote, proverb, drama, census, allegory—all were read as instruction. Henry Lukin declared in a practical vein, "Having hitherto endeavoured to shew how we may find out the true *literal* sence of Scripture, I shall now consider how we may reduce all to use and practice, which is the chief end for which God hath revealed his will to us."[9] He went on to say that even those things most "notional" and "speculative" are reducible to practice. The Bible as guidebook was, to practical intents, the *logos* of doctrine, and of road signs and statute books one expects unambiguousness. Such an orientation and its outworking would inevitably have conspicuous effects on a work as consciously scriptural as *The Pilgrim's Progress*.

The Word as *Logos:* Implications for Poetry and Parable

If biblical history was implicit doctrine, biblical poetry was doctrine made explicit. In imagery, affectivity, rhetorical lineaments, and indirection, one might have expected to find recognized the equivocality of *mythos*, but instead, the Puritan sees biblical poetry as the most straightforward and economic statement of doctrine. When William Perkins listed the four books, Psalms through the Song of Songs, as "Dogmaticall" and described them as those "which teach and prescribe the Doctrine of Divinitie,"[1] he made a truly remarkable adjustment to the difficulty to which Nehemiah Rogers alludes in saying, "for what is the maine cause so many speake against Poetrie, but an ignorant misconceit they have thereof imagining it to be but a vaine invention of man, and an unfitting language for to express holy and sacred matters and mysteries

---

9. Henry Lukin, *An Introduction to the Holy Scriptures* (London, 1669), p. 171.
1. *The Arte of Prophecying*, p. 733.

by."[2] Making a strength out of weakness, Puritan hermeneutics went on to glory in the succinctness of poetic statement. Samuel Smith averred that the Psalms are "an epitome of the whole Bible, teaching us what we are to believe and to do both to God and man."[3] And Rogers said of the same book, "For what are they but a *Compendium* of both *Testaments*?"[4] The poetic character of the Psalms was not utterly obscured, for their lyricism made them usable as song in the worship service; but the requirements for song were quite stringently defined:

> Concerning the *matter* of our songs: It must be first *good* and *wholesome; spirituall* and *heavenly:* Such songs we must sing as are either already in the word, or else composed according to the word. 2. It must be *fitting*, that it may *edifie: It must teach and admonish:* and therefore wisdom is required even in *chusing* of a *Psalme*, that it may be fitting the occasion. (pp. 29-30)

To require that a song "*teach* and *admonish*" is to rein in its affectivity and limit its import.

In the collection of doctrine from biblical poetry, Puritan hermeneutics displayed considerable ingenuity, making allegory from organic image and innocent metaphor. For example, Samuel Smith, a Puritan pastor in the Prittlewell parish at the time the *Mayflower* sailed and an acquaintance of Richard

---

2. Nehemiah Rogers, *A Strange Vineyard in Palaestina: in an Exposition of Isaiahs Parabolical Song of the Beloved, discovered: To which Gods Vineyard in this our Land is Paralleld* (London, 1623), p. 25.

3. Samuel Smith, *David's Blessed Man: or, a Short Exposition on the first Psalme*, in *Samuel Smith on Psalm I., Thomas Pierson on Psalms XXVII. LXXXIV. LXXXV. LXXXVII. and William Gouge on Psalm CXVI*, Nichol's Series of Commentaries, ed. Thomas Smith (Edinburgh, James Nichol, 1858), p. 7. *David's Blessed Man* was first published in 1635.

4. Rogers, *A Strange Vineyard*, p. 24.

THE WORD AS *Logos* 51

Baxter, wrote a popular exposition of the first psalm which proposed to be a study of the estate and condition of all mankind, in this world and the next. He was astute enough to find 31 doctrines in the six verses of the psalm and to arrange them in a table at the close of his exposition. In a representative collection of doctrine, he says, apropos of the words, "which bringeth forth her fruit in due season":

> even so the godly man being ingrafted into Jesus Christ, as by a river's side, and being a lively member of his mystical body, he bringeth forth much good and pleasant fruit, and that in due season, whenas it may best stand for the glory of God and good of man . . . . Here we see them who are the true and lively members of Jesus Christ, who is a true godly man, and who is planted as this good tree in Jesus Christ the true vine, namely such as be careful and endeavour themselves continually to bring forth the blessed fruit of a godly and Christian life.[5]

The metaphor pressed into doctrine here is actually violated. In the text, "And he shall be like a tree planted by the rivers of water, that bringeth forth his fruit in his season; his leaf also shall not wither, and whatsoever he doeth shall prosper," the metaphor amplifies a single asseveration that the righteous man prospers as the unreflected, natural, and spontaneous outworking of his righteousness, with no hint of that careful even anxious attention to one's fruit which Smith's interpretation suggests.[6] Calvin has also written a commentary upon this

---

5. *David's Blessed Man*, p. 44.
6. Nicholas Byfield, making glancing reference to the psalm in his *An Exposition upon the Epistle to the Colossians*, p. 62, distorts its central image in the same way as does Smith. What is more interesting, he presents the doctrine about heed to fruitfulness as part of a precis of the psalm which suggests that in common usage this psalm was not a song but a digest of Christian instruction. He says, "in the first Psalme are divers rules; first, We must not sit with wicked men: secondly, we must

psalm, and it is interesting to note that his treatment of this verse shows much more respect to the figure than the Puritan Smith's. He summarily rejects a specific exegesis that may be more ingenious than Smith's but is obviously in the same category of those collections which, to "resolve" the biblical figure into doctrines, break it into fragments which were never meant to be taken separately:

> Those who explain the figure of the faithful *bringing forth their fruit in season,* as meaning that they wisely discern when a thing ought to be done so as to be done well, in my opinion, show more acuteness than judgment, by putting a meaning upon the words of the prophet which he never intended. He obviously meant nothing more than that the children of God constantly flourish, and are always watered with the secret influences of divine grace, so that whatever may befall them is conducive to their salvation; while, on the other hand, the ungodly are carried away by the sudden tempest, or consumed by the scorching heat.[7]

Calvin discerns the latent doctrine but does not have to make an allegory out of the flourishing tree to present it. Every detail in the image is not treated as the first member of an equation.

Smith's skill as allegorist is even better seen in his handling of the first words of the verse: "He shall be like a tree." He commences:

privately and constantly exercise ourselves in the Word of God: thirdly, wee must seate our selves under the powerfull ministerie of the word, neere the Rivers of these waters of life: and lastly, we must take heede of procrastination, delay no time, but with great heedfulnesse respect the season, or due time of fruit: all the yeere is not Seeds-time or Harvest."

7. John Calvin, *Commentary on the Book of Psalms,* trans. from the Latin by Rev. James Anderson (4 vols. Edinburgh, Calvin Translation Society, 1845), *1,* 5–6. The Commentary on Psalms comprises vols. 8–12 of the Works, published in 52 vols.

[O]bserve by this similitude, that man is compared to a tree, and in three things especially,—the shape, the growth, and the state of a tree.

1. Man may well be compared to a tree in respect of his shape; for as a tree consists of the root, the stock, and the boughs, or branches, even so doth man, this mystical tree. He hath his head, which is the root, and hair as small roots, his body as the stock, and his arms and legs as so many boughs, and fingers and toes as lesser twigs. Only the difference between the natural tree, and man this mystical tree, is this: the natural tree is rooted in the earth . . . but man, this heavenly plant, derives not his juice and nourishment from the fatness of the earth, but from heaven above.[8]

He proceeds to discuss the state and growth of a tree, as they correspond to man, the mystical tree, and then considers the phrase, "planted by the rivers of water": "This part of the similitude doth signify unto us our implanting and ingrafting into Jesus Christ his mystical body, by the work of God's Spirit, and by the means of a true and lively faith."[9] The method has become tacit allegorization, and it is clear that a heavy didacticism, in which every Scriptural similitude was treated as full-dress allegory, insured the multiplicity of doctrine, though it sacrificed the unitary import of image or parable.

Details in biblical parable were handled in a very similar way: they were construed as building up not a picture, but rather a system of truths. Thomas Goodwin declared that in the interpretation of parables, while the "general scope" is usually annexed by Christ, Christ leaves the reader, in the light of the analogy of faith and the general sense provided, "to

8. *David's Blessed Man*, p. 37.
9. Ibid., pp. 39–40.

apply the several particulars" himself, "according to that resemblance that unto spiritual reason doth appear."[1] For a certain taste, it is likely that the "general scope" provided by Christ would have been sufficient (indeed, the parable being what it is, one must ask whether more than the single-pronged application would be intended), but the parables of Jesus, like the similitudes of David, were made allegories so that doctrine might abound. Here again Puritanism set aside the exegetical conservatism of Calvin, who had condemned such excess. Calvin insisted that "there is nothing more profitable, than to adhere strictly to the natural treatment of things." If the scriptural account made plain, for example, that the ark of the covenant was a type of the Church, let it be accepted as such; "but to accommodate its several parts to the Church, is by no means suitable."[2] This, if we may apply in judgment the words of a Puritan uttered in another context, was "to mingle the Word with mens devises."

Bunyan himself was well acquainted with Puritan procedure in making simple similitude into allegory, and the connections with his practice as allegorist in *The Pilgrim's Progress* are plain enough. In his sermon on "The Barren Fig-Tree," he observes, "In parables there are two things to be taken notice of, and to be inquired into of them that read. *First*, The metaphors made use of. *Second*, The doctrine or mysteries couched under such metaphors."[3] He then lists the six metaphors of the parable, by which he means the basic details, including characters and actions, of the story, and declares, "*The doctrine*, or mystery, couched under these words is to show us

1. Thomas Goodwin, *A Discourse of Election, The Works* (12 vols. Edinburgh, James Nichol, 1861–66), *9*, 50. *A Discourse* was first published in 1682.
2. *Commentaries on . . . Genesis, 1*, 257, 258.
3. John Bunyan, *The Works,* ed. George Offor (3 vols. London, Blackie and Son, 1856), *3*, 562.

what is like to become of a fruitless or formal professor." When he proceeds to a statement of 12 allegorical identifications, most of them cast as doctrines, he confesses, in all candor, that he is breaking the parable "into pieces." To change the metaphor, we might say that the parable, like biblical history and poetry in the standard practice, is stretched on the tenterhooks of a didactic frame. Only too often an allegorical regimentation of import is the consequence. Yet the insatiate appetite of the Puritan for doctrine had to be gratified.

Revelatory Word: A Note on Puritan Semantics

The Puritan conception of revelation as *logos*, or knowledge mediated by words to the human understanding, raises several vexing issues. The crucial affirmation that "God spoke" witnessed to the belief that communication in words between Creator and creature was not only possible, but also unquestionably superior to that way of communication which lay through events with meaning unglossed by statement. Words enjoyed a definitude foreign to events, whose outlines tended to fade into a confusion of implication. While words stated connections discursively, sanctioning certain relationships among their referents and disallowing others, objects were related massively, or associatively, in the viewing imagination. Calvin's words, from his commentary upon Isaiah's vision in the temple, are typical:

> Figures are illusory without an explanation. If the vision only had been offered to the eye of the prophet, and no voice of God had followed, what would have been the advantage? But when God confirmed the vision by His Word, the Prophet is enabled to say with advantage, "I have seen the glory of God." And this can be transferred to the sacraments, because if signs only are pre-

sented to our eyes, they will be, as it were, dead images.[4]

The inevitable question is, How could words convey any truth which had not been invested in them by their entanglements with events? How, that is, could revelation in words escape being ersatz revelation through "dead images," with all the ambiguity of the latter?

The general belief was that a kind of fixing of words as chaste symbols fit for revelatory ends was achieved by the understanding's collation and refinement of ordinary deliverances of the imagination. This belief was grounded in the Puritan understanding of perception. It recognized that in perception an object was apprehended by the senses and passed as image to the understanding, but since the imagination was a seat of false judgment as well as of pictorializing, it was apt to distort its pictures in keeping with its shallow evaluations; therefore, the understanding, by setting specific images within the context of other apprehensions of the original object and by invoking the funded wisdom of past evaluations of that object, was expected to strip away from the image the error of inappropriate evaluation and to present the object in its true shape and colors to the memory for storage or to the will for action. Richard Sibbes speaks of imagination "apprehending things upon shallow ground; from whence springs *affectation*, whereby we desire glory in things above our own strength & measure, and make shew of *that*, the truth whereof is wanting in us." In contrast, the higher faculty of *"True judgement"* discerns the "true reasons of things."[5] And Thomas Adams, speaking to the same point, says confidently that the understanding "apprehendeth things according to their right natures."[6] This standard conception of the workings of

---

4. Cited by Wallace, p. 73.
5. Richard Sibbes, *The Soules Conflict* (London, 1635), p. 286.
6. Thomas Adams, *Mysticall Bedlam, The Workes* (London, 1629), p. 493.

imagination and understanding, which has antecedents in medieval Catholic tradition, was quite congenial to the Puritan semantics of the revealed word. If, indeed, the understanding was equal to the task of correcting the imagination so as to grasp things in their "right natures," the words it employed to name these would share with them a certain chasteness, carrying no penumbra of delusive connotations, and could serve as precise vehicles of revelatory communication. This confidence in words as tools adequate to the sum of truth is evident in the remarks of Richard Alleine, the Puritan author of the ascetic tract, *The World Conquered*. As he disengages thought from imagination, it becomes apparent that the "thoughts" he defends as a way for apprehending truth must be verbal in nature. He is not careful to order the processes of perception temporally, but his conformity to the position popular in the time is apparent:

> The soul goes forth, *to view, to taste,* and *to chuse* for it self; the thoughts *take a view,* the affections and senses *taste and take the relish,* and then accordingly the will *chuses:* The will should nakedly follow the understanding, and chuse only what the unbyassed judgment tells it is good; but it does too ordinarily follow the affections and senses; these blind the reason, and so ingage the will; we chuse what we love, and what pleases, rather then what upon an impartial deliberation, we judge to be good.[7]

Since there was no truth in the image *per se*, it had to be discounted; the truth lay in an abstraction from the image, an abstraction that might be equated to word, and that abstraction in turn had as its referent the *true* object, which was an abstraction from the object as it existed in protean variousness

---

7. Richard Alleine, *The World Conquered* (London, 1668), pp. 286–87.

for the imagination. Revelation, bypassing images entirely, might use words which related referents without taint of distortion or ambiguity. In reading the words of Christ, "I am the true shepherd," one did not dwell on the image of shepherd with its visual particulars, but sought the essential truth present in the abstraction, or idea. In the process, of course, even such rich religious symbols as spirit, blood, life, lamb, might lose all their concreteness.

Two questions arise apropos of this position: Are words ever in fact so decontaminated, so completely free of the emotional colorations of their specific ordinary usages? And, more basically, *is* the human understanding capable of discerning things in their right natures? Plainly the conception of revelation presented in words rather than events committed Puritanism to an unqualified acceptance of the rationality of the human creature receiving revelation. Sibbes was voicing a representative position when he said, "Now *imagination* hurteth us . . . by preventing *reason*, and so usurping a censure of things, before our *judgements* try them." The astonishing but common conviction was that the reason could in fact not err if it were able for the moment of judgment to cast off the distractions of sense and imagination. Sibbes, upon listing several questions ("Soliloquies") the reader should address to himself before passing judgment upon temptations, says: "Here . . . is a speciall use of these Soliloquies, to awake the *soule*, and to stirre up *reason* cast asleepe by Sathans *charmes*, that so scattering the *clouds* through which things seeme otherwise than they are, wee may discerne and judge of things according to their true and constant nature." [8] Here is none of that uncertainty or pessimism which Freud and Hume, Darwin and Marx have obtruded upon modern thinking about the reason. For the Puritan, reason was no pawn of instinct or imbibed convention, no chance product of blind process,

8. *The Soules Conflict*, pp. 236, 285.

whether biological struggle or historical dialectic; it was the faculty which bore the stamp of the divine image, which God could address in revelation. As Richard Baxter remarked:

> The use of the Word, and all ordinances and providences, is first to Rectifie Reason, and thereby the Will, and thereby the Life. Faith it self is an Act of Reason: or else it is a brutish act, and not humane. The stronger any mans Reason is, the stronglier is he perswaded that God is true, and that he cannot lye; and therefore whatsoever he saith must needs be true, though Reason cannot discern the thing in its own Evidence. He that hath the Rightest Reason, hath the most grace.[9]

Much the same attitude was voiced by Thomas Goodwin: "The more rationally the preacher discourseth out of the word, and lays open the meaning thereof in a rational way, so much the better, because it is suited to the minds of men.[1] These observations only confirm the received critical opinion that Puritanism was in fact a matrix of eighteenth-century

---

9. Richard Baxter, *The Saints Everlasting Rest* (4th ed. London, 1653), Pt. 2, p. 207. This title will hereafter be abbreviated to *SER*.

Baxter's rationalistic orientation is hinted by the titles of some of his less-known works: *The Unreasonableness of Infidelity* (1655); *The Reasons of the Christian Religion* (1666), with its two parts, *Natural Religion, or Godliness*, and *Of Christianity, and Supernatural Revelation*; and *More Reasons for the Christian Religion* (1671). The first part of his *Reasons of the Christian Religion* is overtly patterned on a Cartesian model, with its methodological reduction of certainties to the *cogito ergo sum*. The same procedure is implicit in his *More Reasons*. Baxter assuredly deserves more consideration than he has yet been given as a precursor of the natural theologians of the eighteenth century, and as a purveyor of Cartesian thought to the theological world. In him we have a convincing demonstration that a Renaissance confidence in reason and an orthodox Puritan piety could co-exist harmoniously in an individual Christian. Milton was a rationalist like Baxter, but his flights of ratiocination, it is now commonplace to say, took him beyond the pales of orthodoxy.

1. *Of the Object and Acts of Justifying Faith, The Works*, 8, 264.

deism and natural theology, a point that H. G. Good makes in his article on Puritanism in Hastings' *Encyclopedia*,[2] which directs attention to the Puritan sermon as an "appeal to the reason of the common man."

2. H. G. Good, "Puritanism," *Encyclopedia of Religion and Ethics* (13 vols. Edinburgh, T. and T. Clark, 1908–27), *10*, 514.

3

THE HOUSE OF INTERPRETER

Faith, the Word, and the Holy Spirit

Christian's stop at the House of Interpreter comes when he is still a callow novice in the way, immediately after his entrance through the Wicket Gate, but before his great trials in the Valleys of Humiliation and the Shadow of Death, and before he loses his burden at the cross. The episode, which presents the stiffening of his resolution as pilgrim, enjoys special weight not only by virtue of its position in the narrative, but also by virtue of its amplitude. The fact that Bunyan gives twice as much substance to it as to the episode of the Valley of the Shadow and half again as much as to the episode of Doubting Castle may not be a very reliable criterion, but it does suggest that he was working with a particularly congenial situation, expansively relaxing with materials that were both familiar and of intrinsic narrative significance.

Christian is received into the House after repeated knocking, and his host at once assures him, "I will shew thee that which will be profitable to thee" (p. 28). Significantly, he has a candle lit—which Bunyan glosses in the margin as Illumination—and it shortly becomes evident that the episode represents for Christian a crucial confrontation with the Word as it was understood within Puritanism. Christian is given a brief training in hermeneutical procedure, as well as simple lessons illustrating the several categories of edification popular in the current hermeneutics. In both matters, the episode is necessary preparation of the neophyte for the exacting road ahead.

The House is the Word; and, in keeping with Puritan belief about its perspicuity, in it dwells its own sure interpreter, the Holy Spirit. Christian may be exposed to dark riddles in his exploration of the Word, but single authoritative interpretation is ever at his elbow in the person of his host. For his part, Christian must respond in faith to the ministrations of the Spirit. While the latter point of the allegorical reticulum was certainly apparent enough to Bunyan's first readers, it is perhaps lost on modern readers and is worth reclaiming. Any attentive reader has undoubtedly noted the formula Bunyan employs in moving from scene to scene of the episode: "Then he [Interpreter] took him by the hand, and led him into a very large *Parlour* that was full of dust"; "the *Interpreter* took him by the hand, and had [sic] him into a little Room, where sat two little Children"; "Then I saw in my Dream, that the *Interpreter* took *Christian* by the hand, and led him into a place, where was a Fire burning against a Wall"; "I saw also that the *Interpreter* took him again by the hand, and led him into a pleasant place, where was builded a stately Palace"; "So he took him by the hand again, and led him into a very dark Room, where there sat a Man in an Iron Cage"; and, finally, "So he took Christian by the hand again, and led him into a Chamber, where there was one a rising out of Bed." By its very repetition, the detail of Interpreter's taking Christian's hand in leading him from each scene to the next, assumes heavy stress. When one juxtaposes with this judgment the facts that a cliché of seventeenth-century Puritanism was the identification of hand with faith and that this identification is one of the constants of the allegory in *The Pilgrim's Progress*, the detail takes on some consequence.

Among its less complicated meanings, the repeated act is undoubtedly a mark of tender solicitude on Interpreter's part: the way through his house is one that he can be judged to know better than his guest, and he must give guidance, especially since he knows the fitting sequence of scenes to be followed. The taking of the hand in association with the initial lighting of a candle, moreover, suggests that the way is dark, and that Christian may stumble, which is consonant with our general reading of the episode; the Word, while it may be trusted to yield its secrets to the humblest in grace, is obscure and dark in the sense that its truths must be searched out, emptied from riddles and mysteries, drawn up from the deeps, and in every case sought in pureness of intention.

Exposition of the Word, indeed, was the true locus of revelatory action on God's part. If God did not insure that His riddles were read properly, His speaking was in vain. So Thomas Adams insists "all right and sober exposition is of God. *Dan.* 2.28. *It is God in heaven that revealeth secrets.*" [1] William Perkins, in avowing that the "principall interpreter of the Scripture is the holy Ghost," [2] provides ample reason to believe that Bunyan's Interpreter is a type of God the Holy Spirit disclosing the dark truths of his Word and thereby consummating the latent revelation for Christian, one of the elect. This specification of Christian as elect is not gratuitous, for William Pemble's assurance that "the truth of Scriptures is knowne unto them for whose benefit they were written, namely the elect," [3] reminds us that in one somber respect, the Puritan never repudiated belief in the obscurity of the Word, though he was not apt to bring this reservation into

---

1. Thomas Adams, *A Commentary or, Exposition upon the Divine Second Epistle Generall, written by the Blessed Apostle St. Peter* (London, 1633), p. 366.
2. Perkins, *The Arte of Prophecying*, p. 737.
3. William Pemble, *Vindiciae Gratiae; a Plea for Grace* (London, 1627), p. 217.

polemic against the Catholic on the question of the Word's clarity.[4] The Word was on its own testimony dark to those who were lost, and this gave license to question the state of grace of those who complained too bitterly of its mysteries. Even for the elect, the chambers of Interpreter's House are *secret* chambers, and the way is dark for the unaided eye. Thus Christian's hand must be taken both to guide him and to protect him from stumbling, but the meaning of the gesture is much richer than this. There can be no doubt about the identification of Interpreter's taking of Christian's hand as the Spirit's appealing to and evoking the faith of the novice in his training. When Christian is wounded in his hand by Apollyon in the Valley of Humiliation, Bunyan explains in the margin that he is wounded in his faith, and when, in the second part, Christiana's boy Matthew takes the medication prepared by Mr. Skill for his stomach ache, Bunyan explains that the pill in his hand is "A word of God in the hand of his faith." A less explicit example of this identification is the occasion when Evangelist is chiding Christian for leaving the way after taking Worldly Wiseman's advice:

> *Christian* fell down at his foot as dead, crying, "Woe is me, for I am undone": at the sight of which *Evangelist* caught him by the right hand, saying, "All manner of sin and blasphemies shall be forgiven unto men; be not faithless, but believing." (p. 22).

---

4. Cf. Pemble's tergiversation on this point, though apropos of a different argument: "All things revealed in the Scriptures, whether they be Doctrinall, Historicall, or Propheticall, may be knowne in the evidence of the Narration, not only by such as are truly sanctified, but by those also, who, remaining unregenerate, enjoy only the benefit of common illumination." He points out that this conclusion is to be brought to bear against "that injurious accusation wherewith those of the Romish Church have slandered God and his written Word, that the Bible is an obscure booke not to be understood." (p. 176)

The identification of hand with faith is apt, of course, since faith is conceived of not simply as passive trust during one's exile from the spiritual world, but as active grasping, that apprehension of present, palpable, spiritual realities, which is also described as vision, or seeing with the eye of faith. Faith was no salutary pretense; it was a way of establishing contact with immediate, if transcendent, reality.

Christian's progress through Interpreter's House demands the constant exercise of faith. It was only to faith, of course, that revealed interpretations could address themselves, and to faith the Spirit sealed interpretation as authoritative, the very word of God. Apropos of this matter, it is interesting that, while Bunyan's age abounds in learned attempts to evince proofs of the infallibility of Scripture which would be convincing to the skeptical, there was general admission of the inadequacy of such proofs. John Preston, for example, presented a formidable list of the standard proofs in his *Life Eternal* but concluded by saying, "I confesse all this which hath been said is not enough, unlesse *God* infuseth an inward light by his Spirit to worke this faith." [5] John Owen, in his ambitious *Of the Divine Originall, Authority, self-evidencing Light, and Power of the Scriptures,* was forced to qualify one of the claims made in his title by admitting that the proofs of Scripture "conclude to a *probability* only, and are suited to beget a *firme opinion* at best, where the principle intended to be evinced is *de fide,* and must be believed with faith divine,

---

5. John Preston, *Life Eternall* (2nd ed. London, 1631), p. 57. It is of interest that when Christian is first brought into the house and taken to see the picture of Evangelist, no mention is made of Interpreter's taking his hand. A candle is lit (which, as we have noted, Bunyan glosses marginally as the provision of illumination) but is not mentioned subsequently. This opening accords well with Preston's explication of the relationship of illumination to faith and reading. Once one's faith had been "worked" by illumination, the reader was prepared to proceed in faith to matters of explication.

and supernaturall." [6] In the last analysis, the Scripture commended itself as divine revelation to a faith divinely imparted to the reader—and that faith was a vital adjunct to reading. Baxter dares to say, "Though few complain of their not believing *Scripture,* yet I conceive it to be the commonest part of unbelief, and the very root of *bitterness,* which spoileth our Graces." [7] Such had to be remedied before one could hope to profit from the Word.

If faith in the Scripture as infallible divine Word was necessary to proper exegesis, so also was faith that God would reward diligence in searching with specific expositions sealed by His Spirit. The first species of faith shaped one's general intellectual predisposition, the second sharpened one's alertness to particular truths, and both were hinted in the statement of Hebrews: "But without faith it is impossible to please him: for he that cometh to God must believe that he is, and that he is a rewarder of them that diligently seek him" (Hebrews 11:6). The careful iteration of the detail of Interpreter's taking Christian's hand probably indicates in particular that the second species of faith is being called into play. As Christian is shown a number of doctrines dramatized, he must be willing to accept the normative exegesis which Interpreter supplies, and his faith is prerequisite to his learning.[8] While renouncing the Catholic "mysteries" of equivocal event, the Puritan retained a fond interest in the mysteries of doctrine. Every detail of Scripture could be conceived of as a verbal brushpile, concealing some truth alive with edifying vitality,

---

6. Owen, *Of the Divine Originall, Authority, self-evidencing Light, and Power of the Scriptures* (Oxford, 1659), p. 122.

7. Baxter, *SER,* Pt. 4, p. 188.

8. When Calvin says that the words of Scripture "will not obtain full credit in the hearts of men, until they are sealed by the inward testimony of the Spirit" (*Institutes, 1,* 72; 1.7.4), he calls attention to this precise interaction of Spirit and faith that is so plainly allegorized in Interpreter's guidance of Christian.

and to apprehend that truth, one courted in faith the ministry of the Holy Spirit. But not for a moment, to be sure, could one neglect those rational procedures for extricating meaning which were presumably the ones which God honored and sanctified, since they led to plain, authoritative statement of doctrine.

The exercise of Christian's faith as adjunct to exegesis is, then, a fitting element in the links among the several scenes of his tour. Christian leaves singing, and he indicates that he has glimpsed the importance of faith, when he says, "I have seen things . . . to make me stable / In what I have began [sic] to take in hand." The things he retains he keeps in the hand of faith.

Example and Precept, Promise and Threatening: The Seven Scenes

Christian is shown seven subjects for interpretation: a picture of Evangelist gracing the wall of the first room; the sweeping and sprinkling of a dusty parlor; the children Patience and Passion behaving in a manner consonant with their names; a fire mysteriously maintained; a man taking the castle of the Kingdom by storm; a hopeless sinner in an iron cage; and a man who has dreamed of the Judgment. All these scenes support a reading of the House as the Word, provided that the equivalences are not applied too rigorously. The identification served as a kind of model for Bunyan's fabrication of the episode, a model more or less embodied in its structure and detail, and the degree of embodiment conceded by the reader depends upon how persuasive he finds the evidence. That the equation plainly was an organizing model is indicated by the fact that Interpreter presents Evangelist, whose picture Christian is shown initially, as "the only Man, whom the Lord of the Place whither thou art going, hath Authorized, to be thy Guide in all difficult places thou mayest meet with in the way"

(p. 29). Evangelist is, of course, himself the divine Word, peripatetic, seeking men out where they are, and guiding them aright in their Christian walk. In particular, as Evangel, or good news, he is a necessary counterpoise to the staticity of the Word as it is allegorized by Interpreter's House, and there is good reason for his likeness to be shown at the beginning of Christian's tour. The second scene presenting an effective way to clean a dusty room, contrasts the Law, which merely stirs up corruption, and the Gospel, which cleanses it away; the contrast between the dispensation of Law and the dispensation of the Gospel is that between the two chief categories of the Word, historically considered. The five scenes which follow may be related to the simple categories of edification which the Puritan reader employed in searching the Scripture: example and precept, promise and threatening.

In order to establish and adumbrate Bunyan's debt at this point, we should note the ways in which these categories figured in Puritan collection of doctrine. "Example" was a broad category, strategically useful to the exegete in his implementation of convictions about the Word as *logos*. The term could be conveniently applied to any datum of Scripture—character, action, trope, or image—which for the ends of edification was seen as the vehicle of implicit precept. Constituting the immediate fabric of much of Scripture (though some of it was, after all, explicit doctrine), examples were intermediate between the particular and the abstract and claimed affinity to both levels. The terms "promise" and "threatening" are transparently related to the covenant theology of Calvinism and together embodied the sanctions and energizing and ordering ends of precept whether implicit or explicit. The promises were covenants which an absolute and arbitrary Sovereign offered to seal with man, and as such beyond price as binding obligations and defining limits upon the Deity, while threatening was simply promise in a negative formulation.

When John Bartlet, in his manual of piety entitled *The Practical Christian*, urges the Christian carefully to consider the good things of the Word, he lists the four we have been discussing. He puts precept first, then promise and threatening, and example last, but the importance of example is hinted in his statement relating the other three categories to it. He asks the reader to meditate "On the Examples in the word of mercy, and goodness to the obedient, and Justice and Severity to the disobedient; and when you meditate on them, to take notice, there is no Example in it [the Word] but is for instruction; and hath a promise, or a threatning in the Bowels, and Bosom, of it, *Rom.* 15.4. II. *Cor.* 10.11."[9] When Richard Baxter and Henry Lukin reduce Scripture to precepts, promises, and threatenings,[1] we are entitled to assume that for them, as for Bartlet, any and all of these might in fact occur in Scripture in the implicit form of example.

It is true that the presence in Scripture of doctrine in anything but explicit forms was a matter receiving repeated explanation. In their vigorous defenses of "example," Puritan divines betrayed an uneasiness that implied certain assumptions about the proper vehicle of truth. The customary procedure was to defend example as precept incremented by evidence of its practicability. Henry Lukin says:

9. John Bartlet, *The Practical Christian* (London, 1670), pp. 41–42.
1. See Baxter, *The Life of Faith, The Practical Works*, ed. William Orme (23 vols. London, James Duncan, 1830), *12*, 359: "Exercise your faith upon all the holy Scriptures, precepts, promises and threatenings, and not on one of them alone"; Henry Lukin, *An Introduction to the Holy Scriptures*, p. 174: "The Doctrine of the Scripture consists of *Precepts*, which teach and enjoyn our Duty, and of such *sanctions* as do enforce these precepts, that is, *Promises* whereby we are encouraged to our Duty, or *Threatnings* whereby we are awed so as to keep within the bounds of it."

> The actions of *Men* in Scripture are either *good,* or *evil,* or of a *doubtful nature* by their good actions, we see not only what we should do, as we do by Precepts, but also what we may do? [The confusing punctuation is the text's.] for what one does, another may through the assistance of Gods grace do likewise. Hence it is, that Examples are of greater force than Precepts, and do in a sort *compel,* Gal. 2. 14.[2]

In the Puritan purview, Scripture might well have been delivered as a compendium of general directives. But that God had chosen to do otherwise did not, could not, vitiate the conception of Scripture as rules. Richard Sibbes amplifies upon the point made by Lukin. Examples show, first,

> that *the things commanded are possible to be done.* Then they shew us the *way and means more plainly, how to do them.* Thirdly, they shew *how graceful and acceptable they are when they are done.* So as the Scriptures are not penned altogether in a commanding fashion, but have mingled sweet alluring examples. For there are four ways of teaching: rule, reason, similitudes, and examples. The two former enjoins, but works not on the affections. Similitudes are but slight; only examples conforms us in a most sweet alluring manner.[3]

Richard Baxter echoes the conviction voiced by Sibbes, that the exemplification of precept is a strength of the divinely given guidebook; it is, he says, "a mercy that the Scripture is written historically: and therefore we should remember such particular examples as suit our own case." He urges caution, however, in the use of examples. We are to "Understand well the different nature and use of Scripture examples; how some

---

2. Lukin, p. 210.
3. Sibbes, *The Christian Work, Works,* 5, 122–23.

of them have the nature of a divine revelation and a law; and others are only motives to obedience, and others of them are evils to be avoided by us."[4] Example could be related to precept in a number of ways, and once it was assumed that in fact all details of Scripture *would* have edifying import, human ingenuity could see to it that the necessary connections with precept were made. Exemplification might relate to precept in either a positive or a negative manner. To provide motives for obedience it might present law or portray the advantages of obedience to law. In any case, precept was immediately accessible in the example.

William Perkins sums up quite nicely the rationale of the collection of doctrine from example:

> [W]e must specially remember that an example in his own kind, that is, an Ethique, Oeconomique, Politique, Ordinarie, and Extraordinarie example hath the vertue of a generall rule in Ethique, Oeconomique, Politique, Ordinarie, and Extraordinarie matters. The examples of the fathers are patterns for us. 1. *Cor.* 10.12 . . . . And it is a Principle in Logicke, that the *Genus* is actually in all the *species:* & a rule in the Optikes, that the generall species of things are perceived before the particular.[5]

Such an emphasis upon the exemplary features of the biblical events need not, it is true, have done any violence to the events. Appreciated as part of the penumbra of implication surrounding event, doctrine could be discerned with no reduction of the central core, and all learning from experience certainly implies a discernment of promise and warning in particular happenings When such an emphasis upon the general present in the particular becomes extreme, however, the particular may suffer from a pressure to forget the determinate

---

4. *The Life of Faith*, pp. 233, 231.
5. *The Arte of Prophecying*, pp. 750–51.

singularity of the individual which is the mark of its real existence and to exalt its typicality and universality—in short, its symbolic value. One thinks of Kenneth Burke's identification of the symbolic with the *statistical*. A King David seen only as a nexus of general representations of truth has become, for practical purposes, a symbol, as the term is used for a figure in allegory, and, without question, the approach to biblical circumstance as example invited allegorical interpretation.[6]

We have noted above how the two opening scenes can be related to an understanding of the House as the Word. The five scenes that constitute the remainder of Christian's course in his tour of Interpreter's House illustrate in transparent fashion the basic categories of the current hermeneutics. As didactic actions offering promise and threatening are framed for Christian's scrutiny, his tour becomes much like a brief meditation on the Word, a suggestion to which the evidence

---

6. The natural tendency of the search for doctrine to encourage allegorical interpretation was recognized in medieval Catholic hermeneutics. Indeed, doctrine was described as the allegorical sense. John McCall, in a discussion of John Cassian (*Christ and Apollo*, supplement 4, p. 220) observes that for Cassian (d. 435 A.D.) the spiritual meanings of Scripture are threefold: tropology, anagogy, and "allegory or doctrinal significance." And he translates this conclusion from G. Paré, A. Brunet, and F. Tremblay's *La Renaissance du XIIe Siècle: les écoles et l'enseignement*: "But one recognizes quickly on reading Hugh St. Victor, and the authors who talk about the allegorical sense, that by this they understand the doctrinal content of Scriptures." Though allegorical interpretation is difficult, it explores "the body of the doctrinal edifice." Catholic and Puritan might not come to agreement on the relationship of such doctrine to the literal sense, and Hugh St. Victor is perhaps more vehement in his asseveration of the problems in discerning the allegorical sense than the Puritan, intent on collecting doctrine as the perfection of the literal sense, would be. Curiously, in insisting upon doctrine as the fullest realization of the literal meaning, the Puritan cultivated a situation in which heavy didacticism would obscure the historicity of the materials. The Catholic, in keeping literal and secondary meanings more or less separate, could stress both the uncomplicated literal-historical and the doctrinal-allegorical meanings without allowing the latter to crowd the former from attention.

of the opening section of this chapter lends some weight. It is certain that scriptural example was the class of didactic action most familiar to Bunyan and it is to this category that one should look first for the glossing of his practice.

As a propaedeutic to pilgrimage, the scenes quite properly constitute encouraging and admonitory examples apropos of patience, divine support, determination, all of which Christian will need in full measure. The scenes involving Patience and Passion, the fire mysteriously maintained, and a soldier taking the Castle of the Kingdom by storm deal clearly with promise, comprise the epitasis of the allegorical sequence, and move toward the genuine climax of the taking of the Castle, with Christian's "recognition" of the soldier as a type of himself. There is a sure hand behind the symmetrical ordering of the sequence around the three scenes of promise, which are prefaced by two presenting the Word as central motif for the whole and followed by two that develop threatening as the conjugate of promise.

Patience and Passion are examples of the pilgrim and his antitype. Interpreter explains their relevance to wondering Christian:

> These two Lads are Figures; *Passion*, of the Men of *this* World; and *Patience*, of the Men of *that* which is to come: For as here thou seest, *Passion will have all now*, this year; that is to say, in *this* World; *So* are the Men of this World: they must have all their good things now, they cannot stay till next *Year;* that is, untill the *next* World, for their Portion of good. (p. 31)

With a dexterity and wit almost metaphysical, Bunyan points out, by way of Interpreter, the latent promise:

> Therefore *Passion* had not so much reason to laugh at *Patience*, because he had his good things first, as *Patience* will have to laugh at *Passion*, because he had his best

> things *last*; for *first* must give place to *last*, because *last* must have his time to come, but *last* gives place to *nothing*; for there is not another to succeed: he therefore that hath his Portion *first*, must needs have a time to spend it; but he that has his Portion *last*, must have it lastingly. (pp. 31–32)

If this scene presents a contribution which the human creature can make to the success of his pilgrimage, the next presents the mysterious but indispensable contribution of God. Christian is shown a fire burning against a wall. A figure stands by it, casting water on it, but it is not quenched; indeed, it burns higher and hotter. Interpreter explains:

> This fire is the work of Grace that is wrought in the heart; he that casts Water upon it, to extinguish and put it out, is the *Devil:* but in that thou seest the fire, notwithstanding, burn higher and hotter, thou shalt also see the reason of that: So he had him about to the back side of the Wall, where he saw a Man with a Vessel of Oyl in his hand, of the which he did also continually cast, but secretly, into the fire. Then said *Christian*, *What means this?* The *Interpreter* answered, This is *Christ*, who continually with the Oyl of his Grace, maintains the work already begun in the heart; by the means of which, notwithstanding what the Devil can do, the souls of his people prove gracious still. (p. 32)

The scene, like the earlier one, has its problematic aspect—it is startling to find a character in the spectacle summarily identified as Christ, just as in the previous episode the time scheme in which Passion wastes all her goods in a moment is enigmatic—but it clearly exemplifies a promise: the work of grace is maintained by inscrutable process, despite the efforts of the Evil One. The pilgrim need not fear.

The third scene is an obvious paradigm of successful pilgrimage. In fact, it is pilgrimage in microcosm, with the stress, as in the first scene, upon a human contribution to success, in this case determination. The scene sc closely simulates Christian's projected pilgrimage that he needs no assistance in reading himself in the example. A group of men crowd the entranceway of a castle, desirous of entering, but they are restrained by other men in armor. A little distance from the door sits a man with a book:

> *Christian* saw a man of a very stout countenance come up to the Man that sat there to write; saying, *Set down my Name Sir;* the which when he had done, he saw the Man draw his Sword, and put an Helmet upon his Head, and rush toward the door upon the Armed Men, who laid upon him with deadly force; but the Man, not at all discouraged, fell to cutting and hacking most fiercely; so after he had received and given many wounds to those that attempted to keep him out, he cut his way through them all, and pressed forward into the Palace; at which there was a pleasant voice heard from those that were within, even of the Three that walked upon the top of the Palace, saying,
>
> > *Come in, Come in;*
> > *Eternal Glory thou shalt win.*
>
> So he went in, and was cloathed with such Garments as they. Then *Christian* smiled, and said, I think verily I know the meaning of this. (pp. 33–34)

Having discerned the implicit promise (eternal glory goes to the overcomer) in this example of determination in the Christian warfare, Christian conceives himself to be sufficiently girded for his pilgrimage. He has battened on promise, and in a swell of confidence, he entreats Interpreter, "Now . . . let me go hence."

But there is more to the Word than promise, and more to

pilgrimage than pursuit. The two concluding scenes of Christian's tour are portentous with warning. The hopeless sinner in the iron cage and the reprobate who has dreamed of the Last Judgment are uncomplicated examples of dereliction. Indeed, the utter simplicity of their signification perhaps presents more clearly than the involved nuances of earlier scenes Bunyan's adroit use of "example" as it was understood in hermeneutics. (The reader was to glean precept from character and incident, but when an exemplary action of Scripture was very complex, it might offer complex precepts. Though the scene with Patience and Passion does not present coercive evidence of its connections with the "example" of hermeneutics, it is readily assimilable to that category in the context of a sequence of framed exemplary actions.)

Before both of the last two scenes Interpreter has to resist Christian's pleas and urge him to stay for the completion of his curriculum, for the full development of his course of study demands that he learn to interpret minatory examples. Led into a very dark room, Christian learns from his dialogue with the man in the iron cage that he was once a "fair and flourishing Professor" of righteousness. When Christian asks how he came to this condition, the man replies:

> I left off to watch, and be sober; I laid the reins upon the neck of my lusts; I sinned against the light of the Word, and the goodness of God: I have grieved the Spirit, and he is gone; I tempted the Devil, and he is come to me; I have provoked God to anger, and he has left me; I have so hardened my heart, that I *cannot repent*. (p. 34)

Christian inquires of Interpreter if there is any hope for the man, and Interpreter has him ask the derelict himself. The derelict replies:

> I have Crucified him [Christ] to my self afresh, I have despised his Person, I have despised his Righteousness, I have counted his Blood an unholy thing, I have done despite to the Spirit of Grace: Therefore I have shut my self out of all the Promises; and there now remains to me nothing but threatnings, dreadful threatnings, fearful threatnings, of certain Judgement and firy Indignation, which shall devour me as an Adversary.

Interpreter's counsel is pointed: "Let this mans misery be remembered by thee, and be an everlasting caution to thee." One's election was a fact verified only by a successful consummation to his pilgrimage. Unqualified hope marked the superficial mind, such as Bunyan so pathetically portrayed in the lad Talkative, and later in Ignorance, who stumbles down to perdition from the very gates of Heaven. So, when Interpreter asks, after the final scene, *"Hast thou considered all these things?"* Christian replies, "Yes, and they put me in *hope* and *fear*."

It is difficult to appreciate the terror which that final scene of Christian's tour must have evoked for the devout Puritan. For the present age Doomsday does not ordinarily portend the auditing of individual accounts, with the possibility of an infinite loss sustained by finite creature, but suggests, rather, the merciful indiscriminateness of genocide; since it is impersonal, it is not truly tragic. But Bunyan and his audience tacitly assumed the enormity of a grim abyss of eternal dereliction opening at the edge of the individual world, and if the death of the Christian saint lies vexatiously outside the purview of tragedy, the death of the Christian reprobate represents tragedy with certain of its elements evolved to infinity. The derelict of the closing scene describes to Christian his dream of the return of Christ as judge. The good are taken, but he is left. Christian asks what he found frightening in the sight, and the derelict answers:

> Why, I thought that the day of Judgement was come, and that I was not ready for it: but this frighted me most, that the Angels gathered up several, and left me behind; also the pit of Hell opened her mouth just where I stood: my Conscience too within afflicted me; and as I thought, the Judge had always his eye upon me, shewing indignation in his countenance. (p. 37)

It is that intense personal attention of the divine eye which is so awful, and which is perhaps the galvanizing energy of threatening in the Puritan account. The intimacy of address which made promise rich encouragement could well render threatening unbearable. Another detail of the passage, the integrality of the opening of Hell's mouth at the derelict's feet to his terror, is of some significance, for in Christian's later journey through the Valley of the Shadow of Death, Hell's mouth opens near the way. The dread imagery of final judgment on sin as present threat to the individual is a natural part of Christian's walk. Indeed, all the eschatalogical realities —death, judgment, and hell as well as heaven—are to be immediate and palpable pressures upon the wayfarer.

Promise and threatening, as the motivating adjuncts of precept, are a vital part of pilgrimage. Interpreter says as much in his closing words to Christian: "Well, keep all things so in thy mind, that they may be as a *Goad* in thy sides, to prick thee forward in the way thou must go." And his very last statement to the departing pilgrim presents a fitting conclusion to Christian's tour of the House of the Word. There must be a continuity in the operation of the Holy Spirit in his pilgrimage. In leaving Interpreter behind, he cannot leave behind the Holy Spirit, anymore than in leaving the House, he can leave the Word. Bunyan is plainly aware of the problem. The Holy

Spirit who guided him in Interpreter's House will continue to guide him in another persona, just as Evangelist, the Word peripatetic, continues to instruct him: "Then *Christian* began to gird up his loins, and to address himself to his Journey. Then said the *Interpreter*, The Comforter be always with thee good *Christian*, to guide thee in the way that leads to the City" (p. 37). Holy Spirit, erstwhile Interpreter, remains with Christian as Comforter.

Christian's curriculum in Interpreter's House seems tailored to his peculiar needs. He is not shown all the significant rooms, and the lessons he is given are clearly spurs for him in his headlong flight and vigorous pursuit. Later, when Christiana visits the same hostel, her peculiar needs in a pilgrimage much less anxious and headlong are met in different ways. After Christian has been taught something about exploring the Word in faith and shown promises and threatenings, with their germane precepts, he has indeed "closed" with the Word. It is only moments after leaving Interpreter's House that he comes to a Cross, "and a little below in the bottom, a Sepulcher." Here the burden tumbles from his back, and Graceless becomes Christian in surety.

4

EXEMPLARY HISTORY: PARABOLIC DRAMA AND CHARACTER-AS-EXAMPLE IN *THE PILGRIM'S PROGRESS*

The Idea of Exemplary History

The Puritan denominated a scriptural circumstance "example" presumably both to recognize its doctrinal significance and to honor its historicity. Yet the stratagem had its weakness insofar as the latter goal was concerned, for an overly thoroughgoing exploitation of the particular as exemplary moves from history into the atemporal world of logic and idea. But while allegory was a natural terminus toward which such examples tended, it was entirely possible for them to maintain their intermediate state as both idea and event, and the hybrids are noteworthy. Person-as-example in hermeneutics was a didactic entity which preserved historicity while moving in import toward the allegorical type. Event-as-example was a sort of parabolic drama in which action preserved historicity even while the simplicity of prescribed import suggested the simplicity of contrived dramatization.

It is surely no accident that character and event of this sort are typical of *The Pilgrim's Progress*. A variety of inventions in the allegory conflate realistic particularity and doctrinal import in ways that show a striking similarity to the character and event of exemplary history in Scripture. Indeed, Bunyan on occasion makes explicit reference to "example" of this kind.

An understanding of this matter can clear up confusions of long standing about the nature of the scenes Christian witnesses in Interpreter's House. The simple categorization of them as emblems, such as Rosemary Freeman and Roger Sharrock have encouraged, misses the crucial point that the scenes are not tableaux[1] but dramas, the very point which so distressed Coleridge, who saw grave incoherence in the time scheme of one of these dramas. In settling these problems by describing the exemplary history of Scripture as it was understood in Puritan hermeneutics, incidental illumination will be cast on the more general question of character and action in Bunyan's allegory.

William Perkins, voicing a popular judgment, declares that the Old Testament "is distinguished by bookes, which are either Historicall, or Dogmaticall, or Propheticall." The historical books, which include all those from Genesis through Job, are "stories of things done, for the illustration and confirmation of that doctrine which is propounded in other bookes. 1. *Cor.* 10.11. *Now all these things came upon them for ensamples; and were written to admonish us.*"[2] It scarcely needs to be observed that this approach to event as *illustration* of doctrine threatens to reduce it to allegory, with the intended doctrine the *logos* or animating principle in the events. The events are no less real, but their signification is much more contrived, more univocal, than might have been supposed. They happened, to paraphrase Romans 15.4, which Perkins quotes in this context, for our learning. The remarks of Richard Rogers, in

1. Cf. Sharrock's note on the passage, *The Pilgrim's Progress*, p. 317.
2. Perkins, *The Arte of Prophecying, The Works*, 3, 732.

his *A Commentary upon the Whole Booke of Judges* are similar:

> I intended [in the *Commentary*] . . . to benefit Students and Preachers . . . so they may learne how to make use of the historicall part of the Bible, and learne to draw doctrine and instruction out of the examples thereof, fit for the people (and that out of the bad as well as the good) even as well as out of other Scripture: which all have not learned to doe, neither have attained unto: and therefore doe oft times offer violence to the Scriptures, by making allegories of them, and so wresting them to another sense then the Holy Ghost hath made of them.[3]

There is some irony in Roger's failure to discern the readiness with which his own procedure could implement allegorical reduction. As the attention is tacitly shifted from thing to word, the event is not left to speak for itself. Commenting on the opening seven verses of Judges, Roger says:

> In that this people was now constrained to looke about them, and (now Joshua was dead) to doe that themselves for their peace and quiet, which hee was wont to doe for them: we are taught, that when chiefe & speciall persons are taken away, who were wont to beare the burden for many others, then they who were left behinde, must put forth themselves, and take the more paine, and be put to greater plondges then they were before.[4]

As the reader contemplates "chiefe & speciall persons" and all those who suffer the loss of their solicitous leaders, Joshua and the Israelites remain at the fringe of his awareness, but they are out of focus. His attention is centered upon an abstract and

3. Richard Rogers, *A Commentary upon the Whole Booke of Judges*, verso of the first leaf of the unpaginated introduction.
4. Ibid., p. 2.

general truth. Taking the representative Puritan belief that "the very *History* of Scripture is *Doctrinal*" [5] and bringing to bear the judgment that exemplification of doctrine is a demand upon history calculated to schematize and circumscribe its import, one has little difficulty in concluding that the character and action of exemplary history must be of peculiar kinds, reflecting the impositions from without, whether of divine allegorist or human seeker after doctrine.

Parabolic Drama in *The Pilgrim's Progress*

A natural approach to the matter of parabolic drama, or event-as-example, in *The Pilgrim's Progress*, is by way of Coleridge's frequently cited criticism of the scene enacted by Patience and Passion in Interpreter's House. The offending paragraphs read:

> I [Bunyan] saw moreover in my Dream, that the *Interpreter* took him by the hand, and had him into a little Room, where sat two little Children, each one in his Chair: The name of the eldest was *Passion*, and of the other, *Patience*; *Passion* seemed to be much discontent, but *Patience* was very quiet. Then *Christian* asked, What is the reason of the discontent of *Passion*? The *Interpreter* answered, The Governour of them would have him stay for his best things till the beginning of the next year; but he will have all now: But *Patience* is willing to wait.
>
> Then I saw that one came to *Passion* and brought him a Bag of Treasure, and poured it down at his feet; the which he took up, and rejoyced therein, and withall, laughed *Patience* to scorn: But I beheld but a while, and he had lavished all away, and had nothing left him but Rags. (pp. 30–31)

---

5. Cf. the remarks of Henry Lukin, *An Introduction to the Holy Scripture*, p. 174.

Coleridge cites this as "one of the not many instances of faulty allegory" in *The Pilgrim's Progress* and insists that it is in fact no allegory at all:

> The beholding "but awhile," and the change into "nothing but rags," is not legitimately imaginable." [The redundant quotation mark is the text's.] A longer time and more interlinks are requisite. It is a hybrid compost of usual images and generalised words, like the Nile-born nondescript, with a head or tail of organised flesh, and a lump of semi-mud for the body.[6]

If he is intent upon singling out such cases of fractured time as flaws in the allegory, however, it is curious that he does not reprehend other scenes as well. All but the first, which is in fact a portrait, present an animated parable the time and space of which are self-contained and discontinuous with the world of Interpreter and Christian.

When Christiana and her group come to Interpreter's House in Part Two, they are shown much which Christian did not see. But they are pilgrims, too, and first among the many things they view are those very scenes which Christian witnessed: Wondrous to say, again the courageous soldier takes the castle, again the man wakes with a fearful dream fresh in mind. One is tempted to think, *mutatis mutandi*, of those funhouses in amusement parks where, regardless of the number of trips one has made through their circuitous passages, the same little dramas and surprises will be staged at certain junctures: piled boxes begin to fall, creatures start from hiding, or doors open and shut ominously. Coleridge's protest about the mixing of temporal schemes becomes irrelevant once it is apparent that the action of these scenes is not meant to be seen as continuous with the action of Interpreter and his guests. These "events"

---

6. Coleridge, *Notes on English Divines*, ed. Rev. Derwent Coleridge (2 vols. London, Edward Moxon, 1853), *1*, 339.

which transpire in the Significant Rooms are *sui generis*, and the "mixing" is a mistaken concept of the viewer who will not make the concession of faith needed to appreciate such dramatizations.

These actions, assuredly, are not *mythos*. They are univocal statements in deed, and their only *raison d'etre* is to dramatize that simple rational truth which Interpreter or his guest can read to their good. They are, in short, significantly akin to biblical example as construed in the then current Puritan hermeneutical practice. Just as one could go to the Word and find univocal truths acted out, with the didactic events redramatized as many times as one cared to return to the page, so univocal truths were reproduced, dramatically, as many times as one set the process in motion by entering a Significant Room. If the reader remains a trifle uneasy about the nature of the actors in the parables—are they clockwork automata or beings of the same reality as Christian who do this as edifying playacting?—his qualms are perhaps to be respected as a judgment upon the limitations of the Puritan approach to event as *logos*. The covert wish that Christian had the chance to question one of these parabolic figures about his private life, when he was not obliged to act his part, evidences that refractory human interest in the human mysteries and the darkness of events that entails a dim prognosis for the exegetical system which slights them.

Common to Bunyan's parabolic dramas, and scriptural event-as-example, then, is the reader's impression that characters act roles to present a parabolic truth. When characters which are realistically developed (or which enjoy a certain realism by their association with realistic characters in the same narrative framework) are forced into the straitened gesturings and posings of action conceded to have a single evident message, realism must assert itself by persuading the reader that he witnesses a dramatic presentation. The various scenes in the

Interpreter's House impress one in that way, as do biblical events when the reader takes at all seriously the historicity of a character whose actions are read as exemplified doctrine. Insofar as such a reading presses action into unnatural univocality of import, the realism of character exercises its energies by hinting that the character has an *assumed* simplicity of role in the episode. The tragic story of the prophet Hosea's taking a prostitute to wife provides a ready illustration of such a drama which owes its parabolic aspect not to the imposition of the reader but to the explicit design of the writer.[7] The contrivedness of the prophet's dealings with Gomer, which dramatize so starkly and lucidly the truth of Israel's conduct toward her God, shows just that role-playing which in the great host of biblical episodes subtly marks the character whose actions are read as parabolic but who is too real to be seen as type. In these latter cirumstances, however, such role-playing cannot truly be assigned to the character. Such ascription is merely the reader's compensatory reflex in reconciling character and doctrine.

As Christian proceeds on his pilgrimage, he is involved in several further happenings which ask to be described as parabolic dramas. For example, as they compare their experiences after meeting on the far side of the Valley of the Shadow of Death, Christian and Faithful discuss a strange assault which Faithful suffered at the foot of the Hill Difficulty. Faithful tells his story thus:

> When I came to the foot of the Hill called *Difficulty*, I met with a very aged Man, who asked me, *What I was, and whither bound?* I told him that I was a Pilgrim, going to the Coelestial City: Then said the old Man, *Thou lookest like an honest fellow; Wilt thou be content to dwell with me, for the wages that I shall give thee?* Then I asked

---

7. Cf. especially chapters 1 and 3 of the book.

him his name, and where he dwelt? He said his name was *Adam the first, and I dwell in the Town of Deceit.* (p. 69)

He resists old Adam's entreaties and is quickly assured that he will be punished by an assailant sent after him, who will make his way bitter to his soul. Adam is as good as his word. The assailant sweeps up, swift as the wind, knocks Faithful down, and leaves him for dead. "He had doubtless made an end of me," Faithful observes, "But that one came by, and bid him forbear." Christian asks who this was:

> *Faith.* I did not know him at first, but as he went by, I perceived the holes in his hands and his side; then I concluded that he was our Lord. So I went up the Hill.
> *Chr. That Man that overtook you, was Moses, he spareth none, neither knoweth he how to shew mercy to those that transgress his Law.* (p. 71)

The appearance of Adam, Moses, and Christ here certainly quickens attention and raises sundry questions, and the following section will discuss Bunyan's transplanting of character from Scripture to allegorical landscape. With respect to the issue at hand, however, all we need notice is that the signification of these characters, whose names suggest a historical fullness of individuality, is contrivedly narrow. In fact, they are the agents as well as the terms of a simple parabolic presentation. Characters having the individuality of Christian and Faithful combined with the clockwork articulation and movement of the suffered action and the plainly truncated import of the agents provide all the elements of parabolic drama. When an action happens solely for the learning of the pilgrims, much as all events of scriptural history happened for the exemplification of doctrine, the nuance that simplicity of meaning owes to an assumed simplicity of role on the part of agent is inescapable.

Even when the figures in these dramas bear typic names, their commerce with a character as real as Bunyan's Christian makes the reader loath to write them off as animated abstractions. Once a measure of reality is conceded them, the episodes of which they are part take on a pronounced dramatic aspect. Consider, for example, Christian and Hopeful's encounter with Flatterer:

> They went then till they came at a place where they saw a *way* put it self into their *way*, and seemed withal, to lie as straight as the way which they should go; and here they know not which of the two to take, for both seemed straight before them, therefore here they stood still to consider. And as they were thinking about the way, behold, a man black of flesh, but covered with a very light Robe, came to them, and asked them, why they stood there? They answered, They were going to the Coelestial City, but knew not which of these ways to take. Follow me, said the man, it is thither that I am going. So they followed him in the way that but now came into the road, which by degrees turned, and turned them so from the City that they desired to go to, that in little time their faces were turned away from it; yet they followed him. But by and by, before they were aware, he led them both within the compass of a Net, in which they were both so entangled, that they knew not what to do; and with that, *the white robe fell off the black mans back:* then they saw where they were. (pp. 132–33)

Christian's memory is jogged, and he recalls the counsel of the Shepherds apropos of flatterers. "As is the saying of the Wise man," he concludes, "so we have found it this day: *A man that flattereth his Neighbour, spreadeth a Net for his feet.*" This "man black of flesh" who so completely deceives Christian and his companion is, like those figures in the scenes in Interpreter's House, both term and agent, and he is obliged to enact a parabolic drama for any pilgrim passing through his territory who is careless enough to collaborate with him.

Admittedly the issue of parabolic drama is not an adequate measure of the relevance of the hermeneutical conception of exemplary history to Bunyan's practice, for it concerns at best a handful of episodes in *The Pilgrim's Progress*. To do justice to the extent of the influence of this conception on Bunyan, certain features of Bunyan's portrayal of character must be studied. Exemplary character is at the center of most of the actions of *The Pilgrim's Progress*, whether or not they are parabolic dramas.

Character-as-Example in *The Pilgrim's Progress*

The basic stratagem of allegory, that of substituting one set of terms for another, fosters a diversity of kinds of character in allegorical narrative. A character used as a symbol may be made to stand for concrete agent, for abstraction, or hybrids of the two. To be more specific, it may represent a particular person, unnamed but identifiable in his disguise, or a particular concrete nonhuman agency—animal, spirit, or physical force. It may also represent a variety of kinds of abstraction—moral quality, idea, attitude. Whatever opinion one holds of C. S. Lewis' argument in *The Allegory of Love* that allegory enjoys a special affinity with moral abstraction since *ab origine* it was used to objectify and allow the scrutiny of individual moral conflict, it is evident that allegory shows its peculiar strengths when it is used to explore mental states rather than to present in disguised form (say, for satiric purposes) historical events.[8] As an important factor in the special ability

---

8. This is no covert thrust at the allegory of Swift in *Gulliver's Travels, Book One*, in order to magnify the virtues of a Bunyan or Spenser. Swift does all that one could ask him to do with allegory as history-in-disguise, and presumably he could have gone on to prove the limits of allegory by using it to dramatize moral consciousness, but he finds it

of allegory to handle mental quantities, character-symbols are ordinarily used to objectify abstractions.

The consequences are interesting indeed when moral allegory is wedded to a hearty particularization of character, as in *The Pilgrim's Progress*. Hybrid character—palpable abstraction or symbolic person—is the inevitable if paradoxical result. But the fact that the characters of *The Pilgrim's Progress* have impressed so many readers as enigmatic meetings of person and abstraction surely asks for a careful attack upon the questions of definition and precedents. Both are supplied plain answers, though undoubtedly not the only ones, by the hermeneutical context, and the concept central to this explanation is character-as-example. In a sense, all that is required is an effort to think rigorously about the nature of didactic character when the didacticism is intrinsic to realistic figure rather than adumbrated by contrived action or by relationships among symbolic types.

Perhaps the most important point about the bulk of Bunyan's characters is that they are real individuals who do not incarnate but exemplify a particular quality. There is a profound difference between type and example. Consider the oft-quoted words of Bunyan's character Honest when he is identified by Great-Heart as old Honesty and replies, blushing, "Not Honesty in the *Abstract*, but *Honest*, is my Name, and I wish that my *Nature* shall agree to what I am called" (p. 247). Something of this sort might be said by every one of Bunyan's wayfarers, whose names, incidentally, like that of Honest, are more often than not adjectival in nature rather than substantival, and hence hint at attribute rather than essence. Moreover, Christian is not Man but one among men, and, in his preserved particularity, he is an example for the reader's emulation. There is nothing vicarious about his pilgrimage.

more congenial, apparently, to handle such exploration by way of extended conversation among characters.

Everyone in history must travel the way individually, if he travels it at all.

But the sincere wayfarer is only one variety of character. There are also insincere wayfarers like Talkative and Atheist, the former an engaging addlepate and the latter a lusty old cynic, who are individualized and exemplary in a pejorative sense. There are figures like Gaius, Demas, and Madame Wanton (identified with Potiphar's wife) who are drawn from biblical history but who in their exemplary features have somehow escaped time and live immortally as part of the landscape of Christian's pilgrimage. Still other prop characters, such as Discretion, Charity, and the Evangelist, are close to simple types rather than real exemplary characters. And, finally, characters like Sloth, Presumption, and Heedless, as former pilgrims who have left the way, are preserved in a peculiar undecayed immortality alongside the way as exemplary memorials. The effects of the Puritan estimate of Scripture as doctrine upon the Puritan understanding of biblical character can be easily traced. While it was taken for granted that the men and women of Scripture were historical, it was also assumed that their lives were illustrative of doctrine. Character in Scripture and in *The Pilgrim's Progress* was didactic example, and it is worth exploring the pronouncements of several influential Puritans of Bunyan's century on this concept.

Nicholas Byfield, a Puritan pastor at Chester, in his commentary on Colossians, has occasion to discuss Onesimus, the slave boy befriended by the apostle Paul. Onesimus is visible for a moment as a historical corporeality, but he is soon transformed into much much more as the doctrines are collected from his exemplary qualities:

> This *Onesimus* was the theevish and fugitive servant of *Philemon*, who comming to Rome, was converted by Paul in prison, and is now for honours sake sent with *Tichicus*. From hence divers things may be noted.

1 That hatefull and unfaithfull persons may be converted, and made worthy, faithfull, and beloved.

2 That religion and the word doth not marre, but make good servants . . . .

3 That no mans sinnes, of which they have repented before God and the Church, ought to be charged upon them as any disparagement in subsequent times. . . .

4 It is a good worke, to grace and credit such as by repentance returne from their former evill waies.

5 Repentance and true grace is the surest way to credit.[9]

Treated as an example, Onesimus, in the multiplication of doctrines, has become the Converted and Renovated Slave, a paradigm to be commended to all men.

Another specimen of this practice is found in John Owen's *An Exposition of the Epistle to the Hebrews.* Commenting upon Hebrews 11:31, which lauds the faith of Rahab the harlot, who was instrumental in the Israelites' conquest of Jericho, he says:

> 1. This Rahab was by nature a Gentile, an alien from the stock and covenant of Abraham. Wherefore, as her conversion unto God was an act of free grace and mercy in a peculiar manner, so it was a type and pledge of calling a church from among the Gentiles; . . . .
>
> 2. She was not only a *Gentile,* but an *Amorite;* of that race and seed which in general was devoted unto utter destruction. She was therefore an instance of God's sovereignty in dispensing with his positive laws as it seems good unto him . . . .
>
> 3. She was a *harlot;* . . . . And herein have we a blessed instance both of the sovereignty of God's grace

---

9. Nicholas Byfield, *An Exposition upon the Epistle to the Colossians* (London, 1615), p. 177.

and of its power;—of its freedom and sovereignty, in the calling and conversion of a person given up by her own choice to the vilest of sins; and of its power, in the conversion of one engaged in the serving of that lust . . . which of all others is the most effectual in detaining persons under its power.[1]

Doctrine, to be most effective, must have a generality of reference, and historical figures are most useful to practice when they can be made to illustrate broad classes. It is ironic that in many cases those very defining marks which, taken as a configuration and with no pressure toward the generic, constitute the individuality of a person can, if taken *seriatim* and treated as typical of classes, obscure the uniqueness of the individual.

The literature of Puritan hermeneutics offers a wealth of references to character as example, and, not surprisingly, the evidence indicates that the predisposition exerted influence far beyond the pages of Scripture. The assiduous Christian saw character in every circumstance as somehow exemplary. Richard Sibbes says:

> *We are to look to every one that hath any good things worthy of imitation*, as those that delight in gardens, hear of any choice flowers, they will have a slip for their own garden. Thus it should be with us; where we see any flower of any grace, get that and place it in our own gardens. In every Christian there is something imitable, and something that may further us; and therefore this apostle longed to see the Romans, that he might be comforted by their faith, Rom. i. 12. It is with the church as with the firmament, ever some are rising and some are

---

[1]. Owen, *An Exposition of the Epistle to the Hebrews, Works, 16*, 177–78.

setting. Let us look to the stars of our time, and walk by their light.²

Elsewhere he sets the injunction in ominous context. The divine purpose in the matter is to be recognized and honored:

> And let us know that we shall be countable for those good examples which we have from others. There is not an example of an humble, holy, and industrious life, but shall be laid to our charge; for God doth purposely let them shine in our eyes, that we might take example by them.³

Manifestly, Puritan piety and the hermeneutics with which it was organically related gave powerful impetus to a didactic conception of character which effectively wedded historicity to plain instructive import and generality of reference. Despite the nisus toward the allegorical in such an approach, the perils, and difficulty, in ignoring historicity of biblical figure or of neighbor helped to keep exemplary character a genuine hybrid, paradoxical and intriguing in its dynamic equilibrium.

Four basic kinds of character in *The Pilgrim's Progress* to which an appreciation of the hermeneutical category of "example" is especially relevant deserve individual attention. These were suggested at the opening of this section: sincere wayfarer, insincere wayfarer, biblical wayside character, and wayside "memorial." In the framework of Bunyan's allegory, with its landscape of symbolic exigencies, it is not surprising that wayfarers like Christian and Faithful should on occasion be lumped by the inattentive reader with such prop figures as Experience and Giant Despair as allegorical and no more. But if Honest bears the name of a virtue he hopes to attain—a virtue which is not his very substance but a goal in pursuit of

---

2. Sibbes, *The Christian Work, Works*, 5, 124.
3. Sibbes, *Divine Meditations and Holy Contemplations, Works*, 7, 193.

which he is exemplary—so Christian and Faithful, Christiana, Mercy, Hopeful, Fearing, Valiant-for-the-Truth, and their fellows are exemplary figures of distinguishable personality rather than shades whose countenances are the featureless masks of a unitary essence. The prototypes for such characters are abundantly present in Word and experience as interpreted by a moralistic Puritanism. Moreover, it should not be forgotten that Bunyan in his Apology presents his allegory as the story of a man individualized enough to secure the reader's identification; it is a *man* who speaks from the clouds, not a disembodied idea.

The way he travels, moreover, has a history of real human wayfarers. Christian keeps company with David and Joseph and Abraham, and Bunyan tells us that the ditch running along at his right in the Valley of the Shadow once received the erring King David. Wanton, who troubles Faithful, had erstwhile troubled Joseph when he traveled the way. At House Beautiful, Christiana is taken to the Mount where Abraham had offered Isaac. Christian, like his biblical antecedents, is exemplary individual.

One of the best illustrations of sincere wayfarer as example is provided by Mercy, the secondary heroine of Part Two, where Bunyan is deeply concerned with remedying the impression given by Part One that no one but redoubtable and toughened Christians may hope for a successful pilgrimage. The Puritan was only too ready to seize upon personal weakness as a sign of reprobation. Christian had triumphed, but any fool could see he was a man of uncommon parts. Bunyan's roster of pilgrims in the second part, ranging from Fearing to Despondancie, corrects this notion, not only presenting Christiana as a fit example of woman on pilgrimage, but using her companion, Mercy, to pull together and epitomize his whole emphasis. In an interesting play upon her name, Bunyan makes her, not the abstraction Mercy, not even an example of human mercy. Example she is, and Mercy she is, but neither in the most obvious sense. In this character, Bunyan indeed seems to present with most dexterous equivocation God's merciful acceptance of one who, by all the signs the human eye can judge, was not of the elect. If this was the case, her acceptance was of course consummate mercy.

At the Wicket Gate, where the women are grievously frightened by the devil's dog, the Keeper who is Christ takes Christiana in by the hand, but Mercy is left without. After a time Christiana remembers and intercedes for her companion: "And she said, my Lord, I have a Companion of mine that stands yet without, that is come hither upon the same account as my self. One that is much dejected in her mind, for that she comes, as she thinks, without sending for, whereas I was sent to, by my Husbands King, to come" (p. 189). When the Keeper then opens the gate and questions Mercy about why she has come, she replies: "I am come, for *that*, unto which I was never invited, as my Friend *Christiana* was. *Hers* was from the King, and *mine* was but from *her:* Wherefore I fear I presume." But the Keeper welcomes her, with words which Bunyan asterisks and comments upon in the margin with the injunction "*mark this*": "I pray for all them that believe on me, by what means soever they come unto me." The issue of prevenient grace is nicely obfuscated here, for, while Bunyan does not categorically say that Mercy came uncalled, he plainly wants to present the broadest possible construction of the divine invitation. That this conception of Mercy as exemplifier of divine mercy is warranted is confirmed by the words of old Honest when he learns her story upon meeting Christiana's group late in the pilgrimage: "At that the old *Honest* man [sic] said, *Mercie*, is thy Name? by *Mercie* shalt thou be sustained, and carried through all those Difficulties that shall assault thee in thy way; till thou come thither where thou shalt look the Fountain of Mercie in the Face with Comfort" (p.

248). He has broadened the original point which Bunyan makes at the Wicket Gate. Not only in Mercy's entrance upon the Way, but in all the circumstances of her perseverance, we see illustration of the divine mercy. But she functions illustratively without sacrificing a whit of her fullness and corporeality as character. Before the journey is over, she has married Christiana's oldest son, Mathew, given him children, and relaxed in the sundry amenities of what G. K. Chesterton calls more walking tour than pilgrimage.

Biblical example, to be sure, presented itself in negative as well as positive formulations, offering admonition as well as prompting emulation. The worst of Biblical characters were in some sense exemplary. Henry Lukin manages to go beyond the discernment of warning in his consideration of such example: "When we read the *evil* actions, or miscarriages of men in Scripture, we see what is in our own nature, for there are in us the seeds of the same sins, which would bring forth the like fruit, were it not for the *renewing* or *restraining grace* of God."[4] Such examples are germane to Bunyan's portrayal of the insincere pilgrim, where he presents the same conflation of individuality and admonitory nuance which biblical character offered the Puritan reader.

When Coleridge raised a question about the legitimacy of presenting insincere pilgrims traveling the same true Way with Christian, he found a crux in an episode early in the first part. Shortly after Christian is relieved at the Cross of the burden on his back, he encounters two men who come "tumbling over the Wall, on the left hand of the narrow way." Their names are Formalist and Hypocrisie, and Christian at once enters into conversation with them, for they seem to be on the way, though they have conveniently evaded all those tests and harassments which he has undergone. Their defense is in one respect unassailable, for they *are* on the way:

4. Lukin, *An Introduction to the Holy Scripture*, p. 212.

> They told him, That Custom of climbing over the wall, it being of so long a standing, as above a thousand years, would doubtless now be admitted as a thing legal, by any Impartial Judge. And besides, said they, so be we get into the way, what's matter which way we get in; if we are in, we are in: thou art but in the way, who, as we perceive, came in at the Gate; and we are also in the way that came tumbling over the wall: Wherein now is thy condition better then ours? (p. 40)

Coleridge criticizes the passage by saying, "The allegory is clearly defective, inasmuch as the 'way' represents two diverse meanings: (1) the outward profession of Christianity, and (2) the inward and spiritual grace." So that the only right answer for Christian to make his interrogators is " 'No! you are not in the same "way" with me though you are walking in the same road.' " [5]

The presence of two diverse meanings for the way which Coleridge finds here does not deserve to be so readily and patronizingly dismissed as pun. Christian's answer—"I walk by the Rule of my Master, you walk by the rude working of your fancies"—directs attention to the inner man and isolates a criterion for judging true wayfaring which is basic to the workings of the allegory. Coleridge might have pointed to a score of other pilgrims who walk the way with Christian for

---

5. Sharrock cites this criticism in his note on the passage, *The Pilgrim's Progress*, p. 320.

Coleridge's designation of the primary meaning of the way is somewhat loose. A shabby renegade like Atheist, encountered by Christian on the way, is in no sense making a "profession of Christianity." But insofar as he walks the way he perhaps conforms to some element or another of the corporate Puritan tradition it memorializes. Being on the way at one juncture, certainly, does not imply a profession of everything Christianity, or more precisely Puritan Christianity, prescribes. See the second section of Chapter 5 for a discussion of the way as a memorialization of Puritan experience.

a shorter or longer spell but are in no sense elected to grace, any one of whom might have raised the same argument that Formalist and Hypocrisie do. In the remonstrance of these two insincere pilgrims, Bunyan makes explicit a question in order to show its impropriety. None of his wayfarers, sincere or insincere, is of that kind whose worth and import may be judged by reference to the containing reticulum of ordained meanings allegorized as landscape. The wayfarers are gifted with inner depths of motive and intention, an understanding of which is absolutely essential to the reader's judgment of them. In a word, for characters such as Bunyan's, merely being on the way could not possibly serve as an adequate test of the wayfarer. A character like Ignorance can take the way to its very end, conforming, we may suppose, to the whole gamut of demands which the way presents, but he is damned at last. His *heart* was not right! Formalist and Hypocrisie are on the way, but since they follow their fancies, the inner man is in error.[6]

The dichotomy Bunyan is here recognizing is implicit in the equivocal phrase "on the way." To say that one was on the way to the Celestial City could indicate an appraisal of immediate stance or a statement of purpose and direction. Borrowing a pair of terms from mechanics, we might say that the phrase denotes either a *vector*, i.e. a directed quantity, or a *scalar*, an undirected one. Atheist, standing in the way and deriding Christian, may be on the way as quantity with mass but without direction, but the true pilgrims are on the way to the Celestial City with respect to both immediate locus and inner determination. As such, of course, they are distinguishable not only from all insincere pilgrims, whose determination is impure and merely in fancy directed toward the true ends of pilgrimage, but also from prop characters—the residents of Vanity Fair, Madame Wanton, and the rest—who may from time to time step on *the* way to the Celestial City, but who are in no

6. Cf. Bunyan's presentation of Talkative, pp. 75–85.

wise on *their* way to the Celestial City. An appropriate inner purpose has not reconciled such travelers to the way.[7]

The wayside characters, on the other hand, exist in a timeless world, as might be expected. Travelers on the way are immersed in time, for pilgrimage is among other things, the career of a human life. The figures on the wayside are essentially static, with the eternity and ideality of abstraction. Such characters forever act a particular limited role in contrast with the multifarious action of pilgrims or are in some way fixed forever as examples. In this category are both the prop characters, such as Discretion, Charity, Experience, and Gaius the host, and the wayside memorials, erstwhile pilgrims who left the way and are preserved undecayed at wayside as admonitions.

Among the prop characters, those who are particularly relevant to the hermeneutical category of example are the biblical figures lifted bodily from sacred history and transplanted to the timeless realm bordering the pilgrims' way. Bunyan, dares to make figures like Demas, Gaius, Mnason, and the wife of Potiphar, who lived and died as a matter of record, function as props in his allegory, but his daring is unextraordinary. Biblical character seen as example was readily manipulatable in this way, when its "lesson" was taken with special seriousness. Such emphasis pressed it toward abstraction, giving it something of abstraction's tractability and timelessness.

In their travel, Christian and Hopeful come upon the Hill Lucre where a silver mine offers treasure to those who will leave the way and dig. Demas, whom the apostle Paul immortalized by a passing reference to him as a lover of the world, appears as a promoter of the mine, but the pilgrims resist his overtures and Christian denounces him roundly: "*Demas*, Thou art an Enemy to the right ways of the Lord of

---

7. Wayside figure *could* become sincere wayfarer. Hopeful leaves his home in the town of Vanity and joins Christian as companion, after the martyrdom of Faithful.

this way, and hast been already condemned for thine own turning aside, by one of his Majesties Judges; and why seekest thou to bring us into the like condemnation?" (p. 107) He continues with a stout reading of Demas' pedigree, and a most striking pedigree it is, with its concatenation of historical individuals related only as a family of examples:

> I know you, *Gehazi* [the greedy servant of Elisha] was your Great Grandfather, and *Judas* your Father, and you have trod their steps. It is but a devilish prank that thou usest: Thy Father was hanged for a Traitor, and thou deservest no better reward. (p. 108)

All three figures named are examples of greed and betrayal of trust. Demas as example is perfectly compatible with his wayside context of timelessness and ideality, for even in his original context of Scripture, as the Puritan read it, he was blend of abstract and particular.

Much the same may be said of the other biblical characters who inhabit the wayside in Bunyan's allegory. Gaius, who entertains Christiana's group in Part Two, is the exemplary host of Paul's letter to the Romans and, as example, is immortal. So too is Mnason, an old disciple who plays host to the group in the town of Vanity; appropriately, he had once played host to Paul in Jerusalem, another city which in light of its treatment of Paul, Bunyan may have regarded as inimical to pilgrimage. Madam Wanton will be discussed in a later chapter, but here we may note that Bunyan's identification of her with the promiscuous wife of Potiphar, which treats her as an example of salaciousness, allows her to be at once historical and timeless.

Finally, the memorials which in profusion mark the wayside of Christian's and Christiana's pilgrimages constitute one of the most interesting outworkings of the Puritan conception of character as example and the last one we are to consider.

Character as a conflation of person and doctrine was always susceptible to a reduction which divested it of its dynamic qualities. An even more thoroughgoing kind of stasis than that of the prop characters is offered by the memorials. They are not only timeless, but immobile and lifeless. Having perished as persons, they live as words, a literature of admonition inscribed by the way.

Christian and Faithful have scarcely broken away from Demas, with his urgings to turn aside to the world, when they come upon a grim reminder of what such disobedience entails in the pillar of salt that was once the wife of Lot. Indeed, Coleridge might have cited this incident rather than the scene of Passion and Patience as a defect in the allegory, since, like the scenes in Interpreter's House, its implied plane of action (albeit past action) is out of focus with the principal one, and in this case the discontinuity is not immediately justified by the framework. Christian reads the Hebrew inscription on the pillar (Bunyan explains to our surprise that Christian was "learned") and comments: "Ah my Brother, this is a seasonable sight, it came opportunely to us after the invitation which *Demas* gave us to come over to view the Hill *Lucre:* and had we gone over as he desired us, and as thou wast inclining to do (my Brother) we had, for ought I know, been made our selves a spectacle for those that shall come after to behold" (p. 109). The two have a moment before concluded that this is Lot's wife, changed to salt as she fled Sodom, and while the reference makes the geography of the scene extremely problematic, it is plain that biblical "example" is present here as timeless and immutable warning. When Christian draws out the doctrine by saying "Let us take notice of what we see here, for our help for time to come: *This* woman escaped one Judgment; for she fell not by the destruction of *Sodom,* yet she was destroyed by another," Hopeful replies, "True, and she may be to us both *Caution,* and *Example.*" This reduction of the biblical episode is perhaps unfortunate since to remember the end of Lot's wife merely as an example of judgment is to miss the poignancy of the original, in which a human being looked back to see for one last time everything that had comprised her life. But such participation in the story, of course, weakens its didactic thrust, and we are reminded of the motives which prompted Puritanism to repudiate Biblical circumstance as *mythos*.

If we make the necessary allowances for vexed geography, the encounter with a memorial in salt ending several millennia is not dreadfully taxing on poetic faith. Other memorials, which involve corpses preserved at wayside for centuries, make heavier demands—or, should we say, render especially useful an understanding of the legitimizing assumptions involved. Consider the scene shown to Christian and Hopeful by the Shepherds from the top of the Hill Errour:

> So *Christian* and *Hopeful* lookt down, and saw at the bottom several men, dashed all to pieces by a fall that they had from the top. Then said *Christian*, What meaneth this? The Shepherds answered; Have you not heard of them that were made to err, by hearkening to *Hymeneus*, and *Philetus*, as concerning the faith of the Resurrection of the Body? They answered, Yes. Then said the Shepherds, Those that you see lie dashed in pieces at the bottom of this Mountain, *are they:* and they have continued to this day unburied (as you see) for an example to others to take heed how they clamber too high, or how they come too near the brink of this Mountain. (pp. 120–21)

That their bodies be preserved undecayed for 1600 years is not so much a miracle of mummification as evidence of their status as admonitory message, exemplary character collapsed into word.

The same observation can be made of the scene in the second

part when in the Valley of the Shadow of Death, Christiana's company finds itself among the snares and gins that harassed Christian:

> Now when they were come among the Snares, they espyed a Man cast into the Ditch on the left hand, with his flesh all rent and torn. Then said the *Guide*, that is one *Heedless*, that was agoing this way; he has lain there a great while . . . . You cannot imagine how many are killed here about, and yet men are so foolishly venturous, as to set out lightly on Pilgrimage, and to come without a *Guide*. (pp. 243-44)

Heedless is preserved as warning example, to discourage such presumptive venturing. Mention might be made too of Simple, Sloth, and Presumption, whom Christiana's company finds hanging at wayside, though their demise must have come long years previous, for they were on the way when Christian was a pilgrim. Concerning them, Christiana asks a leading question of Great-Heart: "But had it not been well if their Crimes had been ingraven in some Plate of Iron or Brass, and left here, even where they did their Mischiefs, for a caution to other bad Men?" (p. 214) Great-Heart assures her that indeed such inscriptions are to be found at the nearby wall. But Mercy discerns that the most fitting statement is that presented in these most strangely incorporeal corpses and makes a song:

> Now then, you three, hang there and be a Sign
> To all that shall against the Truth combine:
> And let him that comes after, fear this end,
> If unto Pilgrims he is not a Friend.
>   And thou my Soul of all such men beware,
> That unto Holiness Opposers are.

These memorials, like Heedless and Lot's wife, are the casualties of wayfaring. They show only too vividly that off the way lies perpetual stasis, that disobedience means loss of freedom and immobility. In a sense, such figures are the damned who mark the Hell which fringes the way from start to end, a Hell suggestive of the constricted center of Dante's *Inferno*, where Satan is fixed in ice. They, along with the biblical wayside agents like Gaius and both the sincere and insincere wayfarers, represent Bunyan's adaptation to his own purposes of the category of character-as-example popular in Puritan hermeneutics of the time.

5

THE ANALOGY OF FAITH AND THE UNITY OF *THE PILGRIM'S PROGRESS*

The Pilgrim's Progress opens with a distinction between outer and inner landscape. Bunyan says: "As I walk'd through the wilderness of this world, I lighted on a certain place, where was a Denn; And I laid me down in that place to sleep: And as I slept I dreamed a Dream." There is a significant difference between the world of Bunyan's waking life and the world of his dream. Whatever else the world of his dream is, it is *not* wilderness. Rather, it is an ordered spiritual realm in which good and evil, though in continual warfare, are in a strife where all battle lines are clearly drawn. Christian's universe is one of unambiguous meaning, of polarities which reduce every decision to a clear choice. The world indeed is one of such implicit meaning that right conduct is, with only rare exceptions (e.g. the episode with Flatterer), a function of the good will rather than of acute discernment.

Christian has more than a clear way, however. When first encountered, he is reading a book which convincingly predicts for him the whole future of his present course. Not long thereafter, he meets Evangelist, who has perfect counsel on what he must do to be saved. This collaboration of book and Evangelist is the Word both in its convicting and instructive power and in its exemplification of an accessible body of truth wholly adequate to one's spiritual pilgrimage. Equipped with the Word and walking the way he does, Christian is without excuse, should he digress.

Not surprisingly, *The Pilgrim's Progress* presents a conspicuous superimposition of stasis and linear movement—a feature expected in allegory that develops a determinate structure of beliefs—and such a narrative appears to lack genuine contingency. Suspense grows out of the reader's interest in the varied guises or costumery which the anticipated terms of the shaping system assume when they appear in the action. The linear development, then, is a program of implementation answering the question "How?" rather than a course involving emergence of true novelty answering the question "What?" But even as we generalize upon the peculiar design *The Pilgrim's Progress* presents, on the assumption that it is not unique, we are obliged to admit that in the world of *belles lettres*, works which enjoy an intimacy of connection with a canon of truth believed entire, such as *The Pilgrim's Progress* enjoys with the Christian Scriptures, are rare. This intimacy is precarious: narrative so ordered is apt to be wholly assimilated to idea (in which case movement collapses into static structure) or to betray the informing truth by allowing the action to exercise its autonomous energies. Neither *The Divine Comedy* nor *The Faerie Queene* offers the kind of connections between canon and narrative that are present in Bunyan's allegory, and in neither do movement and resolution seem in some sense illusory.

Given its problematic dynamics, the unity of *The Pilgrim's Progress* is to a great extent a reflection of the unity of Puritan religious experience as it was wrought in the eminently practical struggle to define a body of practice that could assimilate and be assimilated to the Word while, at the same time, maintaining a coherence adequate to the variety of historical pressures exerted on it. In hermeneutical practice, this concern showed itself in the heavy stress upon the analogy, or proportion, of faith—that is, the Word that stood luminous and coherent behind the convolutions of the letter as the perfectly unified disclosure of the mind of God. The common assumption within Puritanism was that all Scripture could be reduced to a consistent body of doctrine. The susceptibility of Scripture to such a reduction meant that it could be seen simultaneously as a *fait accompli,* one complete thought in the mind of God, and as a dynamic unfolding, and this superimposition of stasis and cursus is a paradigm for *The Pilgrim's Progress.* The fact, incidentally, that the analogy of faith, reflecting a supposed *a priori* unity of the Word as well as an achieved coherence of practice, proved itself a generally useful hermeneutical device suggests that Puritanism had early attained a fair measure of internal consistency, whatever judgments may be brought against the adequacy or stability of the synthesis.

William Perkins gives a succinct description of this strategic criterion in *The Arte of Prophecying.* It is, he says, "a certain *abridgement* or *summe* of the Scriptures, collected out of most manifest & familiar places. The parts thereof are two. The first concerneth faith, which is handled in the Apostles Creede. The second concerneth charitie or love, which is explicated in the ten Commandements." [1] Among the several assumptions implicit in this practice the most important was the simple belief that scriptural doctrine *did* comprise a unity. If the import of a passage tugged in a direction opposite to the approved consensus, it was not allowed to qualify the consensus but was manipulated into agreement.[2] Furthermore the identity of the

---

1. Perkins, *The Arte of Prophecying, The Works,* 3, 737.
2. Cf. Perkins, p. 740. "*If the native (or naturall) signification of the words doe manifestly disagree with either the analogy of faith, or very perspicuous places of the Scripture: then the other meaning which is given of the place propounded, is naturall & proper, if it agree with contrarie and like places,*" etc. Cf. also John Owen, ΣΥΝΕΣΙΣ

analogy of faith with the summary of beliefs held by the Puritan to be important was assumed to bear witness to the derivation of the latter from the former. The possibility that the analogy of faith simply represented a kind of exegetical gerrymandering, carried out to authorize practice, was not entertained. These primary assumptions are well illustrated in the following passages from John Owen. Speaking on the unity of the Word, Owen says: "In our search after truth our minds are greatly to be influenced and guided by the analogy of Faith . . . . There is a harmony, an answerableness, and a proportion, in the whole system of faith, or things to be believed. Particular places are so to be interpreted as that they do not break or disturb this order, or fall in upon their due relation to one another." [3] All the Scripture, he adds, "is from the same spring of divine inspiration, and is in all things perfectly consistent with itself." Regarding the second assumption implicit in this hermeneutical practice, Owen says: "And this *analogy* or 'proportion of faith' is what is taught plainly and uniformly in the whole Scripture as the rule of our faith and obedience." [4] Right conduct, or obedience, was conceived as consequent to the clear apprehension of the divine will, as stated in the proportion of faith. Yet it was quite possible, even if the possibility were overlooked, that favored modes of conduct—ritual, devotional, and the like—prompted the searching of Scripture for the doctrines that would confirm them.[5]

ΠΝΕΥΜΑΤΙΚΗ or, *The Causes, Ways, and Means of Understanding the Mind of God as Revealed in His Word*, *Works* (London, 1678) 4, 197. "The rule in this case is That we *affix no sense unto any obscure or difficult passage of Scripture but what is materially true and consonant unto other express and plain testimonies*" (p. 740).

3. Owen, *An Exposition of the Epistle to the Hebrews*, *Works*, *13*, 315.

4. Owen, ΣΥΝΕΣΙΣ ΠΝΕΥΜΑΤΙΚΗ, *Works*, *4*, 198.

5. Insensitivity to the reciprocal dependence of Word and practice led to the grave irony of invoking the analogy of faith when clearly it did not point to a résumé of belief which recommended itself to all men. We may make this point simply by juxtaposing a statement by Owen

If the Reformation inspired a conception of the church universal as invisible rather than visible entity, it also encouraged a conception of the unity of doctrine in the Word which rested not so much on coerced sense as upon faith. Paul Baynes, who succeeded William Perkins in the pulpit of Great St. Andrews at Cambridge, put the profession in words which suggest its underpinnings in something other than direct observation. After declaring that the law and the gospel reveal a single "matter and substance," he affirms that "the true churches of God profess one and the self-same doctrine, and therefore must hold in spiritual concord one with another." This is the case since "There is but one Christian doctrine which the visible church can embrace and hold; for God and Christ were 'yesterday, to-day, and will be the same for ever,' Heb. xiii. 8. And as the church of God hath had one, so all the churches now have one and the same." [6]

---

with one by George Tavard, a twentieth-century Catholic theologian. Says Owen, in *An Exposition of . . . Hebrews:* "Want of a due attendance unto this rule [the analogy of faith] is that which hath produced the most pestilent heresies in the church. Thus the Papists, taking up these words, 'This is my body,' without a due consideration of the analogy of faith about the human nature of Christ, the spirituality of the union and communion of believers with him, the nature of sacramental expressions and actions, which are elsewhere evidently declared, by which the interpretation, according to the apostle's rule, is to be regulated and squared, have from them fancied the monstrous figment of their transubstantiation, absolutely destructive of them all." The analogy of faith, however, says Tavard in his *Holy Writ or Holy Church* (New York, Harper and Brothers, 1959), p. 95, can be nothing less than a reflection of the consensus of believers, and it is less than clear how the Reformers paid heed to the issue of consensus. His position is in bold conflict with Owen's. "In breaking through the analogy of faith, the Reformation became neither scriptural nor traditional . . . . Only the totality of the Church's tradition, universal in time and space, guided by the inspiring presence of the Paraclete, reflected in the consciences of believers, is adequate to the totality of Scripture" (p. 316).

6. Paul Baynes, *An Entire Commentary upon the Whole Epistle of St. Paul to the Ephesians* (Edinburgh, James Nichol, 1866), p. 246.

THE UNITY OF *The Pilgrim's Progress*

With substantial motivations for assembling a body of doctrine that would be clear, harmonious, and authoritative, it is not surprising that the Puritan refined procedures for discerning latent doctrine, such as would dovetail to form the desired unity. Some attention has already been given to this in the discussion of the techniques of collection. Puritan hermeneutics never hesitated to go beyond the letter to the Word of doctrine. A representative utterance of Thomas Adams will clearly demonstrate how the freedom exercised in the quest of doctrine afforded ample opportunity to press literal meaning into a system predetermined according to the dictates of coherence. The Scripture, he says, "is the golden pot of *Manna*; the words, that is the golden pot: the sense, that is the *Manna*. It is not enough to take what offers it selfe at the first proposed; but to digge deepe. God that is rich in the veines of nature, is not poore in the veines of Scripture: excellent in the historie, more excellent in the mysterie."[7] Adams hints that a doctrinal richness in Scripture licenses a certain freedom of movement. Though his freedom was materially limited by the bias against *mythos*, the interpreter still had scope for synthesis, for pulling together compatible teachings, and the presence in Scripture of "mysterie," understood in this way, had weighty implications for mystery in human experience. If the mystery of the Word could in fact be articulated in an authoritative and coherent body of doctrine, such as Ames attempted in *The Marrow of Sacred Divinity* and Samuel Willard in his *Compleat Body of Divinity*, then the mysteries confronting man in daily experience were of no consequence. For practical purposes, the mystery of the Word cancelled the mystery of experience.

While this notion is basic to an appreciation of the dynamics of *The Pilgrim's Progress*, it runs so counter to many modern conceptions of man's relation to truth that it warrants amplification. When Christian at the story's opening asks "What must

7. Adams, *A Commentary or, Exposition upon . . . St. Peter*, p. 287.

I do to be saved?" all answers which are not present in the book he holds in his hands are presumably accessible in the person of Evangelist. Christian is of course the ectype of his creator, who can sit in Bedford Jail and, without moving from his cell, go on pilgrimage in a static exploration of the meanings of the Christian vision of truth. Truth was for Christian, for Bunyan, and for every Puritan, an *a priori* deliverance, at least in theory. And whereas the modern pilgrim sails his odyssey in the hopes of finding truth somewhere in his peregrinations, the Puritan pilgrim of the seventeenth century felt assured that truth was early and always seeking him, in the form of a revealed word. The modern reader can perhaps be forgiven for his impression that in a pilgrimage that is in large measure the exfoliation of a Word once and for all delivered, events only seem to be happening. Movement is paradoxically at once cursus and stasis. Behind event is discerned the Word, behind act the animating Truth, and the progress takes on the quality of illusion, while the static changeless truth is apprehended as reality.

We do not make this point at the expense of a commendation of Bunyan's mythic realism, but neither do we defend too simple a conception of Bunyan's relationship to Puritan practice. Bunyan knew well that the interpretive method that wrought doctrine from Scripture in Puritan hermeneutics, that delighted in reducing event to moral and action to statement, plainly undercut the dynamics of narrative. If unreduced action gave too much scope to the transient, to discrepancy, and plurality of viewpoint—the very features historical criticism, which takes the dynamic perspective for granted, does in fact discover—reduced action provided a perfected monolithic unimpeachable unity. But that unity was essentially static, devoid of the strengths as well as the weaknesses of the dynamic perspective. Bunyan is capable of qualifying this hermeneutics in his handling of scriptural event and metaphor, but it is necessary to point out that the peculiar dynamics of his narrative are indebted to the Puritan conception of reading the Word as static system. Not only is such a system present behind the action, but it is related to Christian and his pilgrimage as prevenient truth in the shape of Evangelist and the book.

This point is borne out by a nuance of Bunyan's characterization. The typical reader who, like Coleridge, finds himself following along with the characters of Christian's pilgrimage as human folk nicknamed by their neighbors is apt to be disturbed by the severity of Bunyan's handling of that "very brisk Lad" Ignorance. When Christian and Hopeful first meet him after they descend from the Hill Clear, not far from the Celestial City, it takes Christian only a moment to discover that there is little hope for the fellow. Ignorance falls behind but later rejoins the two before they reach Enchanted Ground. The conversation is heavy with remonstrance, to which Ignorance is impervious, and the last glimpse of the obtuse fellow is at the close, when Bunyan makes of him a final grim "example." The same King who receives Christian and Hopeful orders two shining ones to go out and "take *Ignorance* and bind him hand and foot, and have him away. Then they took him up, and carried him through the air to the door that I saw in the side of the Hill, and put him in there. Then I saw that there was a way to Hell, even from the Gates of Heaven, as well as from the City of *Destruction*" (p. 163). Such a summary disposition of Ignorance would certainly have occasioned no remorse for the Puritan reader, for his fate was in keeping with the Puritan conception of truth as so accessible to every man as to render inexcusable the ignorant. What is perhaps so startling in Bunyan's account is not his disposal of one deluded pilgrim named Ignorance, but the fact that he dares to disassociate his other pilgrims from this most human of traits, precipitating it out into one poor wretch and throwing it away at the last. Implicit in such a procedure is the understanding of truth, discussed above, that is integral to the unity of *The Pilgrim's Progress*. The shaping doctrine of the work has something of the imposing poise and weight of the timeless axiom or a heavenly Jerusalem delivered intact to an awed creaturedom, and such structures stand above the impeachments of time. The unity of such tranquil fabrications, is that impressive one of *a priori* deliverance. Plainly, the unity of *The Pilgrim's Progress* may be traced to its informing brief, which assumed the Word was a single structure of doctrine and religious experience a fitting witness to that structure.

The analogy of faith, of course, represented the fruitful corroboration of Word by way. The body of doctrine requiring acceptance was the Word as it had meaningfully addressed itself to the peculiar contours of Puritan life. Even if there was hesitation about admitting the reciprocal influence here, it was natural to associate ordered life with ordered doctrine. Baxter uses strong language in commenting on the association: "There are so few Christians that have a true method of faith or divinity in their understandings, even in the great points which they know disorderly, that it is no wonder if there be lamentable defectiveness and deformity, in those inward and outward duties, which should be harmoniously performed, by the light of this harmonious truth." [8] It must be apparent, however, that when ordered life and ordered doctrine were conjugate, the Word would be read as license and vindication. So in *The Pilgrim's Progress* it is impossible to disengage Word from Way, especially when the focus is the coherence of the entire work.

Whatever else it may be, the way Christian goes is a canonization of Puritan religious experience, and its unity is the historically refined wholeness of that experience. It is important to note that in Bunyan's allegory, way and wayfarer reciprocally define the other. If to be a Christian is to travel

---

8. Baxter, *The Life of Faith, The Practical Works, 12*, 390.

the way, it is equally true that the Way names the course which the Christian takes. The correct route to the Celestial City reflects, presumably, not only the *de jure* pronouncements of its King, but also the practical discoveries of pilgrims about the efficient ways to get from terminus to terminus. A review of the whole course of Christian's journey—the Slough of Despond, the Burning Mount, the little wicket gate, Interpreter's House, the two valleys, Vanity Fair, Doubting Castle, Enchanted Ground, Beulah Land, the river of death—cannot help but persuade one that in all features Bunyan sets forth the way canonized by consensus. It was the way that Puritan pilgrims did in fact travel, beset by the peculiar temptations of doubt, despair, legalism, and rationalism, encouraged by the Word, the sharing of experiences, the sweet breezes of Beulah (the land of the marriage covenant), and the vision of an eternal city discontinuous with the *civitas terenna*. The Way is as much descriptive as prescriptive.

I concede that it is natural and popular to take Christian as the classic paradigm of man the lonely voyager, the embattled individual, in contrast with Christiana of Part Two, who makes her pilgrimage as part of a churchly entourage.[9] But even as Wayfarer Christian is ingredient in tradition, one of a host whose wayfaring has helped inscribe in the landscape the road he walks. Indeed, he himself helps to define the road to be walked. To read the two parts of the allegory in close sequence is to be convinced of the multitude of ways Christian prepares the way for his wife and family. By instructive markers, by decisive victories over besetting enemies, by the impalpable influence of reputation, he transforms the way he covers. The reader can conjecture that it was the same with all pilgrims before him. Yet it is possible to fall into error here, since the basic outlines of the way were fixed before Christian came

---

9. Louis Martz, for one, points attention to this contrast in his introduction to the Rinehart edition of *The Pilgrim's Progress*.

to it and endured after he left it behind. This general shape witnessed to the *a posteriori* achieved unity of Puritan experience, serving as a containing structure for individual pilgrimage and the natural correlate of the *a priori* unity of the Word. On the one hand, the coherent Word, implied in the analogy of faith, contributes to the impression of stasis in *The Pilgrim's Progress* by functioning as the prevenient knowledge undercutting the exigency in Christian's pilgrimage as well as by providing the timeless structure of idea standing behind the flickering play of action. On the other hand, coherent experience, similarly implied in the analogy of faith, is a unifying influence upon Bunyan's narrative insofar as it insures that the Way is coherent.

While the unity of the way is humanly achieved, it is important to indicate the way in which it is also presumably dictated by God. The features of this imposition offer a close analogy with the workings and consequences of prevenient knowledge. In view of Bunyan's Calvinism, we can scarcely avoid speaking of Christian the pilgrim as one of God's elect, whose willing must sooner or later be related to the fact of prevenient and sustaining grace. But prevenient grace, like prevenient knowledge, if too evident in the springs of narrative, is likely to destroy the illusion of a dynamic career.

As Christian, the elect, goes on pilgrimage, the reader is encouraged to see that the most important criterion for judging one's prospects on the way is the condition of the will, and the inner self of the pilgrim thus becomes the real locus of conflict. Christian's success will depend on the quality of his intent rather than the external challenges that he meets. But when the locus of conflict is the will, and that will is in fact fixed by divine grace, there can be no contingency. There is, however, sufficient novelty in the implementation of divine grace, and Christian's experimental exfoliation of the divine Word, to tug the reader onward. It must be admitted, too, that

Bunyan is not at great pains to keep before the reader this element of his theological brief: Christian and the other pilgrims of the first and second parts spend no time worrying about the illusoriness of their freedom.

This scrutiny of the Word and the way and their relations to questions of coherence and dynamics in *The Pilgrim's Progress* discloses, we may observe, Bunyan's indebtedness to the Puritan understanding of the analogy of faith, which argued the unity of the Word and of the correlate Puritan experience which it illuminated and by which it was construed. An appreciation of the unity of Word and of way is basic to an understanding of the unity of Bunyan's allegory.

6

TWO DIVERGENT TRADITIONS IN PURITAN MEDITATION

The reader's first glimpse of Christian finds him in anguished meditation, standing in a field, with a book in his hand. The scene happily dramatizes a notable motif of Puritan discussions of meditation. The two Old Testament texts most often cited in justification of meditation were the first Psalm, with its description of the righteous man who reflects on the law both day and night, and the brief statement in Genesis (24:63) about Isaac's going into the field at evening to meditate. The biblical account presents Isaac's meditation as incidental to the action, which is his meeting with Rebekah, but for the defenders of formal meditation it was a sturdy evidence and was often cited as a kind of license. Isaac was a patriarch of the faith in that dawn of the world when God moved more freely among His creatures. If Isaac saw fit to improve the time with this practical support to faith, how much more should the children of a later age in which faith was seldom reinforced by sight?[1]

---

1. Cf. Richard Rogers, *Seaven Treatises* (London, 1610) p. 252. For what may be regarded as permutations of the basic image, see Baxter, *SER*, Pt. 4, p. 153, and Sibbes, *The Soules Conflict*, p. 257.

It is wholly appropriate that Bunyan's narrative should open with such a posture for the hero. In Part Two, when Prudence catechizes Christiana's boys, she says, "Especially be much in the Meditation of that Book that was the cause of your Fathers becoming a pilgrim" (p. 226). Christian's conviction of sin is the outgrowth of his meditative confrontation with an indicting Scripture. Bunyan's beginning, moreover, hints at the place of meditation in shaping the substance and method of *The Pilgrim's Progress*.

The numerous Puritan advocates of meditation made high claims for the practice, claims which reflected the conventional valuation placed upon "closing" with the Word and which encouraged widespread exercise of a particular devotional methodology. Bearing in mind the enormous significance of the Puritan sermon, one must consider seriously Bishop Ussher's statement in his *A Method for Meditation* that "every Sermon is but a preparation for meditation," [2] especially since his judgment is not uncommon. Richard Rogers can insist that "this spirituall exercise of meditation is even that which putteth life and strength into all other duties, and parts of Gods worship." [3] And Edmund Calamy makes the point with a detailed metaphor:

> The reason why *all the Sermons we hear do us no more good, is for want of Divine meditation;* for it is with Sermons as it is with meat, it is not the having of meat upon your table will feed you, but you must eat it; and not only eat it, but concoct it, and digest it, or else your meat will do you no good . . . . And *one* Sermon well digested, well meditated upon, is better than *twenty* Sermons without meditation.[4]

2. Ussher, *A Method for Meditation* (London, 1657), p. 49.
3. Rogers, loc. cit.
4. *The Art of Divine Meditation* (London, 1680), p. 31.

Meditation was by no means limited to the digesting of sermons, but it is worth noticing that Puritan homiletics, enjoying a relationship to exegesis in Puritan hermeneutics that paralleled the relationship of devotion to exegesis in Catholic hermeneutics, was of great influence in winning Puritan devotion away from its prerogative of imaginative freedom to the same rational and didactic ends which determined the hermeneutical approaches to Scripture. A literal hermeneutics, oriented toward *logos*, plainly would do much to narrow the conception of the Word which the meditative Puritan brought to his practice. Moreover, a hermeneutics which incorporated homiletics might be expected to encourage homiletical meditation. Simply stated, meditation tended to handle Scripture as homily and to conceive of its own method as that of preaching to the self. Such meditation could not sustain the kind of imaginative reading and reconstruction of the Word found in Bunyan, but it was the foil to a special development within Puritan devotion, i.e. the tradition of heavenly meditation, which did in all likelihood influence aesthetic practice. It is, moreover, of considerable relevance to two other traditions in Puritan meditation—occasional meditation and meditation on experience—which, because of their special subjects and methods, were handled as distinct entities by Puritan writers and are therefore most conveniently discussed separately in an examination of certain features of the narrative substance of *The Pilgrim's Progress*.

The Line of Joseph Hall

The central tradition in formal Puritan meditation may be said to begin with Joseph Hall, Bishop of Exeter and Norwich, who was a Puritan in theological orientation though not in church polity. In its categories and emphases, his *Art of Divine Meditation*, which first appeared in 1606 and went through two more editions by 1609, proved the source of a stream of influence that extended the length of the seventeenth century. Indeed, it is convenient to speak of "the line of Hall," since his work was appropriated wholesale by Isaac Ambrose, writing in the 1650s,[5] and Edmund Calamy, writing a generation later.[6] Besides his influence upon these major figures, which we shall examine in detail, Hall apparently had a wide influence upon minor writers, as well as upon Richard Baxter who, however, does not belong to the line of Hall as we are using the term.

Hall's treatise on meditation represents a carefully reasoned implementation of the orientation toward *logos* in the area of private devotion. Louis Martz, in *The Poetry of Meditation*, shows that Hall, who deviates from the Ignatian tradition by making no provision for use of the imagination in meditation, goes back to the pre-Ignatian Catholic writer Joannes Mauburnus in order to construct a program for exciting the affections toward holy ends. Mauburnus had borrowed in turn from the *Scala Meditationis* of Johan Wessel Gansfort.[7] The *Scala*, as a matter of fact, is an elaborate device for using the understanding as well as the affections in the process of meditation, but Hall discards the eight-point program for the understanding on the grounds that it is flawed by both "*Darkenesse* and *Coincidence*."

---

5. Isaac Ambrose's *Prima, Media, & Ultima* (London, 1654) is a most useful though little known compendium of Puritan theology and devotion. Ambrose borrowed heavily without specific acknowledgment from a number of his better known predecessors and contemporaries in keeping with the widespread Puritan practice of treating the extant works of edification as a kind of common fund of spiritual nourishment. So, while one may not be sure from what source Ambrose is borrowing at any point, he can appreciate Ambrose's work as a mid-century summary of Puritan spirituality. For convenience, we shall refer to this work hereafter simply as *PMU*.

6. *The Art of Divine Meditation*.

7. Louis Martz, *The Poetry of Meditation* (New Haven, Yale University Press, 1954), pp. 331–33.

While it is of some importance that Hall, in the first place, skipped over the whole Ignatian tradition to rediscover Mauburnus, a precursor of that tradition, it is of even greater importance that in lieu of Mauburnus "dark" program for the understanding, he should have decided to dip into the schoolboy rhetoric books of the time and to exploit nothing more nor less than "all, or the principall of those places which natural reason doth afford us." [8] These "places" are the heads of argumentation. The order as Hall gives them is: description, division, causes, fruits and effects, the subject wherein or whereabout it is, appendances and qualities, contraries, comparisons and similitudes, titles and names, testimonies.[9] The ordinary use of these heads is described well by Sister Miriam Joseph in her *Shakespeare's Use of the Arts of Language:*

> In the Renaissance, as in earlier times, educated men amplified a subject by drawing it as a matter of course through the topics of invention. The topics provide a systematic and exhaustive analysis. A definition expresses the nature or essence of the subject under discussion by telling to what class or genus it belongs and how it differs from other species within that genus. The contrary or contradictory illuminates by contrast. Comparison of the subject with members of the same species shows it to be greater, equal, or less; with those of a different species, similar or dissimilar. The subject may be considered in its parts, and in relation to its characteristics or adjuncts. One may further consider its causes, its effects, its antecedents, its consequents. Its name may reflect its nature, and re-

---

8. *The Art of Divine Meditation* (London, 1607), p. 88. Hereafter this work shall be referred to as *ADM*. Though a like abbreviation will be used for Edmund Calamy's work of the same title, the context will indicate which is meant.

9. Hall, pp. 95–145.

lated names signify related realities, as for instance, to act justly signifies that one is just or possesses justice.

From these sixteen topics intrinsic to the subject under discussion—definition, division, genus, species, contraries, contradictories, comparison, similarity, dissimilarity, adjuncts, cause, effect, antecedent, consequent, notation, and conjugates—are drawn artificial arguments, so called because they are discoverable through the art of topical investigation. Besides these there are extrinsic arguments, which are called inartificial because they do not depend upon the art of the investigator, but are furnished to him by the testimony of others.[1]

A brief comparison of the topics listed by Sister Miriam Joseph with the heads of Bishop Hall will show the remarkable degree of correspondence. The order of use of these categories was securely fixed in the rhetorical tradition of the time. Thomas Wilson in his *Rule of Reason* declares, "one question is eight waies examined, and the manner taught thereby to frame it in dewe ordre, so that he whiche kepeth wel this trade, cannot faile in any cause that he taketh in hande." He goes on to list these "eight waies."

    i. whether it be, or no.
    ii. what it is.
    iii. what the partes are.
    iiii. what the causes are.
    v. what are the effectes, or propre woorkyng.
    vi. what are next adioignyng, what are like, what happen thereby.
    vii. what dooe disagre, or what contrarie.
    viii. what example there is, or aucthoritie to prove it.[2]

---

[1]. *Shakespeare's Use of the Arts of Language* (New York, Columbia University Press, 1947), p. 308.
[2]. *The Rule of Reason* (London, 1553), fol. 17, verso.

The ordering of these questions corresponds precisely with Hall's arrangement, though Hall does not include the first and Wilson omits two of his, "appendances and qualities" and "titles and names."

In order to grasp the full significance of Hall's choice of procedure, it should be understood that he elected not to use the imagination and senses. Instead, he began the process of meditation with the understanding and chose to exploit the familiar and time-worn categories for artificial argumentation in order to insure a thorough examination of the topic at hand, before the affections were worked upon. Transparently behind this choice is the Calvinist orientation toward *logos*. The emphasis which looms largest in Hall's procedures is this demand that the subject be examined in an eminently orderly and logical fashion. The process is carefully reined in and controlled by the reason, and the suspect imagination is granted no opportunity to introduce a contraband intuition that might transcend the logical categories.

That Puritan practice on this issue owed more to a positive emphasis which displaced the use of the imagination, than to the simple working out of a prejudice against that faculty is argued by the fact that Catholicism and Puritanism did not differ in their basic evaluation of the imagination, though Catholic devotion employed the faculty in meditation. Luis de Granada in his *Sinner's Guide* observes:

> Imagination . . . is called a power of our soule, greatly weakened through sinne, & which is very haggard to be subjected unto reason. For oftentimes as a fugitive servant that departeth without licence, it rusheth out of dores, and wandereth throughout the whole world before we understand where it is. It is a faculty also very greedy, in excogitating or searching out any matter, which it hath a desire to: and it imitateth hungry doggs, who tosse and turn all things upside downe, and thrust their snowt into

every dish, now lapping of this, now of that: and although they are beate from it, yet always they returne to their repast fore-tasted. This faculty also is very glib and fleeting, as a wild and an untamed beast, flying very swiftly from one mountaine to another, least it should be taken and restrayned: for it cannot abide a bridle or a bit: neither is it willing to be governed or managed of man.[3]

A Puritan could not have stated the case more strongly, but Luis de Granada could still encourage in his treatise, *Of Prayer, and Meditation*, "After reading, it followeth that we doe Meditate upon the place that we have read. Concerninge which pointe it is to be knowen, that this Meditation is sometimes upon thinges that maie be figured with the imagination, as are al the pointes of the lyfe & Passion of our Saviour Christ."[4] The imagination, though the "fool of the household" as St. Teresa put it, might prove a useful servant in the process of meditation. The Catholic position is implicit in these words attributed to Augustine: "When any sinful Imagination sollicites me, I strait take Sanctuary in my Saviour's Wounds. When the Flesh weighs down my Soul, the remembrance of his Sufferings breaks all my Fetters, and sets me free by heavenly Thoughts again . . . . In his Wounds I can lay me down and sleep securely."[5] In this simple procedure, when the fleshly imagination distracts, one deals with the problem by putting that very faculty to work upon spiritual matters. The faculty may be marred by sin, but it can do no ill so long as it is working with the proper materials.

The obvious question is, Why did not the Puritan put the

---

3. *The Sinner's Guide*, trans. from the French by Francis Meres (London, 1614), pp. 454-55.
4. *Of Prayer, and Meditation* (Rouen, 1584), p. 595.
5. *Pious Breathings. Being the Meditations of St. Augustine, His Treatises of the Love of God, Soliloquies and Manual*, trans. George Stanhope. (6th ed. London, 1728), p. 269.

imagination into harness and tame it by using it? The answer is implicit in the Puritan orientation toward *logos*. The Reformers' need for unambiguous authority in the written Word, an authority investing specific instruction or rules, meant that when the Puritan set about meditating on the Word, he would seek for inspiration in a certain kind of subject and through a particular process; to this task the imagination constituted not so much feeble instrument to be sanctified and used despite its weakness as an utter irrelevancy. The Puritan was not likely to meditate upon events in the life of Christ but rather upon doctrines or specific propositions of Scripture. The antithesis which Thomas Hooker sets up in his *Application of Redemption* grants no scope to imagination: "To preserve our minds from windy and vain imaginations, is to have our understandings fully taken up with the blessed Truths of God as our dayly and appointed food." [6] The unseemly possibility that Hooker rules out is that the understanding might with profit be taken up with holy imaginations, as one variety or representation of "the blessed Truths of God." Shortly before, Hooker had made explicit what these Truths would be: "let thy mind be furnished and fraught with the rich and precious Promises, Commands, and Comforts of the Word; let them be ballasted with these, and they will make thy thoughts steady and setled in thy constant dayly imployments." [7]

Since imagination had no proper place in the process in which man confronted the revealed Word, the Puritan was especially chary of that kind of meditation which came to full bloom in the continental Catholic tradition. Into the tradition of Catholic meditation upon the life of Christ, imagination had entered as an integral part, the Word being regarded as an outline to be expanded upon by the imagination so that the person in

6. *The Application of Redemption. The Ninth and Tenth Books* (London, 1657), p. 232.
7. Ibid.

meditation might enter fully into the scriptural scene. This passage from St. Anselm is illustrative:

> When, therefore, your mind has been purged from tumultuous thoughts by that practical exercise of virtues, then turn your cleansed eyes back to the past, and first of all enter with blessed Mary into her chamber, and unroll the sacred books in which are foretold a virgin's maternity and the birth of Christ. Then wait, expecting the arrival of the angel, that you may see him enter, and hear him salute her; that then, transported with ecstasy and wonder, you may with the greeting angel greet Mary, thy dearest Queen.[8]

But the Puritan's earnest Calvinism obliged him to regard the event as secondary to the voice, or voices, speaking in the event. Treating the Annunciation, he would not, like Anselm, reconstruct the scene but ponder the words of Gabriel and the Magnificat. The Scripture as revealed Word offered no purchase for imagination.

Richard Greenham makes the point vigorously, in words we have quoted earlier. In meditating, "Let the word be the object, and beware of mingling it with mens devises: Psalm. 1.2.26: 119.99."[9] Moreover, "Before and in all wee must pray that the spirit may bee given us, that we neither adde nor detract, that wee goe not too farre, nor come not too short."[1] John Owen in his preface to *Meditations and Discourses on the Glory of Christ* of 1864 makes the point as effectively as it could be:

> His glory is incomprehensible, and his praises are inutterable. Some things an illuminated mind may conceive of it;

---

8. St. Anselm, *Book of Meditations and Prayers*, trans. from the Latin by M. R. London (London, Burn and Oates, 1872), p. 199.
9. *The Workes*, p. 40.
1. Ibid., p. 41.

but what we can express in comparison of what it is in itself, is even less than nothing. But as for those who have forsaken the only true guide herein, endeavouring to be wise above what is written, and to raise their contemplations by fancy and imagination above Scripture revelation (as many have done), they have darkened counsel without knowledge, uttering things which they understand not, which have no substance or spiritual food of faith in them.[2]

The invoking of imagination in contemplation was darkening counsel without knowledge. The "spiritual food of faith" did not consist of anything the imagination could provide.

Thus the Puritan's failure to use imagination in meditation may be understood to have grown out of his conviction that the way of the imagination represented an inferior way to truth, since God had revealed all the supremely important things in words. The imagination could not relay truth to the understanding as word and was therefore left unexploited. Not only did the orientation toward *logos* lead the Puritan to doctrines, promises, commands—truth of any kind so long as it could be put into words—but it involved the explicit abjuration of meditation upon revelatory events, such as the Passion. Such events were not considered open to exploration by the imagination of the meditator but were regarded as carriers of doctrines, to be appreciated by reason and faith.

If the imagination had strikingly divergent roles in Catholic and Puritan meditation, no less is to be said for the implementation of the understanding in the two traditions. The energy which the Catholic channeled into the exercise of the imagination, the Puritan diverted to the exercise of the understanding. True, the Jesuit Puente, who fits into the Ignatian tradition, anticipates Hall's use of the logical categories when he suggests the rule:

2. *The Works*, 1, 275.

with the understanding to make severall discourses, and considerations about that mysterie, inquyring, and searching out the Verities comprehended therein, with all the causes, proprieties, effectes, and circumstances that it hath, pondering them very particularly. In such sort that the Understanding may forme a true, proper, and entire concept of the thing that it meditateth, and may remaine convinced, and persuaded to receive, and to embrace, those truthes that it hath meditated, to propound them to the Will, and to move it therby to exercize its Actions.[3]

Puente makes no attempt, however, to outline a restraining and comprehensive program of meditation using the logical heads. More importantly, he employs the understanding in a role dependent upon the prior use of the imagination, which in his sequence calls up profound mysteries from the memory for contemplation. The term "mystery," except insofar as it stood for doctrine, was alien to Puritan meditation.

Though Hall finds in Mauburnus an elaborate scale for employing the understanding, it was obviously inadequate for his purposes on other counts than the darkness and coincidence which he mentions. Mauburnus supplies eight steps, but our listing of only the first two should be sufficient for making the desired point. These are "Commemoration. An actual thinking upon the matter elected," and "Consideration. A redoubled Commemoration of the same, till it be fully knowen."[4] Curiously, though Mauburnus does suggest later in his scale that the use of similitudes may help in the understanding of the subject, his description of consideration implies that the sub-

---

3. Luis de la Puente, *Meditations upon the Mysteries of our Holie Faith, with the Practise of Mental Prayer touching the same* (2 vols. St. Omer, 1619), *1*, 3–4. This is cited by Martz, p. 34.
4. Hall, p. 87. Hall furnishes a translation of the relevant section of Mauburnus' scale in the margin of his treatise.

ject will be fully known before any of the six subsequent steps are even brought into use. This inference is confirmed by the fact that his later steps, vague and overlapping, are scarcely designed as tools of analysis. The general impression given by Mauburnus' scale is that he is using the understanding, at the outset at least, much as the later Ignatian tradition made use of the imagination and memory—namely as a faculty for bringing the far-ranging and restless mind into a narrow focus, where the will can then use the mind's concentrated energies to excite the emotions. But in the Ignatian tradition, and to an even greater extent in that Puritan tradition of meditation which began with Hall, the understanding was regarded as a keen-edged blade for cutting to the heart of the subject under meditation. It did more than bring a subject into focus; it explored it thoroughly.

Hall's methodology proved immensely attractive to the Puritan mind. Its rationality and orderliness, its careful skirting of the pitfalls of intuition and imagination, and, not least important, its familiarity by virtue of its sources in the rhetoric texts of the time assured it a lasting influence. Because Hall's work was so important in dictating the main line of thought in Puritan meditation in the century, it is only proper to sketch in the direct line of his influence.

In 1654 Isaac Ambrose published a treatise on meditation as part of the second volume in his series, *Prima, Media, & Ultima: The first, Middle and Last things: in Three Treatises*. Not only did Ambrose borrow whole paragraphs from Baxter's *Saint's Everlasting Rest*, but he adopted Hall's methodology *in toto* without giving credit to his benefactor. He used the logical categories—description, distribution, causes, effects, opposites, comparisons, and testimony—as Hall had recommended (*PMU*, 2, 222), deviating only by omitting three of the heads. However, this omission is inconsequential when one considers the borrowings in his introduction, where he urges:

> That we be not too curious in prosecution of these Logical places; the end of this *Duty* is not to practise Logick, but to exercise Religion, and to kindle Piety and Devotion: Besides every theam will not afford all these places; as when we *meditate* of God, there is no room for *Causes and Comparisons:* it will therefore be sufficient; if we take the most pregnant and voluntary places. (*PMU*, 2, 222-23)

In his treatise, Hall had urged:

> That whosoever applieth himself to this direction, think him not necessarily tyed to the prosecution of all these Logical places . . . so as his Meditation should be lame and imperfect without the whole number: for ther are some Themes which wil not beare all these; as when we meditate of God, there is no roume for *Causes* or *Comparisons;* & others yeeld them with such difficultie, that their search interrupteth the chiefe work intended. It shalbe [sic] sufficient if we take the most pregnant, & voluntary. (*ADM*, pp. 91-92)

When Ambrose passes to the second stage in meditation, following use of the understanding, he says, "Concerning that part which is in the affection, it is good to follow that course which the common places of Rhetorick do lead us unto: These are six" (*PMU*, p. 223) and proceeds to list the six steps which Hall had given under procedures for the affections. Though one can only guess about Ambrose's motives for ascribing his steps to the rhetorical tradition instead of to Hall, the six steps—relish, complaint, wish, confession, petition, confidence —do *not* occur as commonplaces in the rhetoric books of the time. They are a patent borrowing from Hall, who had borrowed them from Mauburnus, who had borrowed them from Gansfort.

In his *Art of Divine Meditation*, published in 1680, Edmund

Calamy, whose name may be remembered for having provided the "e" and the "c" in "Smectymnuus," borrows heavily from Hall, too. In giving his rules for proceeding with the understanding, he says:

> Now here I must tell you I shall be somewhat difficult and hard to be understood, this is the knottiest and difficultest part of Meditation; and therefore learned men that write of this subject, that labour to teach the art of *Divine Meditation*, do give in nine *common-place-heads*, as so many several ways of the enlarging the understanding in the consideration of the Truths that they meditate upon. (*ADM*, p. 176)

By combining two of Hall's categories, he devises nine steps instead of ten, but his indebtedness is apparent here and also in his borrowing of Hall's program for the affections. However, while Calamy certainly belongs to the line of Hall, it is plain that he does not feel perfectly at ease with Hall's categories. He attempts to reveal the practical value of meditation for the man of little education, and in presenting Hall's steps, he repeatedly excuses himself for offering something so difficult by noting that he is borrowing from "learned men." After supplying Hall's program for both the understanding and the affections, Calamy continues:

> Now because these *Logical heads* are somewhat difficult, I will give you some *plainer rules*, for helping ordinary Christians, those that are babes in the school of Grace, and are not able to enlarge their thoughts upon any subject; I will give you briefly five easie Rules to help you to enlarge your thoughts upon what *subjects* you chuse to meditate on. (*ADM*, p. 184)

Calamy's move toward a simplification of Hall is significant. He pays his respect to what has become an established tradition by giving it a superficial coverage, but he is not content to leave it unrevised. With the Restoration, of course, there came a profound change in the intellectual temper of Puritanism. The Puritan who refused to be assimilated into a society dedicated to moderation found himself and his children denied access to the institutions of public learning. Nonconformity ceased to attract and enlist the services of the intellectually elite, and the Puritan readership declined in sophistication.

Heavenly Meditation

Had the Puritan orientation toward *logos* never been qualified, Bunyan might have had sufficient inspiration, and license, to write pedestrian sequels to his *Solomon's Temple Spiritualized*—perhaps a *Bedford Jail Spiritualized*—since the considerable talent for unimaginative "spiritualizing" cultivated by the Puritan displayed itself both in the discernment of elaborate typology in unlikely spots in the Old Testament and in the reading of the individual life as a detailed commentary upon Scripture. But a Bunyan wholly committed to *logos* would have produced a drastically truncated *Pilgrim's Progress*, if he had produced one at all. The qualification of prevailing attitudes which renders explicable Bunyan's achievement came in a tradition in Puritan meditation sharply divergent from the line of Hall.

Though the Puritan's pilgrimage was given shape by his vision of heaven, it was only too easy for vision to decay into heuristic fiction, the celestial spires fading out among the wavering verticals of common day. Understandably, the conception of life as pilgrimage was only as coercive as the vision of its end. Christian, we recall, is taken to the summit of the Hill Clear for a glimpse of the distant Celestial City, much as Moses was shown the promised land from the top of Mount Pisgah. We can be sure that had his vision of the end ever dimmed, not even the powerful energies of his revulsion from the City of Destruction would have been enough to prod him safely through his many hazards, which included Enchanted Ground, that slumberous graveyard for pilgrims who had safely escaped the perils of their origins but had forgotten what they were striving for.

The Puritan literature on heaven is enormous, the natural outgrowth of that paradoxical Christian asceticism which to an Oriental eye might perhaps not be construed as asceticism at all, since renunciation appears as an abbreviated prologue and way to an eternal banquet. The literature is plainly designed to keep the anticipated reward ever new and attractive to the wayfarer. Isaac Ambrose avows:

> Did we but think on this glorious place, wherein are those heavenly mansions prepared for us, did we spend many thoughts upon it, and ever and anon sigh and seek after it, untill we came to the fingering and possession of it; O how would these heavenly *meditations* ravish our souls, as if Heaven entred into us, before we entred into Heaven! (*PMU, 3,* 227–28)

And the pleasure derived was no end but constituted rather the quickening of objectives.

The utility of such practice is clearly set out by Sibbes: "The life of a Christian is wondrously ruled in this world, by the consideration, and meditation of the life of another world." Nothing does more to steer the course of the Christian than careful consideration of the life to come. It disposes and frames a man to all courses that are good. "There is no grace of the spirit (in a manner)," Sibbes says, "But it is set on worke by the consideration of the estate that is to come, no not one." [5] Certainly, "if we have interest in Christ, who is in glory 'at the right hand of God,'" our souls will be raised to heaven "in our affections before we be there in our bodies." [6]

5. *A Glance of Heaven* (London, 1638), p. 88.
6. *Light from Heaven* (London, 1638), p. 194.

The consummation which the Puritan pursued in his pilgrimage was an end perfectly capable of reducing all antecedent experience to the status of means, and in so uncomplicated a circumstance lies the clue to an understanding of how developments in Puritan meditation reinstated the imagination as a faculty worthy of respect, germane to the reading of experience and Word. The crucial doctrine that the sincere pilgrim did not allow himself to "love" any earthly thing but found for every earthly thing some use was implemented in the tradition of heavenly meditation, which sees its finest embodiment in the work of Richard Sibbes and Richard Baxter. But when remembered experience was used, not as instruction, but as foretaste of heavenly experience, with the intent of making the heavenly goal more winsome, it was natural that the faculty for reproducing experience in affective dress, i.e. the imagination, would be deployed and sanctioned.

Significantly, Baxter's treatise on meditation, which constituted Part Four of his *Saint's Everlasting Rest*, is actually a treatise on "Heavenly Meditation," as the reader who looks no further than the separate title page for Part Four will gather. While Baxter courts his audience by declaring that he expands upon an "Excellent unknown Duty," the truth is that he is moving within a tradition of program and emphasis to which virtually every Puritan writer on meditation contributed and which developed explicit respect for the imagination at the hands of Richard Sibbes, whose *Soules Conflict* was almost certainly an inspiration for Baxter. In his ground-breaking work, *The Poetry of Meditation*, Louis Martz gives deserved attention to Baxter's role in bringing Puritan meditation closer in practice to Catholic meditation, yet Baxter's amplification of "heavenly" meditation is part of a tradition in which that rapprochement was taking place well before he gave it the thrust of his genius. Martz's suggestion that Baxter's work must be relevant to Bunyan's work of a generation later is a sound one.[7] The exploration of that relevance, however, takes one back to the beginnings of those developments to which Baxter gave special impetus.

The Puritan saw the present world as a realm of means. Bishop Hall could exclaim that Christianity had taught the believer nothing if he had not learned this. One must learn to be a hermit at home. "Begin with your own heart; estrange and wean it from the love, not from the use of the world."[8] The preservation of such an attitude was surely demanding, and much experience was undoubtedly prevented from assuming its proper aesthetic fulness, since such fulness has a distressing way of claiming finality of a sort. But virtue could be made of grim necessity. While one steadfastly refused to rest in the immediate, he could cultivate forbearance and love of the transcendent ends. One might learn love for the Giver by refusing to love the gifts. As Sibbes indicates, "If we walk aright in God's ways, let us have heaven daily in our eye, and the day of judgment, and times to come, and this will stern the course of our lives, and breed love in the use of means, and patience to undergo all conditions."[9] He goes on to warn that a man may be sure he loves the world if he is more concerned about acquiring than "using," but the question that arises is, of course, how certain experiences are to be *used*. The sensuous world forces itself upon one in a thousand and one ways—fragrances, tastes, textures, cadences. To such a basic question as whether one could in fact make use of the unreduced experience of smelling a rose, heavenly meditation sanguinely answered, "Yes." The enjoyment of the rose might be taken as a forecast of what the enjoyment of heavenly blooms might be. Thus all earthly pleasures were prophecies, and all earthly pains, foils.

7. Martz, pp. 172–73.
8. *Epistles, The Sixth Decade, Works*, ed. Philip Wynter (8 vols. London, Oxford University Press, 1863), 6, 284.
9. *Divine Meditations, Works*, 7, 189.

One of the two books which Bunyan's wife brought as dowry to the conjugal home was Bishop Lewis Bayly's *Practice of Pietie*, a chunky compendium of devotional aids that touches, among a host of other matters, upon heavenly mindedness. The construction Bayly imposes upon immediate experience is conventional: "And if our loving God hath . . . provided us so many excellent delights, for our passage through this *Bochim*, or valley of teares; what are those pleasures which he hath prepared for us, when we shall enter into the *Palace* of our *Masters joy?*"[1] In an antecedent discussion, Bayly shows how such meditation might proceed, though his references to the heavenly life are indirect, the explicit reference being to heaven's sovereign: "When wee taste things that are deliciously *sweet*, let us say to our selves, O how *sweete* is that God, from whom *all* these creatures have received this *sweetnesse!* When wee behold the admirable colours which are in Flowers and Birds, and the lovely *Beautie of Women:* let us say, How *Faire* is that God, that made these so faire!"[2]

Further illustration of how experience could be used to promote heavenly-mindedness is provided by Thomas Adams, the silver-tongued Puritan preacher referred to by Southey as a prose Shakespeare. Adams tells of his reading:

> That a reverend Preacher sitting among other Divines, and hearing a sweet consort of Musicke as if his soule had been borne up to Heaven, tooke occasion to thinke and speake thus; *What Musicke may we thinke there is in Heaven? A friend of* mine viewing attentively the great pompe and state of Court, on a solemne day, spake not without some admiration: *What shall we thinke of the glory in the Court of God?* Happy object, and well observed, that betters the soule in grace.[3]

1. *The Practice of Pietie* (London, 1628), p. 152.
2. Ibid.
3. *The Sinners Passing-Bell, Works*, p. 253.

Sibbes and Baxter, coming later, with a more programmatic approach to heavenly-mindedness, and giving overt recognition to the imagination in its responsible involvement, both defend this use of experience. Both, indeed, employ the strikingly apt metaphor of the grapes of Kadesh-Barnea. Sibbes observes in his *A Glance of Heaven* (1638): "So that by a grape wee may know what Canaan is: as the spies, they brought of the grapes of *Canaan* into the desert: we may know by this little taste, what those excellent things are." [4] And Baxter exhorts: "Thus take thy *heart* into the *Land of Promise;* shew it the pleasant hills, and fruitful valleys; Shew it the clusters of Grapes which thou hast gathered; & by those convince it that it is a blessed Land, flowing with better then milk and honey" (*SER*, Pt. 4, p. 205). He later makes his point in more detail:

> Judge of the Lion by the Paw, and of the Ocean of Joy, by that drop which thou hast tasted: .... Hath not God sometime revealed himself extraordinarily to thy soul, and let a drop of glory fall upon it? Hast thou not been ready to say, O that it might be thus with my soul continually, and that I might alwaies feel what I feel sometimes! ... Why think with thy self then, what is this earnest to the full Inheritance? Alas, all this light that so amazeth, and rejoyceth me, is but a Candle lighted from Heaven, to lead me thither through this word of darkness! (*SER*, Pt. 4, pp. 241–42)

These statements explicitly yoke the images of pilgrimage and reward which we have noted as basic to the rationale of heavenly-mindedness.

Such a sampling of Puritan statements upon the "heavenly" use of experience in one's pilgrimage can do no more than hint at how the devotional practice encouraged a recovery of

4. Sibbes, pp. 72–73.

the imagination. But since it is not really until the work of Sibbes that we find overt recognition of what heavenly-minded meditation implied for the imagination, we shall conveniently take up the achievement of Sibbes and Baxter together under a separate rubric. In them the problematic relationship of *love* to *use* is clarified, and the imagination is carefully set to work. The perils in counterposing the love of and the use of creaturely experience are plain: if one was too careful not to love, the experience was apt to be truncated, the pleasure dissipated, and the circumstance no real foretaste of heavenly life. Indeed, it seemed impossible to *use* experience while one was an engrossed subject, for action and moral reflection interfere with one another. The vital clarification needed was the observation that heavenly use belongs to the imaginative *recall* of experience and does not constitute a restraint preventing the experience proper from attaining to its natural plenitude. To call up past experience in the fulness of feeling which could effectively forecast heavenly experience plainly required exercise of the imagination, and this fact is grasped in the work of Sibbes and Baxter. As a by-product, the conception of Scripture as *logos* is significantly qualified. Once they had brought imagination into employ, it was perfectly natural for these writers to turn to scriptural experience which in imaginative reconstruction might augment the reader's own experience as foretaste of heaven. And there were no limits upon what scriptural event might prove relevant to this program of imaginative reconstruction.

As an introduction to the achievement of Sibbes and Baxter in this connection, and as a needed qualification of widespread beliefs about the absence of meditation on the earthly life of Christ in Puritanism, we may take up the case of heavenly meditation as a spur to the imaginative recovery of Christ's human life. Louis Martz, citing Helen White, points out that Puritanism by and large manifested very little interest in the human aspect of the Incarnation.[5] Roger Sharrock observes that Christ in his human nature plays little part in Puritan piety.[6] Conceding these observations as statements about comparative emphasis, we may note that the significant exceptions to this general picture appear, where they might be expected, in heavenly meditation.

Sibbes' most pointed discussion of the imaginative recovery of the life of Christ as an adjunct to heavenly-mindedness comes in his work *Light from Heaven* (1638):

> [A]s the soule of man is first sinfull, and then sanctified; first humble, and then raysed: so our meditations of Christ must be in this order; first, thinke of Christ, as abased and crucified: for, the first comfort that the soul hath, is in Christ *manifested in the flesh*, before it come to *received up into glory*. Therefore, if we would have comfortable thoughts of this, Christ *received up in glory*, thinke of him first *manifest in the flesh*: let us have recourse in our thoughts to Christ, in the wombe of the Virgin; to Christ borne, and lying in the Manger; going up and downe, doing good; hungring and thirsting, suffering in the Garden, sweating water and bloud, nayled on the Crosse, crying to his Father, *My God, my God, why hast thou forsaken me;* finishing all upon the Crosse, lying three dayes in the Grave: have recourse to Christ thus abased, and all for us, to expiate our sinne; he obeyed God, to satisfie for our disobedience. Oh, here will be comfortable thoughts for a wounded soule, pierced with the sense of sinne, assaulted by Satan: To thinke thus of Christ, abased for our sinnes; and then, to thinke of him taken *up into glory*. . . . Then thinke of Christ in heaven, appearing

5. Martz, p. 163.
6. *John Bunyan* (London, Hutchinson's University Library, 1954), p. 77.

there for us, keeping that happinesse that he hath purchased by his death for us, and applying the benefit of his death to our soules by his Spirit.[7]

Such meditations, Sibbes assures his reader, are vital to heavenly-mindedness. Indeed, the glorification of the Incarnate Lord was designed to turn man's thoughts heavenward: "Againe, the *Mysterie* [sic] of Christs *Glory* it tends to *godlinesse* in this respect, to stirre us up to heavenly-mindedness. . . . We are for Heaven, and not for this world: this is but a passage to that *glory*, that Christ hath taken up for us; and therefore, why should we have our minds groveling here upon the Earth?"[8] In this particular emphasis upon visualizing the Incarnate Lord glorified in order to bring the place of His glorification nigh, Sibbes is so closely echoed by Baxter that there is a hint of indebtedness. One might consider these passages. Sibbes declares:

> In this manner, and order, we shall have comfortable thoughts of Christ. To thinke of his *glory* in the first place, it would dazle our eyes, it would terrifie us, being sinners, to thinke of his *glory*, being now ascended: but when we thinke of him as descended first, as he sayth, *Who is he that ascended, but he that descended first into the lower parts of the Earth?* So, who is this that is taken up in glory; is it not he that was *manifest in our flesh* before? This will be comfortable.[9]

And Baxter states:

> To conceive no more of God and Glory, but that we cannot conceive them; and to apprehend no more, but that they are past our apprehension; will produce no more

---

7. *Light from Heaven*, pp. 197–98.
8. Ibid., p. 194.
9. Ibid., pp. 198–99.

love but this, To acknowledge that they are so far above us that we cannot love them; and no more Joy but this, That they are above our rejoycing. And therefore put Christ no further from you, then he hath put himself, least the Divine Nature be again inaccessible. Think of Christ as in our own nature glorified; think of our fellow Saints as men there perfected; think of the City and State, as the Spirit hath expressed it, (only with the Caution and Limitations before mentioned). (*SER*, Pt. 4, pp. 219–20)

Baxter, to be sure, could scarcely have picked a finer mentor to emulate and echo. Richard Sibbes is one of the most attractive spirits among Puritan divines of the seventeenth century. In his own day he was known as an astute physician of souls, talented in the presentation of the comforts which the Scriptures had to offer the troubled. His special genius was ministering to the anxieties of those unsure of Election. Baxter refers to him as "that comfortable Doctor" (*SER*, Pt. 3, p. 167) with good reason. A concordance to his works would certainly show an astonishing frequency of occurrence for the word "comfort," and it may be noted that the adjectival form appears twice in the brief passage quoted above. In his immensely popular treatise *The Bruised Reed*, which saw six editions between 1630 and 1638, Sibbes turned the brilliant stroke of making the doubter's very uncertainties evidence of God's special interest by making use of the scriptural statement about the bruised reed's going untrampled. Another sermon of his, *Bowels Opened*, was responsible for the spiritual awakening of Baxter, according to the latter's own testimony.

The Soules Conflict, of special interest to us in the present context, was first published in 1635, and it proved popular enough to warrant three further editions by the end of 1638 and two more in 1651 and 1658. Like a host of other Puritan treatises, the work was a prolonged exposition upon a passage of Scripture, in this case the fifth verse of the forty-second psalm: "Why art thou cast down, O my soul? and why art thou disquieted in me? hope thou in God: for I shall yet praise him for the help of his countenance." Sibbes' elaborate exposition is concerned with a topic of enormous interest to the Puritan Christian, the civil war fought in the soul, and cites the sundry encouragements and stratagems which the Christian can make use of in the war. A work that combined an anatomy of the soul with the pastoral end of good counsel not unnaturally faced the question of how the unruly faculty of soul, imagination, was to be handled. In a lengthy and closely reasoned chapter on the imagination, Sibbes provided what is probably the first detailed engagement with the subject in seventeenth-century Puritanism.

After cataloguing the general varieties of sin that imagination can lead one into, Sibbes takes a new tack in argument by observing, "Sometimes, the ministring of some *excellent thought* from what wee *heare* or *see*, proves a great advantage of spirituall good to the soule." [1] A moment later he declares:

> One seasonable truth falling upon a prepared heart, hath oftentimes a sweet and strong operation; *Luther* confesseth that having heard a grave Divine *Staupicius* say, that *that is kinde repentance which begins from the love of God*, ever after that time the practice of repentance was sweeter to him. This speech of his likewise tooke well with *Luther*, that in doubts of *predestination wee should beginne from the wounds of Christ*, that is, from the sense of Gods love to us in Christ, wee should arise, to the grace given us in *election before the world was*. (*SC*, pp. 255–56)

The curious commentary, an insistence that the evocative thought, beginning with the "wounds of Christ," must be

---

1. *The Soules Conflict*, p. 253. Hereafter the title will be abbreviated to *SC* and references noted in the text.

swallowed up in the appropriate Calvinistic formula, shows that Sibbes is Puritan, but his expansion upon the efficacy of "seasonable truth" shortly leads him onto new ground:

> The putting of *lively* colours upon *common* truthes hath oft a strong working both upon the *fancy*, and our *will* and *affections:* the spirit is *refreshed* with *fresh* things, or old truthes *refreshed;* this made the Preacher *seeke* to finde out *pleasing* and *acceptable words;* and our Saviour Christs manner of *teaching* was, by a lively *representation* to mens *fancies*, to teach them heavenly truths in an earthly sensible manner; and indeed what doe wee *see* or *heare*, but will yeeld matter to a holy heart to raise it selfe higher?
>
> Wee should make our *fancie* serviceable to us in *spirituall* things. (*SC*, p. 256)

Sibbes' argument is the inevitable one, though it is surprising that Jesus' failure to measure up to Puritan norms regarding use of the imagination was noted by so few.

Sibbes then makes his point in detail:

> Seeing God hath condescended to represent *heavenly* things to us under *earthly* termes, we should follow Gods dealings herein: God represents *heaven* to us, under the term of a banquet, and of a *kingdome*, &c. our *union* with Christ under the term of a *mariage*, yea, Christ himselfe, under the name of whatsoever is *lovely* or *comfortable* in heaven or earth. So the Lord sets out *hell* to us by whatsoever is terrible or tormenting. Here is a large field for our imagination to walke in, not onely without *hurt*, but with a great deale of spirituall *gaine;* If the wrath of a *King* be as the *roaring* of a Lion, what is the wrath of the *King of Kings?* If *fire* be so terrible, what is *hell* fire? If a darke *dungeon* bee so lothsome, what is that *eternall* dungeon of darknes? If a *feast* be so pleasing, what is the

continuall feast of a good conscience? If the meeting of *friends* be so comfortable, what will our meeting together in heaven be? The *Scripture* by such like termes, would help our *faith* and *fancie* both at once; a sanctified *fancie* will make every creature a *ladder to heaven.* (SC, pp. 257–58)

It is interesting that Martz, in suggesting that Baxter provided a methodology for Bunyan to follow in writing *The Pilgrim's Progress*, quotes the following passage from *The Saints Everlasting Rest:*

> There is yet another way by which we may make our senses here serviceable to us; and that is, By comparing the objects of Sense with the objects of Faith; and so forcing Sense to afford us that *Medium,* from whence we may conclude the transcendent worth of Glory, By arguing from sensitive delights as from the less to the greater. (*SER*, Pt. 4, p. 221)

But this "comparing the objects of Sense with the objects of Faith" is precisely the procedure that Sibbes was urging fifteen years earlier, providing what is perhaps the first important consolidation of insights native to the tradition of heavenly meditation that are relevant to Bunyan's use of the imagination. Sibbes' case for the imagination, indeed, is the fitting elaboration of the implications of the world seen as means, but it opens the door to a sacramentalism which is something more: "Whilest the soule is joyned with the body, it hath not only a *necessary* but a *holy* use of *imagination,* and of *sensible* things whereupon our imagination worketh; what is the use of the *Sacraments,* but to help our *soules* by our *senses,* and our *faith* by *imagination;* as the soule receives much hurt from imagination, so it may have much good therby" (SC, pp. 258–59). The concession Sibbes makes regarding the joining of soul with body and regarding the use of "sensible things" means that at least one Puritan could appraise his stance and discern that the current orientation toward *logos* left much out of account. If this awareness never broadened into the holy absorption in the creatures which Anglican devotion was capable of, it at least hinted the legitimacy of such sacramentalism.

In *The Saints Everlasting Rest*, Baxter candidly witnesses to his acquaintance with *The Soules Conflict*, though his overt references to it are limited to a discussion of Christian assurance in Part 3.[2] Later Baxter takes an insight which he shares with Sibbes, and which in all probability he derived from him, and elaborates it into a methodology of meditation. In Part 4, after a lengthy exposition of the process of "consideration" or debate with the self, his point of departure for a chapter entitled "Some Advantages and Helps for raising and affecting the Soul by this Meditation" is presented thus:

> It is no easie matter to rejoyce at this which we never saw, nor never knew the man that did see it; and this upon a meer promise which is written in the Bible; and that when we have nothing else to rejoyce in, but all our sensible comforts do fail us: But to rejoyce in that which we see and feel, in that which we have hold of, and possession already; this is not difficult. Well then, what should be done in this case? Why sure it will be a point of our Spiritual prudence, and a singular help to the furthering of the work of Faith, to call in our Sense to its assistance: If we can make us friends of these usual enemies, and make them instruments of raising us to God, which are the

---

2. *SER*, Pt. 3, pp. 157–68. It was Christian assurance, of course, about which Sibbes spoke with such widely conceded grace and authority. The topic was a natural one upon which Baxter might admit indebtedness, in a time when the admission of debt was a matter seldom troubled with.

usual means of drawing us from God, I think we shall perform a very excellent work. (*SER*, Pt. 4, p. 217)

It is true that Baxter turns to the senses and the imagination only after he has proved to himself that the trusted faculties of reason and faith cannot guarantee him all that he demands of meditation. Even after he makes his concession to the senses, his methodology is dominated by an extraordinary emphasis upon rational argumentation, and his meticulous subordination of the senses to the reason testifies to the larger orientation within which he is making his concession. But the novelty of his maneuver is evidenced by his willingness to approach the Scripture as *mythos*. Asking for careful use of the descriptive phrases of Scripture relevant to the meditated subject, he remarks:

> But what is my scope in all this? . . . that we make use of these phrases of the Spirit to quicken our apprehensions & affections, but not to pervert them; and use these low notions as a Glass, in which we must see the things themselves, though the representation be exceeding imperfect, till we come to an immediate and perfect sight; yet still concluding, that these phrases, though useful, are but borrowed and improper. (Pt. 4, pp. 218-19)

Baxter is moving toward acceptance of *mythos* as a subject for meditation, but he has perhaps not escaped a certain bondage to the Word. Imagination is not free to fashion details in filling out the scene so that the meditator can enter wholly into the scene contemplated, as in Ignatius' *Exercises* or Fray Luis de Granada's meditations. Such meditations never achieve that sharpness of focus which is to be found in the Ignatian tradition, primarily because Baxter's intent, to hint at the qualities of heavenly life, presents problems in imaginative construction which are alien to Ignatian meditation on the human life of Christ.

However fully he remained bound to the explicit statement of Scripture, Baxter, like Sibbes, seems to have slipped outside conventional attitudes and to have seen the orientation toward *logos* clearly enough to criticize it. At the center of Baxter's turn toward the senses is the suspicion that revealed knowledge is rather empty without a grounding in the sensory references of the words used. He observes:

> Those conceivings and expressions which we have of Spirits, and things meerly Spiritual, they are commonly but second Notions, without the first; but meer names that are put into our mouths, without any true conceivings of the things which they signifie; or our conceivings which we express by those notions or terms, are meerly negative; what things are not, rather than what they are: As when we mention [Spirits] we mean they are not corporeal substances, but what they are we cannot tell, no more then we know what is *Aristotles Materia Prima*. (SER, Pt. 4, p. 218)

Because this is the case, Baxter is willing to improve conceivings of spiritual matters by enriching abstract terminology with the sensory suggestiveness of scriptural usage. This might not increase the content of truth in such conceivings, but assuredly makes them more useful in the practical matter of exciting spiritual-mindedness.

Baxter, one suspects, has discerned the semantic legerdemain which the Puritan theory of revelation involved. When words rather than events were taken as the vehicle and locus of revelation, with their special merits for the office consisting in large measure of their supposed freedom from the ambiguity of event, the word was in effect robbed of the primary reference which nourished it, given a secondary transcendent reference which was chaste and vacuous. *Spirit* could mean very little when it was separated from the world of wind and breath and the host of meanings, centering in invisible and mysterious agency, those relevant images evoke. Quite understandably, heavenly realities were emasculated in such "second Notions," as Baxter complains.

Between Baxter and Bunyan, an interesting minor figure appears in the tradition of heavenly meditation. The observations of Henry Lukin, whose *Introduction to the Holy Scripture* (1669) has been cited earlier, are noteworthy because they show the currency of the attitudes we have been discussing, at the very time Bunyan was writing *The Pilgrim's Progress*. Lukin says boldly:

> There is nothing more ordinary in Scripture, then to represent *Spiritual* things by *natural*, that we may more clearly apprehend them: all our knowledge beginning at our *senses*. Indeed if we have onely the *Protasis* without the *Apodosis;* or Metaphors and Similitudes without any *Explication* of them, they remain dark and difficult, *Matth.* 13.10, 11. but the Scriptures shewing the *Analogy*, which is between *Natural* things, and Spiritual; and how *the invisible things of God are clearly seen, and understood, from the things that are made*, Rom. 1. 20. they are thereby much illustrated, and made more intelligible, *John* 3.12. *we are likewise more lively affected with such things as are represented to our senses*, Lam 3.51. and this is also a great help to *Heavenly Meditation*, & a singular means to maintain in our thoughts a remembrance of Spiritual things.[3]

Lukin does not develop his observations, but the fact that he presents his comment upon using the senses in heavenly meditation as something of a commonplace, a point that does not need elaboration for the reader, is suggestive. Within the tradition of heavenly meditation, the concession to sense

3. Lukin, p. 101.

and imagination, so foreign to Puritanism at large, was by this time conventional.

Having adumbrated the significant developments within heavenly meditation which have some bearing on the work of Bunyan, we can now turn to specific critical problems raised by *The Pilgrim's Progress*, whose full title, we recall, identifies the pilgrimage as one from "THIS WORLD, TO That which is to come." Bunyan the allegorist was also Bunyan the heavenly-minded, and the emphases and methods of heavenly meditation are conspicuously relevant to the narrative he develops.

7

MEDITATION AND BUNYAN'S IMAGINATIVE REALISM

Bunyan and the Imagination

The Pilgrim's Progress presents itself as a sequence of pictures—a wicket gate, a grim valley, a hostel, a fair, a river edged on the far side by light—and its episodes loom in memory more as image than idea. The fact that the allegorical involvements of the imagery of Bunyan's masterwork always seem of secondary importance is clear witness to the origins of the work in a powerful imagination. Our effort here is to explicate its indebtedness to the developments in Puritan meditation that reclaimed that faculty.

The distinction between image and idea is of course homologous with that between *mythos* and *logos*, between the fruits of imagination and those of reason, and, to broach the several important issues of the ensuing discussion it is convenient to cite, and qualify, certain remarks of Perry Miller:

> By temperament and by deliberate intention the Puritan was less of an "imagist" than the Anglican and more of an "allegorist." He was not insensible to beauty or sublimity, but in the face of every experience he was obliged to ask himself, What does this signify? What is God say-

ing to me at this moment? . . . The result in Puritan writing was an insistent literalness that sometimes, to our eyes, verges on the pedantic; but at its best, as in John Bunyan, achieves a realism that is at the same time an implicit symbolism, becasue the plain statement of fact vibrates with spiritual overtones. The concreteness of *Pilgrim's Progress* and *Mr. Badman*, where a great wealth of observation is employed directly for thematic assertion, is the supreme achievement of this Puritan esthetic.[1]

The observation that the Puritan was less the "imagist" and more the "allegorist" than the Anglican, points up the Puritan's basic orientation toward *logos*. To appreciate a circumstance as a congeries of images was to approach it as *mythos;* but to route its meaning through the reducing valve of the question, "What is God saying to me at this moment?" was to demand meaning that could be verbalized. Miller is certainly correct in suggesting that this reduction of experience to the letter of doctrine eventuated in "an insistent literalism" in Puritan writing. However, the nexus between Puritan literalism and Bunyan's imaginative realism is not axiomatic. Miller's defense of Bunyan's work as the supreme product of Puritanism's allegorical temper, a temper which presumably set it apart from Anglican "imagism," disregards the organic relationship between its realism and its imagery. Bunyan was, like the Anglican, capable of appreciating experience for its images, and the assumption that the allegorical temper which, on the one hand, resulted in an "insistent literalness" received, on the other hand, its finest expression in his realism slights the significant function of the imagination in the creation of realistic narrative. The characteristic Puritan procedure of extracting from objects and events significance that could be verbalized is quite distinct from the process wherein objects

1. *Images or Shadows*, p. 4.

and events are grasped and relished by the imagination and memorialized on the page as images. Since Puritanism rejected the truth of the image and condemned the imagination, the supposition that the "allegorizing" of phenomena might after all provide the writer with a host of images for his use in fashioning realistic fiction renders the distinction between "allegorist" and "imagist" problematic if not meaningless. Miller presumably adduces a nexus between "allegoristic" literalism and the realism of Bunyan's best work simply because he is unaware of the development in Puritan meditation which opened the way for the appreciation both of Scripture and experience as the source of affective images as well as of doctrine.

We have noted that in heavenly meditation the memory functioned as a reservoir of imagery that preserved experience in order to make possible the edifying reenactment basic to the appreciation of experience as foretaste. In his Apology Bunyan relates memory and the imagination in a way that suggests the rationale provided by meditation, but before citing his statement, certain remarks of William Perkins, who speaks for the mainstream of Puritanism in vilifying the image as datum to be preserved in memory, can be presented as foil: Discussing the committing of sermon to memory in his *Arte of Prophecying*, Perkin observes:

> Artificiall memorie, which standeth upon places and images, will very easily without labour teach how to commit sermons to the memorie: but it is not to be approoved. . . . The animation of the image, which is the key of memory, is impious; because it requireth absurd, insolent and prodigious cogitations, and those especially which set an edge upon and kindle the most corrupt affections of the flesh.[2]

2. *Works*, 3, 758.

It is not difficult to surmise that the "cogitations" Perkins is implicating are the workings of the "sensitive" rather than the rational soul, those that deal with images, which show the taint of their fleshly origin, rather than with words and statements, which escape such taint. When Perkins suggests a proper method for memorization, his statement is further indication of Puritan taste in the matter of confronting truth: he urges that the minister "diligently imprint in his minde by the helpe of disposition either axiomaticall, or syllogisticall, or methodicall the severall proofes and applications of the doctrines, the illustrations of the applications, and the order of them all." The following lines from Bunyan's Apology may be contrasted with Perkins' remarks:

> Come, Truth, although in Swadling-clouts, I find
> Informs the Judgement, rectifies the Mind,
> Pleases the Understanding, makes the Will
> Submit; the Memory too it doth fill
> With what doth our Imagination please.
>
> (p. 5, 11. 9–13)

For Bunyan, who suggestively links imagination with memory, truth, stored in memory and pleasing to the imagination, is in one of its species the truth of experience reconstructed in meditation. But for Perkins memory was, properly, an adjunct to the reason, rather than to the imagination.

Indeed Bunyan associates memory and imagination in a way that suggests that he often preserved experience as image rather than verbal construct, and this tendency is confirmed by the evidence of his work, which, as has often been observed, was created in terms of imagery. As Henri Talon put it: "Far from labouring his effects, Bunyan thought in images. He never really grasped his idea until he saw it personified; and so Biblical metaphors came to populate—literally—the universe he created."[3] That Bunyan's creative process was in large part the manipulation of images is supported by the evidence that he actually heard and saw what he was creating and expected the same to hold true for his readers. In his Apology he had affirmed:

> This Book it chaulketh out before thine eyes
> The man that seeks the everlasting prize.
> (p. 6, 11. 23-24)

And indeed the narrative is vividly visualized. In the opening scene of the narrative, for example, Bunyan says: "I dreamed, and behold, *I saw a Man cloathed with Raggs, standing in a certain place, with his face from his own House, a Book in his hand, and a great burden upon his back.* I looked, and saw him open the Book, and Read therein; and as he read, he wept and trembled" (p. 8). The first sentence limns out a silent tableau, confronting the reader with one of the most gripping images of the whole book: a man standing alone in a field, in meditation. The composition is static for only a moment, however, for Bunyan declares, "I looked, and saw him open the Book." His vivifying gaze breaks the charm of immobility, and from this moment the narrative proceeds under his watchful eye. If his creative process was not actually that of dreaming a dream, it was assuredly that of seeing a vision.

But the procedure of creating largely in terms of images was alien to the Puritan aesthetic, and our defense of the tradition of heavenly meditation as a relevant influence is organized about two aspects of Bunyan's art: his undidactic handling of the imagery of scriptural metaphor and his realistic use of the imagery of private experience. Each of these suggests particular developments in the tradition cited, and if the evidence

3. *John Bunyan: The Man and his Works*, trans. from the French by Barbara Wall (Cambridge, Harvard University Press, 1951), p. 182.

available does not warrant the claim of certainty in establishing their influence upon Bunyan, it at least argues the probability of such influence.

Biblical Metaphor in Two Episodes of *The Pilgrim's Progress*

Bunyan's work testifies to an unconventional readiness to allow scriptural metaphor to operate on its own level without reduction for didactic purposes, not to mention an extraordinary deftness in selecting apt metaphors for his needs. In the work of Sibbes and Baxter a methodology for evaluating scriptural metaphors *qua* metaphors was perfected: the metaphor was of value precisely as it brought the whole man into an inspired appreciation of its multiple meanings and warmed the spirit with a glimpse of the reality to which it was related as symbol. Thus Baxter urged that we use "the Spirits figurative expressions" to "quicken our apprehensions & affections, but not to pervert them; and use these low notions as a Glass, in which we must see the things themselves, though the representation be exceeding imperfect" (*SER*, Pt. 4, p. 219), and Sibbes defended scriptural metaphors as serving "*faith* and *fancie* both at once" (*SC*, p. 258). In suggesting that the figurative language of Scripture, with its use of such metaphors as fire, king, and feast for invisibilia, legitimized the imagination as a faculty for glimpsing spiritual realities, Sibbes necessarily gave new status to the metaphor, as Baxter was to discern and make integral to a massive program. Scriptural metaphor was seen, not as the ambush for doctrine, but as genuine symbol, and the inevitable corollary of this approach was that the earthly experience which it tapped had to be explored by all the faculties of the soul before its full value was realized. After all, any meaning of the earthly term, whether grasped by reason or intuition dependent upon the imagination, might conceivably point to a quality of the heavenly referent. It scarcely needs to be pointed out that this evaluation of the metaphor constituted a decisive qualification of the Puritan orientation toward *logos*. Wherever the biblical page offered metaphor which was susceptible to use in heavenly meditation, *logos* was displaced by myth, for such metaphor demanded interpretation in terms of the actual experience to which it referred rather than the doctrine which it directly or indirectly suggested.

Evidence of another kind for a new evaluation of scriptural metaphor in the tradition of heavenly meditation can be discerned in Baxter's reassessment of the use the Christian is to make of the *events* narrated in Scripture. The revaluation of the metaphor was one part of the process in which all scriptural experience was assessed in terms of its meanings for the imagination as well as for the reason. And the metaphors of parable and poetry were bound to be given new status when scriptural experience was approached as Baxter does in such passages as the following:

> O the difference between the last Supper of Christ on earth, and the marriage Supper of the Lamb at the great day! Here he is in an upper room, accompanied with twelve poor selected men, feeding on no curious dainties, but a Paschall Lamb with sowre herbs, and a *Judas* at his table ready to betray him: But then his room will be the Glorious Heavens; his attendants all the Host of Angels and Saints. (*SER*, Pt. 4, p. 232)

With a few words, the scene of the Last Supper is re-created. It is true that Baxter passes quickly from the historical to the heavenly, but the whole vitality of his comparisons stems from the success with which he reconstructs the known, historical factor. Such is the case in this passage:

> If I had seen but *Job* in his sores upon the Dunghil it would have been an excellent sight to see such a mirror of patience: what will it be then to see him in glory praising

that power which did uphold and deliver him? If I had heard but *Paul* and *Sylas* singing in the stocks, it would have been a delightful hearing, what will it be then to hear them sing praises in heaven! If I had heard *David* sing praises on his Lute and Harp, it would have been a pleasing Melody; and that which drove the evil spirit from *Saul*, would sure have driven away the dulness and sadness of my spirit, and have been to me as the musick was to Elishah, that the Spirit of Christ in joy would have come upon me; why, I shall shortly hear that sweet Singer in the heavenly Chore advancing the King of Saints; and will not that be a far more melodious hearing? (*SER*, Pt. 4, p. 233)

In each of these truncated "compositions" Baxter has employed the imagination which he had earlier in his treatise defended as a legitimate help to meditation, and it is noteworthy that the reader is drawn into the life of the biblical events, savoring the emotions which they evoke rather than the doctrine to which they glancingly refer. The incidents are, in short, being appreciated as myth rather than *logos*.

Now if the Psalms could be approached as the record of powerful feeling, if Job could be seen against the vividly imagined background of the ash heap, the time could not be far off when the metaphors of those books which Bunyan used so freely in the construction of his myths could be appreciated as symbols which derived their power from complex and irreducible human experience rather than from vaguely suggested doctrines. By implying an appreciation of certain passages in the Bible as a record of experience in premeditatedly affective and imaginative language, Baxter was resurrecting the genre of poetry in the Bible, a genre which Puritanism at large had all but lost. If he did not completely articulate the implications of his position for the metaphors of the Scripture, those implications were obvious enough to be appreciated by an artist like Bunyan when he had occasion to use the Word in the process of giving abstractions corporeality.

Christian's experience in the Valley of the Shadow of Death is a natural episode to consider in sampling Bunyan's handling of scriptural metaphor. The subject matter may seem remote from the typical concern of heavenly meditation with the forms of eternal felicity—after all, Hell's mouth yawns in the midst of that dreadful vale—but the antitypes were a corollary concern. Sibbes' counsels on the use of "darkness" and "fire" come to mind: in either case one made use of sensory experience better to appreciate the reality of the Hereafter, and it was natural to take up the infernal with its mundane analogues as the proper foil for the heavenly. Moreover, hell was a popular subject for formal meditation outside the tradition at hand, and the importance of such practice should not be overlooked. In fact, Bayly, with whom Bunyan was surely acquainted, and Ambrose, with whom he may have been, made limited place for senses and imagination in the meditation of hell.[4] The subject,

4. Cf. Bayly, *Practice of Pietie*, p. 198: "There thy *lascivious* Eyes shal be afflicted with sights of *ghastly spirits:* thy *curious Eares* shall be affrighted with hideous noyse of *howling Divels,* and the gnashing teeth of *damned Reprobates:* thy *dainty Nose* shall be cloyed with noysome stench of *Sulphur:* thy *delicate Taste* shall be pained with intolerable *hunger:* Thy *drunken Throat* shall be parched with unquenchable thirst." Ambrose may be following Bayly in his description of the same (*PMU*, 2, 244): "the eye shall be tormented with the sight of divels, the eares with the hideous yellings and out-cryes of the damned in flames, the nostrils shall be smothered (as it were) with brimstone, the hand, the foot, the tongue, and every part shall fry in flames of fire: nor onely the body, but the soul shall be tormented; yea the soul-torments, shall exceed all the torments of the body; it was chief in sinning, and therefore must be chief in suffering." It is instructive to note how quickly Ambrose moves beyond the province of the five senses to the nonphysical self whose sufferings do not ask for, or support, imaginative reconstruction. There is convincing evidence to the effect that Ambrose knew the work of Baxter as well as he knew that of Hall (Cf. his "To the Reader" prefacing *Media* in *PMU*), but the fact that he does almost nothing with Baxter's insights suggests something of the power and

like no other in Puritanism at large, invited the imaginative reconstruction integral to Ignatian methodology. But a comparison of the magnificent amplitude and intensity of a Catholic exercise in the genre, so well exemplified in the sermon on hell in James Joyce's *Portrait of the Artist as a Young Man*, with the restraint and imaginative diffuseness of the occasional Puritan effort at reconstruction reveals only too well how necessary to a fruitful deployment of the imagination and to genuine freedom in the handling of biblical metaphor were the developments in the line of Sibbes and Baxter. The episode of the Valley of the Shadow clearly owes something to common formal meditation on hell, but, ironically, it owes even more to meditation on heaven.

In constructing the episode, Bunyan uses seven passages from the Psalms, five from Job, one from Jeremiah, one from Amos, and one from Ephesians. Significantly, he goes to biblical poetry for metaphors which he uses with no attempt at reduction. His first biblical allusion is to Jeremiah, and by way of it he presents the central unifying metaphor of the episode:

> Now at the end of the Valley [of Humiliation], was another, called the Valley of the *Shadow of Death*, and *Christian* must needs go through it, because the way to the Coelestial City lay through the midst of it: Now this Valley is a very solitary place. The Prophet *Jeremiah* thus

vitality of the prevailing emphasis. In another place (*PMU*, 2, 229-30), Ambrose makes a tantalizing beginning in an imaginative reconstruction of the Crucifixion, much as Baxter (or Ignatius) might have, but the focus of his mind's eye becomes uncertain, the image fades, and doctrine comes into focus: "Here! O here is an object (my soul!) well worthy of thy *love!* . . . come and see; this is he whose name is *wonderfull, councellor* . . . [I]f thou know him not by the face, the voyce, the hands, if thou know him not by the tears, and bloody sweat, yet look nearer, thou mayst know him by the heart." But the heart he describes is no picture for the eye, but a theological symbol of love, sorrow, compassion. The meditator's gaze thrusts beneath the surface of the scene to doctrine poignant for conscience.

describes it, *a Wilderness, a Land of desarts, and of Pits, a Land of drought, and of the shadow of death, a Land that no Man* (but a Christian) *passeth through, and where no man dwelt.* (p. 61)

The phrase "the shadow of death" is found in four other places in the Bible, and Bunyan manages to make use of all its occurrences, deploying the metaphor which they contain in his fashioning of an overarching structure whose symbolic suggestiveness never collapses into simple allegory. "The Shadow of Death," that is, does not represent, but suggest. Only once does Bunyan attempt to gloss the detail, and then he elaborates it curiously in terms which preserve it as part of mythic rather than allegorical setting. This elaboration comes in the words of those two men fleeing from the Valley who advise Christian against going further. They observe of the Valley that "death also does always spread his wings over it: in a word, it is every whit dreadful" (p. 62). Bunyan, with his flair for visualization and dramatic interpretation of metaphor, has drawn the interesting conclusion that the Shadow of Death must, of course, be the shadow of some palpable presence, and the image which results is that of an inscrutable horror brooding over the valley. Bunyan has undoubtedly drawn upon certain metaphors of the Psalms but, like his sources, stops short of full visualization with good reason. The suggested metaphors from the Psalms are to be found in verses one and four of Psalm 91, where "wings" and "shadow" are associated: "He that dwelleth in the secret place of the most High shall abide under the shadow of the Almighty" and "He shall cover thee with his feathers, and under his wings shalt thou trust." Bunyan's handling of this picture offers strong evidence of his ability to route the vitality of a scriptural metaphor into dramatic and narrative channels without yielding to the temptation to reduce it to a simple doctrinal truth, as he so easily might have here. The shadow of death remains as narrative fact and multivalent image.

Harold Golder, observing the way in which Bunyan has drawn upon the Scriptures in constructing this episode, suggests that indeed Bunyan was approaching the Word not as doctrine but as "romance." He conjectures, "This attitude of mind with which Bunyan began his reading of the Bible must have affected most interestingly his reaction to certain passages in Job, the Psalms, and the books of the Prophets."[5] One can appreciate the reasons for Golder's conjecture that Bunyan was reading his Bible in a way distinct from that followed by most Puritans, that he was in fact able to enter imaginatively into the images and metaphors of "Job, the Psalms, and the books of the Prophets." Yet there are weaknesses in supposing that after his conversion he would naturally read his Bible as he had read those romances he had put away with the sins of youth. If Puritan conversion meant a hearty abjuration of romances, it also meant an unquestioning acceptance of Holy Writ as a source of edification *sui generis*, with fixed conventions for appropriating its meanings. If we knew no more than that the young Bunyan read romances, we could scarcely conclude that Bunyan the regenerate Christian would approach the Bible as if it were another imaginative narrative. But the complexion of the case changes in the light of our evidence that by the time of the Restoration the imaginative approach to scriptural metaphor and event was, in heavenly meditation, itself a distinct convention. The carryover of attitudes from secular to sacred texts becomes more plausible in the light of the legitimizing of the appreciation of biblical *mythos*.

If the Valley of the Shadow was a glimpse of hell, Beulah Land constitutes a glimpse of heaven. The episode set there is in substance heavenly meditation:

> Now I saw in my Dream, that by this time the Pilgrims were got over the Inchanted Ground, and entering into the Country of *Beulah*, whose Air was very sweet and

---

5. Golder, "Bunyan's Valley of the Shadow," *MP*, 27 (1929), 68–69.

pleasant, the way lying directly through it, they solaced themselves there for a season. Yea, here they heard continually the singing of Birds, and saw every day the flowers appear on the earth, and heard the voice of the Turtle in the Land. In this Countrey the Sun shineth night and day; wherefore this was beyond the Valley of the *shadow of death*, and also out of the reach of Giant *Despair;* neither could they from this place so much as see *Doubting-Castle.* Here they were within sight of the City they were going to: also here met them some of the Inhabitants thereof. For in this Land the shining Ones commonly walked, because it was upon the Borders of Heaven. In this Land also the contract between the Bride and the Bridegroom was renewed: Yea here, *as the Bridegroom rejoyceth over his Bride so did their God rejoyce over them.* Here they had no want of Corn and Wine; for in this place they met with abundance of what they had sought for in all their Pilgrimage. Here they heard voices from out of the City, loud voices, saying, *Say ye to the daughter of Zion, Behold thy Salvation cometh, behold his reward is with him.* Here all the Inhabitants of the Countrey called them, *The holy People, the redeemed of the Lord, Sought out,* &c. (pp. 154-55)

Using imagery borrowed from the poetry of Isaiah 62 and Song of Solomon 2, Bunyan depicts a radiant landscape which perhaps more deserves the epithet of Enchanted Ground than the terrain that adjoins it. Without pressing the imagery into any confining allegorical mode, he has elaborated it around the luminous equation between marriage and covenant. The very name Beulah means marriage, of course, and the Land of Beulah as Bunyan describes it is an appropriate anteroom to Heaven for the people of the Covenant: "In this Land also the contract between the Bride and Bridegroom was renewed." But the theological element of the scene is carefully held in check, for biblical metaphor is an element in the process of painting a landscape, not of elaborating a doctrine.

A curious feature shared by the two episodes just considered, and one which constitutes an independent confirmation of the case for their being visualized myth based upon and inviting imaginative participation in the biblical metaphors, is the palpable presence of the writer in the action. Ordinarily Bunyan the pilgrim, unlike Chaucer the pilgrim, is a benevolent specter who haunts the outskirts of the action, but in both the Valley of the Shadow of Death and Beulah Land the immediacy of his imaginative construction is so overwhelming that he is pulled bodily onto the stage. In the Valley of the Shadow he enjoys a fascinating relationship to Christian: it is as if he moves in and out of superimposition, one moment seeing with Christian's eyes and the next standing at his elbow. After Christian and his unnoticed companion have braved the perils of the first half of the Valley, the narrative proceeds: "About the midst of this Valley, I perceived the mouth of Hell to be, and it stood also hard by the way side: Now thought *Christian*, what shall I do?" (p. 63) Bunyan catches sight of the mouth of hell, but he does not even allow his character to see it for himself, before Christian finds himself framing his question. Here creator and character are one, or at least share the same sensorium. A moment later, however, the author is at Christian's elbow when, after his character cries out for deliverance ("in my hearing," as Bunyan comments) and is beset by a most treacherous peril, he says:

> I took notice that now poor *Christian* was so confounded, that he did not know his own voice: and thus I perceived it: Just when he was come over against the mouth of the burning Pit, one of the wicked ones got behind him, and stept up softly to him, and whisperingly suggested many grievous blasphemies to him, which he verily thought had proceeded from his own mind. (p. 63)

Bunyan is close enough to Christian to catch whispers, and his fiction is plainly of an order capable of absorbing and supporting the reality of the viewer. Similarly, when in Beulah Land Christian and Hopeful take their rest under Bunyan's careful eye, he says:

> Now I beheld in my Dream, that they talked more in their sleep at this time, then ever they did in all their Journey; and being in a muse there-about, the Gardiner said even to me, Wherefore musest thou at the matter? It is the nature of the fruit of the Grapes of these Vineyards to go down so sweetly, as to cause the lips of them that are asleep to speak. (pp. 155–56)

The dreamer has incarnated himself for the eye of other characters in the imagined action. The ease with which the reader accepts this is evidence of the thickness and vitality of Bunyan's created world. Its indigenous creatures do not fade to insubstantial shades when their maker takes the stage with them.

Bunyan's handling of scriptural metaphor in general is quite unfettered by the demands of a reductive didacticism and offers evidence of a readiness to approach the figurative language of the Word as something other than *logos*. Puritan hermeneutics regarded biblical metaphor as a circumlocutory expression of doctrine, while heavenly meditation elaborated a discipline of Bible reading and devotion which accepted the Word as the source of affective images to be used in bringing scriptural reality within the purview of the senses. *The Pilgrim's Progress* offers abundant evidence of the latter approach to scriptural metaphor.

Imagery and Realism in *The Pilgrim's Progress*

Our attention thus far has been given to the probable influence of heavenly meditation upon the way Bunyan approached the Scriptures, but this tradition is also relevant to a second featured element in Bunyan's creative practice; that body of imagery which is not tied to a scriptural source. While it is true that not all of the imagery in this latter category enters into the realism so often discerned in *The Pilgrim's Progress*, a large proportion of it does, and since in the tradition of heavenly meditation can be found propaedeutic for a Puritan literature of realism, the issue of Bunyan's realism serves as a natural focus for the second section of our discussion of that tradition.

We may take as representative of modern interest in Bunyan's realism certain remarks made by J. G. Patrick:

> Not a man or woman in *The Pilgrim's Progress* but has, under the general outline of vice or virtue, the detailed reality of a human being. That is, of course, what makes the power of this great book. No symbolic conflict that between Christian and Apollyon, but a genuine fight in which our hero is not above considering, as the enemy advances, that he has armour only on his breast, none on his back, and therefore cannot turn and flee.[6]

The skirmish with Apollyon is of course a "symbolic conflict," in addition to whatever else it may be, but Patrick shows a sensitivity to those qualities in the narrative which distinguish it from a simple allegory of doctrine. In relating those qualities to Bunyan's use of original imagery, we might well begin with his description of the Slough of Despond, since its analogues in the English countryside have often been cited. Patrick, indeed, believes that a precise source of Bunyan's image can be located:

> Such a spot as would be likely to supply inspiration for the symbol of mire and wretchedness can clearly be traced as nearly as possible halfway between Elstow and Bedford . . . . Although a culvert now prevents the sluggish watercourse, which is crosses, from again becoming

6. Patrick, "The Realism of 'The Pilgrim's Progress,'" *Baptist Quarterly*, *13* (1949–50), 19 ff.

a "slough" to vehicular traffic and pedestrians, such an undrained low-lying spot, with its willows suggestive of damp soil, must, particularly in wet weather, have been a veritable quagmire.

Whatever its source, Bunyan's picture of the Slough lying in Christian's path as he and Pliable flee toward the wicket gate is vividly conceived and memorably described:

> Now I saw in my Dream, that just as they had ended this talk, they drew near to a very *Miry Slough* that was in the midst of the Plain, and they, being heedless, did both fall suddenly into the bogg. The name of the Slow was *Dispond*. Here therefore they wallowed for a time, being grievously bedaubed with the dirt; and *Christian*, because of the burden that was on his back, began to sink in the Mire. (p. 14)

His rescue is effected by Help, while Pliable escapes on that side of the slough "next to his own House."

Now if we were to apply to Bunyan's use of personal observation here the categories which Perry Miller uses to distinguish Puritan from Anglican—"imagist" and "allegorist"—we would not hesitate to designate Bunyan as an "imagist," and thus to set him apart, *per saltum*, from the majority of his Puritan contemporaries. As we shall see more fully when we consider the tradition of occasional meditation in Chapter 8, however, Puritanism's characteristic allegorical temper was evident not only in its hermeneutics but also in its efforts to look beyond the fleeting impressions presented by the creatures to the divine message which they mutely proclaimed. If the Scriptures shadowed forth divine *logos* in a diversity of genres, nature too shadowed forth the divine Word in the multiform objects and events of the real world. The Puritan conviction was well expressed by Joseph Hall when he said, "What is man, to the whole earth? What is earth, to the heaven? What is heaven, to his Maker? I will admire nothing in it self, but all things in God, and God in all things." [7] And the Puritan implemented his *nil admirari*, as applied to nature, by scrupulously looking beyond image to doctrine. Miller observes:

> Everything in experience [for the Puritan] was specifically and continuously ordered by God; the rising of the sun, the blowing of the wind, the very breathing of the lungs, were all, like the decay of the rose, immediate acts of God, ordained for good and sufficient reasons. Events might conform to "laws" of nature, but only because those were God's "usual" methods of acting. To the Puritan, phenomena had significance because they were intentional. In causing this particular rose to be blasted on precisely such and such an evening, God had a purpose. The duty of man was to observe the event and to find out the purpose; most decidedly, it was not to give way to an emotion, whether of admiration or terror, excited by the appearance of things.[8]

Yet, while Bunyan gives ample evidence in *The Pilgrim's Progress* of the Puritan talent for extracting doctrine from appearance, he also shows a hearty interest in the immediately experienced real world. His was a remarkable ability for appreciating appearances.

As important an element in the realism of the Mt. Sinai episode as the following image, for example, may well have been drawn from Bunyan's personal experience:

> So *Christian* turned out of his way to go to Mr. *Legality's* house for help: but behold, when he was got now hard

---

7. *Meditations and Vowes, Divine and Morall, The Second Century* (London, 1620), bound in *A Recollection of such Treatises as have been heretofore severally published and are nowe revised, corrected augmented* (London, 1621), p. 23.

8. *Images or Shadows*, pp. 3-4.

by the *Hill,* it seemed so high, and also that side of it that was next the way side did hang so much over, that Christian was afraid to venture farther, lest the *Hill* should fall on his head: wherefore there he stood still, and wotted not what to do. (p. 20)

The scene is strongly reminiscent of the familiar episode in *Grace Abounding* which describes the time when the youthful Bunyan was convicted by his conscience during his sportive bell-ringing: "but then it came into my head, how if the Steeple it self should fall, and this thought, (it may fall for ought I know) would when I stood and looked on, continually so shake my mind, that I durst not stand at the Steeple door any longer, but was forced to fly, for fear it should fall upon my head." [9] Since in both of these scenes a state of mind is clearly captured in terms of relevant images, presumably it was as vivid pictures that Bunyan entrusted the experiences to memory. It is this and a host of other evidences which prompts Talon to say of Bunyan:

> From his prison he endowed the ideal world of the Bible with the clear forms of the terrestrial universe, and re-created the concrete world, from which he was excluded, with a precision of line if possible greater than there was in fact. He took the real in his vigorous grasp and brought it into his dreams; and this energy of gesture and vision is the better part of his genius.[1]

Bunyan's episode of the Valley of the Shadow offers a variety of evidences of the way he employs images to re-create experience, though in this case the realism is imposed upon admittedly romantic action. His conscious appeals to the senses are legion in this passage:

9. *Grace Abounding,* p. 14.
1. Talon, pp. 183-84.

> About the midst of this Valley, I perceived the mouth of Hell to be, and it stood also hard by the way side: Now thought *Christian*, what shall I do? And ever and anon the flame and smoke would come out in such abundance, with sparks and hideous noises (things that cared not for *Christian's* Sword, as did *Apollyon* before) that he was forced to put up his Sword, and betake himself to another weapon, called *All-Prayer:* so he cried in my hearing, O *Lord I beseech Thee deliver my Soul.* Thus he went on a great while, yet still the flames would be reaching towards him: also he heard doleful voices and rushings too and fro, so that sometimes he thought he should be torn in pieces, or trodden down like mire in the Streets. This frightful sight was seen, and those dreadful noises were heard by him, for several miles together. (p. 63)

The extent to which Bunyan is constructing the scene as an appeal to the imagination through the senses is highlighted by his procedure in describing Christiana's passage through the same valley. Evidently assuming that in Part One he has sufficiently exploited the senses of sight and hearing, he introduces quite a new note in Part Two when, after seeing a pit across their way miraculously removed, Christiana and her group proceed: "Yet they were not got through the Valley; so they went on still, and behold great stinks and loathsome smells, to the great annoyance of them. Then said *Mercie* to *Christiana*, 'there is not such pleasant being here as at the *Gate*, or at the Interpreter's, or at the House where we lay last'" (p. 243). Such appeals to the senses, scarcely the simple vehicles of allegorical meaning, are used to give the quality of flesh-and-blood reality to the experiences of the pilgrims.

A characteristic of Bunyan's art which is readily conceded by most or all readers does not, perhaps, need to be defended at great length here. The passages cited show the expected relationship between his frequently praised realism and his artful exploitation of images, many of which are presumably drawn from his own experience. Furthermore, his readiness to tap the world about him as source of images and to use those images in the creation of realistic if fictive experience represents a deviation from general Puritan practice, but a continuity with the techniques of heavenly meditation. To confirm our case, we may now consider in more detail the particular developments relevant to Bunyan's practice.

At the heart of the qualification of the Puritan aesthetic found in the tradition of heavenly meditation is the assumption that for the individual in meditation to improve his conceptions of things above, he must compare them with things below. Such comparison, significantly, involved an approach to earthly objects and events that used the both senses and the imagination. There could be no better illustration of this point than the detailed quotation from Baxter that urges the individual to:

> Compare also the delights above, with the lawful delights of moderated senses. Think with thy self, how sweet is food to my taste when I am hungry? especially, as *Isaac* said, that which my soul loveth? that which my temperance and appetite do incline to? What delight hath the taste in some pleasant Fruits? in some well relished meats? and in divers Junkets? O what delight then must my soul needs have in feeding upon Christ the living bread? and in eating with him at his Table in his Kingdom? . . . How pleasant is drink in the extremity of thirst? The delight of it to a man in a feaver or other drought, can scarcely be expressed: It will make the strength of *Sampson* revive: O then how delightful will it be to my soul to drink of that fountain of living water, which who so drinks, shall thirst no more? . . . How delightful are pleasant odors to our smell: How delightful is perfect Musick to the ear? how delightful are beauteous

sights to the eye? such as curious pictures; sumptuous, adorned, well-contrived buildings; handsome, necessary rooms, walks, prospects; Gardens stored with variety of beauteous and odoriferous flowers; or pleasant Medows which are natural gardens? O then think every time thou seest or remembrest these, what a fragrant smel hath the precious ointment which is poured on the head of our glorified Saviour, and which must be poured on the heads of all his Saints? which will fill all the room of heaven with its odor and perfume? How delightful is the Musick of the Heavenly Host? How pleasing will be those real beauties above? and how glorious the building not made with hands? and the house that God himself doth dwell in? and the walks and prospects in the City of God? and the beauties and delights in the celestial Paradise? (*SER*, Pt. 4, p. 223)

With unquestionable gusto, Baxter directs his gaze to the things of the flesh, and it is important to note that when he suggests "Think with thy self, how sweet is food to my taste," and so on, he is urging a wholesome interest in the real world not for what it stands for but for what it is in itself. Such an appreciation of the real world is encouraged because its every delight is a truncated statement about the hereafter. It can scarcely be exaggerated how divergent from anterior Puritan "allegorizing" of nature this "comparative" use of nature was; it is approximately the divergence between "allegorist" and "imagist."

The entire section in Baxter's discussion of meditation which deals with use of the senses amplifies this central idea of "comparison" of earthly with heavenly, and in all such comparison we find the real world looked to not for lessons but for images which may be used in the process of stirring the affections. Thus Baxter urges not only that one "Compare . . . the delights above with the lawful delights of moderated senses," but, "Compare also the Excellencies of Heaven with those glorious works of the Creation which our eyes do now behold." The logical expectation that in this exposition the difference between Baxter's use of the creatures and the conventional Puritan use should be clearly defined is not disappointed. Throughout his illustrative examples Baxter is not allegorizing nature but looking to it for the first terms in his heavenly comparisons:

> what a deal of the Majesty of the great Creater doth shine in the face of this fabrick of the world? surely his Works are great and admirable, sought out of them that have pleasure therein. This makes the study of natural Philosophy so pleasant, because the works of God are so excellent: What rare workmanship is in the body of a man? yea, in the body of every beast? which makes the Anatomical studies so delightful; what excellency in every Plant we see? in the beauty of Flowers? in the nature, diversity, and use of Herbs? in Fruits, in Roots, in Minerals, and what not? But especially if we look to the greater works: if we consider the whole body of this earth, and its creatures, and inhabitants; the Ocean of waters, with its motions and dimensions, the variations of the Seasons, and of the face of the earth; the entercourse of Spring and Fall, of Summer and Winter; what wonderful excellency do these contain? Why, think then in thy Meditations, if these things which are but servants to sinful man, are yet so full of mysterious worth; what then is that place where God himself doth dwell and is prepared for the just who are perfected with Christ? . . . This whole earth is but my Fathers footstool; this Thunder is nothing to his dreadful voice; these winds are nothing to the breath of his mouth: So much wisdom and power as appeareth in all these; so much, and far much more greatness and goodness, and loving delights shall I enjoy in the actual fruition of God. Surely, if the Rain which rains, and the Sun which

> shines on the just and unjust, be so wonderful; the Sun then which must shine on none but Saints and Angels, must needs be wonderful and ravishing in glory. (*SER*, Pt. 4, pp. 226–27)

Tacitly assumed in this cataloguing of the creatures is that their "mysterious" worth has been realized and discerned in experience unfettered by a circumscribing didacticism. The very phrase, "mysterious worth," is significant, for conventional Puritanism was interested not in the mystery but in the clear message of the creatures. Baxter's escape from the Puritan impasse of not daring to dwell on the beauty of natural things for fear of losing the spiritual in the corporeal was as simple as it was unoriginal. The entire quickening experience of beauty, untranslated for the reason and mysterious to its core, was oriented within a limiting structure which channeled all its ambiguities in a predetermined direction. All aesthetic experience embodied a *nisus* as it pointed to later terms in the series of which it was the first member and of which all later terms were *invisibilia*.

In this tradition, then, the gaze of the meditator was assiduously turned to the real world. Experience, recapitulated in images for the stirring of the affections, was seen as a limitless reservoir of inspiration. The image had been rescued from limbo and the stage set for the appearance of a genius who would use these techniques of reading the Word and experience in a creative process which would cast eternal truths in a composition of images drawn from the world of sense. It does not seem bold to suggest in light of this evidence that Bunyan's realism is indebted to developments in Puritan meditation.

8

OCCASIONAL MEDITATION AND *THE PILGRIM'S PROGRESS*

Occasional Meditation in Puritan Practice

In Part Two of *The Pilgrim's Progress*, when Christiana's group arrives at the House Beautiful, the boys are catechized by Prudence in a session that closes with her counsel: "You must still harken to your Mother, for she can learn you more. You must also diligently give ear to what good talk you shall hear from others, for for your sakes do they speak good things" (p. 226). Her instruction following these words is significant: "Observe also and that with carefulness, what the Heavens and the Earth do teach you," an injunction that prepares the way for a lengthy dialogue with Mathew which comes shortly thereafter. That dialogue gives ample proof of Bunyan's appreciation of a tradition of meditation that, because of its characteristic matter and manner, the Puritan writers uniformly handled under a separate heading. Known as occasional meditation, it was a method for redeeming the manifold occasions of immediate experience and was often concerned with the "creatures" of the natural order as they offered themselves to observation. When Mathew, having been encouraged by Prudence to ask any questions that came to mind, queries *"What should we learn by seeing the Flame of our Fire go upwards? and by seeing the Beams, and sweet influences of the Sun strike downwards?"* Prudence replies: "By the going up of the Fire, we are taught to ascend to Heaven, by fervent and hot desires. And by the Sun his sending his Heat, Beams, and sweet Influences downwards; we are taught, that the Saviour of the World, tho' high, reaches down with his Grace and Love to us below." The dialogue continues:

> Mathew. *Where have the Clouds their Water?*
> Pru. Out of the Sea.
> Mathew. *What may we learn from that?*
> Pru. That Ministers should fetch their Doctrine from God.
> Mat. *Why do they empty themselves upon the Earth?*
> Pru. To shew that Ministers should give out what they know of God to the World.
> Mat. *Why is the Rainbow caused by the Sun?*
> Prudence. To shew that the Covenant of Gods Grace is confirmed to us in Christ.
> Mat. *Why do the Springs come from the Sea to us, thorough the Earth?*
> Prudence. To shew that the Grace of God comes to us thorough the Body of Christ.
> Mat. *Why do some of the Springs rise out of the tops of high Hills?*
> Prudence. To shew that the Spirit of Grace shall spring up in *some* that are Great and Mighty, as well as in *many* that are Poor and low. (p. 231)

Several features of this dialogue deserve comment. Its extraordinary terseness stems from the formulaic quality of both question and answer. The total effect of the dialogue, indeed, is akin to that produced by many of the elaborate punning scenes in Elizabethan drama; in both cases, at least, the terseness of the interchanges can be traced to the fact that the speakers are availing themselves of the commonplaces of established tradition. Here Bunyan draws upon the conventions of the tradition of occasional meditation and presents a list of observations in a kind of catalogue. It is probable that all of them are clichés of the tradition. Even the one which might seem the most likely to have originated with Bunyan—the observation about the spring in high ground—can be found in William Spurstow's meditation "On a Spring in an high ground," in his *Spiritual Chymist* of 1666, where he declares:

> *Grace* in a poor man is as a *nether spring*, which is not less useful through a defect of Water, but through an incapacity to make any large communication of it, in regard of those circumstances in which he stands: His *wants*, his *paucity* of Friends, the *little notice* the world takes of him, the *slightings* that Poverty exposeth most men unto, are all great obstacles to the *eternal* [sic] diffusions of his grace, though not to his *intrinsecal* fulness of it. But grace in a great Person is like an *upper Spring*, which may convey it self far and near, because of the many advantages which he hath above others.[1]

Occasional meditation appears conspicuously at a number of points in *The Pilgrim's Progress*, and we may profitably devote attention to the background and rationale of this tradition, particularly as it was adapted by Puritanism, for the illumination it can give to Bunyan's allegory. The sources of the tradition are difficult to pinpoint, to be sure, since examples of the didactic use of the creatures are prolific in the Patristic literature; but some idea of the pervasiveness of this approach to nature in the early centuries of the Christian era is given by

---

1. *The Spiritual Chymist: or, Six Decads of Divine Meditations on several Subjects* (London, 1666), pp. 125–26.

the collection of examples which St. Francis de Sales brings together in his *Introduction to a Devoute Life*. He introduces his collection with these words:

> as they that be enamoured with humane and natural love, have almost alway their thoughts fixed upon the parson beloved, their hart full of affection towards her, their mouth flowing with her praises; when their beloved is absent they leese no occasion to testifie their passions by kind letters, and not a tree do they meet with all, but in the barch of it, they engrave the name of their darling: even so such as love God fervently, can never cease thinking upon him, they draw their breath only for him, they sigh and sorrow for their absence from him, all their talk is of him and if it were possible, they would grave the sacred name of our Lord JESUS, upon the brest of all the men in the world.
> . . . And certainly al creatures doe invite them to this, and not one but in its kind, declareth unto them the praises of their beloved: and as S. Augustin sayth (taking it from S. Anthony) all things in this world speak unto us with a kind of language, which though dumbe, in that it is not expressed in words, yet intelligibile enough in regard of their love.[2]

He continues with a host of illustrative examples, drawn from St. Fulgentius, St. Basil, St. Anselm, St. Francis Borgia, and others, and concludes: "See my Philotheus, how easilie and redilie a man may draw good thoughts and holy inspirations, from all things great and small that are presented to our sences and understanding in the varietie of this mortal life." [3]

---

2. St. François de Sales, *An Introduction to a Devoute Life*, trans. John Yakesley (3rd. ed. Rouen, 1614), pp. 155–56.
3. Ibid., pp. 161–62.

This ancient tradition was made to serve characteristically Puritan ends, however, as it was practiced within Puritanism. In the first place, it permitted the congeries of events that made up a day to be approached and evaluated by the reason rather than the treacherous and seductive imagination. Within Puritanism, occasional meditation reduced every "creature" to a statement, every event to a proposition; the "spiritual" ends being pursued by way of the creatures were also thoroughly rational ends. If the Puritan read the Scriptures as *logos*, he proceeded no differently in reading the book of the creatures. Says Thomas Taylor in his *Meditations From the Creatures*, "Thus the creation of the world is a Scripture of God, and the voice of God in all the creatures, and by them all speaketh unto us alwayes & every where." [4] The sundry doctrines were gathered from the lines and letters of miscellaneous circumstance, much as one gathered doctrines from the Scripture. Robert Bolton urges:

> But ever goe about the affaires of thy Calling with a heavenly minde . . . pregnant with heavenly matter and meditation, pickt out of the passages of thy present businesses. For instance; Let the Husbandman in Seedtime, collect this sacred Soliloquie, and heavenly thought; If I now take not the season, I shall have no harvest, but starve in winter. So proportionably: if I gather not Grace in this Sun-shine of the Gospell, and day of my visitation, I shall find nothing but horror upon my bed of death, and burne in Hell for ever hereafter, &c.[5]

For the typical Puritan a creature was only fleetingly appreciated as an image: the flower, or stream, or fire on the hearth were "marginall hands" pointing beyond their elusive and

---

4. *Meditations from the Creatures* (2nd. ed. London, 1629), p. 23.
5. *Some Generall Directions for a Comfortable Walking with God* (London, 1625), p. 70.

fleeting sensory nature to a truth which was the legitimate prize of the reason.

The exploitation of the manifold "occasions" of experience for spiritual instructions, expressed as rational statement, was pursued with a peculiar vehemence in Puritanism as a consequence of a problem which was especially painful to a movement holding to uncompromising ethical standards. For the Puritan, the mercurial stream of consciousness never ceased to provoke ambivalent reactions of awe and fear, as the edifice of righteousness seemed to rest on a fluid foundation. The natural play of the mind represented a gamesomeness that was not wholly subject to the will, and hence even a sanctified will could not guarantee perfect obedience. The fashioning of a godly life was, then, not entirely possible even for the spirit-guided reason; a surd quality was always present. The typical Puritan reaction to this refractoriness of thought can be discerned in an observation made by John Owen: "There is nothing so unaccountable as *the multiplicity of thoughts* of the minds of men. They fall from them like the leaves of trees when they are shaken with the wind in autumn." [6] And Thomas Goodwin is pointed in his diagnosis of the nature of the mind's activity: it is a sign of depravity. He observes that this "foolishness"

> is seene, both in that unsetled wantonnesse and unstayednesse of the minde in thinking, that like quick-silver it cannot fixe, but as *Solomon* sayes, *Proverbs* 17. *verse* 24. *A fooles eyes are in the ends of the earth*, are garish, and runne up and downe from one end of the earth to the other, shooting and streaming, as those Meteors you see sometimes in the ayre . . . [;] our thoughts at best, are as wanton Spaniels, who though indeed they goe with and

---

6. ΦΡΟΝΗΜΑ ΤΟΥ ΠΝΕΥΜΑΤΟΣ or, *The Grace and Duty of Being Spiritually Minded Declared and Practically Improved, Works*, 7, 299. The first edition appeared in 1681.

accompany their Master, and come to their journeys end with him in the end, yet doe run after every Bird, and wildly pursue every flock of sheepe they see. This unsteadinesse, it ariseth from the like curse on the mind of *man*, as was on *Cain*, that it being *driven from the presence of the Lord*, it proves a vagabond, *and so mens eyes are in the ends of the earth*.[7]

The ideal solution to this problem was hinted at by Goodwin. If the structure of righteousness was threatened by the vagrancies of the stream of consciousness, one might hope that the stream could be rigorously controlled. Goodwin touches on this profound aspiration in his extolment of "steadiness":

And though indeed the mind of man is nimble and able thus to run from one end of the earth to another, (which is its strength and excellency) yet GOD would not have this strength and nimblenesse, and metall-spirit in curvetting and tumbling, (as I may call it) but in steady directing all our thoughts straight on to his glory, our owne salvation, and the good of others . . . . As we are to walke in Gods wayes hee calls us to, so every thought, as well as every action, is a step: and therefore ought to bee steady.[8]

Goodwin's suggestion that it may indeed be possible for the individual to rein in his attention in this way, his thoughts displaying a rigorous "steadiness" that bespeaks the effectual government of the reason, has a touch of unreality. In a more practical statement of the possibilities, John Owen argued:

The mighty stream of the evil thoughts of men will admit of no bounds or dams to put a stop unto them. There are

7. *The Vanity of Thoughts Discovered* (London, 1638), pp. 21–22.
8. Ibid., p. 21.

> but two ways of relief from them, the one respecting their *moral evil*, the other their *natural abundance*. The first [is,] by throwing salt into the spring, as Elisha cured the waters of Jericho.—that is, to get the heart and mind seasoned with grace; for the tree must be made good before the fruit will be so. The other is, to turn their streams into new channels, putting new aims and ends upon them, fixing on new objects: so shall we abound in spiritual thoughts; for abound in thoughts we shall, whether we will or no.[9]

Without supposing that the reason has absolute control over the actual processes of mental activity, Owen attacks the problem from the outside by giving the processes conscious focus. His solution, to provide the mind with a generous supply of spiritual objects, could, of course, be implemented in an unusual way by occasional meditation. This methodology of meditation could assure the individual that he would always have spiritual objects for his attention, whatever the surroundings. As Edward Bury says of occasional meditation:

> This keeps the heart in order, . . . it keeps vain thoughts from rising, or at best from roosting: There mans heart is like a mill, if it want grist, it sets it self on fire, and if there be no corn to grinde for God, the devil will throw his tares into the hopper: The heart is always well or ill-employed, and will never be idle; holy meditation puts a man out of satans road, when otherwise he is in continuall danger of falling into his snares.[1]

The explicit assumption that if the mind was not well employed it was ill employed spoke a fearful message to the Puritan concerned with discerning that purity in himself

---

9. ΦPONHMA, p. 300.
1. "To the Reader," *The Husbandmans Companion* (London, 1677), fol. 2, recto and verso.

which was a sign of election. Occasional meditation was undoubtedly recommended strongly to the Puritan conscience by the claims of its defenders that it was indeed a mark of the genuine Christian. The capacity to "spiritualize" all phenomena witnessed to a sanctified heart. Isaac Ambrose observes:

> The heart is an house of common resort, into which multitudes of thoughts, like so many guests, enter, and have free and open accesse; onley if it be sanctified, it ordinarily distils holy, sweet, and useful Meditations out of all objects; as the Bee sucks honey out of every flower, and a good stomack sucks sweet and wholesome nourishment out of what it takes to it self; So doth a holy heart (so far as sanctified) convert and digest all into spiritual and useful thoughts: But on the contrary, if it be wicked, then a world of vain, light, wanton, prophane, and dissolute thoughts lodge there, and defile those rooms they lodge in. (*PMU*, 2, 68–69)

The talent for spiritualizing was emphatically not the gift of ingenuity, as it must appear to many a modern reader, but an indication that grace was operative within the meditator. And of course the operation of grace was a sign of election. In light of these facts, one can appreciate something of the ineluctable appeal of Ambrose's exhortation, or of Goodwin's:

> A heart sanctified, and in whose affections true grace is enkindled, out of all Gods dealings with him, out of all the things he sees and hears, out of all the objects are put into the thoughts, he distilleth holy, and sweet, and usefull meditations: and it naturally doth it, and ordinarily doth it, so farre as it is sanctified.[2]

2. *Vanity*, p. 12.

Similar declarations are made by John Owen and Edmund Calamy. The Puritan's incentive toward a disciplined use of occasional meditation was the strongest possible. The belief that the skill that came with application testified to the effectual working of grace in the heart and was evidence of election and the conviction that the creatures should speak not to the senses and imagination, but to the reason which God had planted in man as an inner ear for hearing his divine voice of revelation, supported the peculiarly zealous appropriation of the ancient tradition of occasional meditation by Puritanism, and it is not surprising that it appears as a conspicuous part of all the major Puritan treatises on meditation, as well as the subject for a host of minor writers such as William Spurstow, Thomas Taylor, Edward Bury, John Flavel, and Henry Lukin.

God's voice was speaking in the creation, as it spoke in the Word, though of course the Word was normative. In discovering these spiritual meanings, man was in fact giving speech to the creatures so that they might "speak" their praises to the Creator; and the notion was peculiarly congenial to a movement oriented to the ear and tongue. Samuel Ward observed:

> The *Hebrewes* have a Canon, that God would be praised in the least Emmet or Gnat, but magnified in the Elephant and Leviathan; admired in the Sunne, Moone, Starres, Comets, Earthquakes, Thunders, and such extraordinarie workes: the praise of his wisdome and power lies asleepe & dead in every Creature, till man actuate and enliven it. The Heavens and the Earth, and all things therein are said to praise God; that is, (saith *Augustine*) when thou considerest their order and beautie, and praisest the invisible Creator, they praise him with thy understanding & thy voice, which have none of their owne, but are dumbe and sencelesse.[3]

3. *A Peace-offring to God, bound* in *A Collection of Such Sermons as have been written by S. Ward* (London, 1627–28), pp. 19–20.

But the "order and beautie" of the creatures—those qualities which spoke praise of their Maker—were actually only a small part of the spiritual meaning one might find in the objective world that forced itself so imperiously upon the senses and imagination. Thus, although such defenders of occasional meditation as Joseph Hall usually found sanction for their methodology in the ancient tradition of meditation upon the creatures, strictly defined—that is, those objects of the creation subordinate to man—in seventeenth-century England the tradition was amplified so that any circumstance in the world outside the reflective spectator might be made to yield spiritual truth. The ingenuity that went into the search for significances is suggested by this selected list of topics from the table of contents in Joseph Hall's *Occasional Meditations:*

> Upon an arme benumbed.
> Upon the putting on of his clothes.
> Upon the change of weather.
> Upon the sight of an harlot carted.
> Upon motes in the sun.
> Upon the sight of a left-handed man.
> Upon the sight of a man yawning.[4]

Since any circumstance, no matter how trivial, might serve as its stimulus, such meditation not infrequently showed a trace of whimsicality, as when Hall, meditating "Upon the sight of a crow pulling off wooll from the backe of a Sheepe," observes, "How well these Creatures know whom they may bee bold with? . . . Meekenesse of spirit commonly drawns on injuries,"[5] or when William Spurstow, in *Spiritual Chymist*, reflects "Upon a Crum going the wrong way":

---

4. *Occasionall Meditations* (3rd ed. [containing 49 meditations not previously published] London, 1633).

5. *Occasionall Meditations*, pp. 71–72.

> What more mean and contemptible thing can there be then a *single Crum* . . . : in the *Mouth* (it is true) it hath scarce substance enough to be felt; but, in the *Throat*, it is such as can hardly be endured. . . . O, how frail and mutable is the Life of Man; which is not only Jeoparded by Instruments of War and Slaughter, which are made to destroy, but by an *Hair*, a *Raisin-Stone*, a *Feather*, a *Crum*, and a thousand such inconsiderable things, which have a power to extinguish Life, but none to preserve it? [6]

Puritan occasional meditation expresses those attitudes toward nature which Baxter in particular took such pains to qualify. One treatise which shows in vivid detail the Puritan methodology of reducing nature to a scripture is Edward Bury's *Husbandmans Companion* of 1677. On several occasions, indeed, Bury catches himself upon the brink of an honest absorption in nature, an absorption unhampered by the attempt to read the significance of the creature; having seen the peril in time, however, he proceeds to a didactic simplification of the experience. In his meditation, "Upon sweet-smelling flowers," for instance, he turns away, almost in consternation, from his spontaneous pleasure and replaces it with a manipulation of chaste abstractions to assist him in turning his thoughts heavenward:

> When I considered what a sweet savour and odoriferous smell, a garden of flowers and hearbs sent forth when it was watered from heaven by a refreshing shower, and cheared again with the sun-beams darted upon it, what a place of pleasure, a paradice of delights it seemed to be, the sight, the smell and savour delighted me, the melodious harmony and birds pleased me, so that my affections began to grow warm, and my fancy to be tickled with it, and I began with *Peter* to say, *it is good being here;* till

6. *Spiritual Chymist*, p. 11.

upon consideration I checkt my self for my folly, for letting out my affection upon such poor objects, and letting them grovel so low upon the ground, and to close with such poor pittiful nothings; then began I to screw my thoughts a little higher, and to say to my self, fool that thou art, is there so much beauty and sweetness in the creature, yea, in these poor pitifull vanishing fading creatures, *which to day are* (saith Christ) *and to morrow are cast into the oven, Mat.* 6. 30. what sweetness then is in the creator, that breathed this sweetness into them; is not he much more sweet and delightfull? and why dost thou not place thy affections upon him, *that is altogether lovely?* [7]

This is a long remove from Baxter's program of meditation, which sanctified aesthetic absorption in the creatures as a preview of heavenly experience. Bury's fear of "losing" himself in the creature and the tacit supposition that this tendency could be checked only by turning from aesthetic appreciation to didactic spiritualizing of the object are characteristic of the mainstream of Puritan thought, but they obviously ignore the alternative which Sibbes and Baxter explored. It was possible, after all, to spiritualize all aspects of the creature, even those which made their appeal to the affections, imagination, and intuition. One could lose himself in a garden to advantage if he were prepared to evaluate the total experience as a meager foretaste of things heavenly.

Occasional Meditation in *The Pilgrim's Progress*

The influence of occasional meditation upon *The Pilgrim's Progress* can be discussed in terms not only of Bunyan's understanding of allegory but also of the occurrences of this kind of meditation as part of the action of the work. The first area of

---

7. Ibid., pp. 120–21.

influence perhaps needs no more than to be mentioned. If one fact above dispute can be deduced from the records of Puritan occasional meditation, it is that through it the Puritan perfected the talent for looking beyond event to word. Caught as he was in the treacherous crosscurrents of beckoning evil and imperfectly understood good, on pilgrimage to heavenly reality, the average Puritan was more interested in objects and events as signposts than as caravanserais; hence their meanings were formulated in statements, as doctrines and instructions. The Puritan approached the creatures in a dialogue in which his questions were met with answers and his reasonings sanctioned by the logic God had woven into the fabric of humble things. As Thomas Adams declared, "A good Christian, that like the Bee workes honey from every flower, suffers no action, demonstration, event, to slip by him without a question. All objects to a meditating *Solomon*, are like wings to reare and mount up his thoughts to Heaven." [8] All the creatures were made to participate in dialogue, and as their meaning was reduced to *logos*, they became allegorical. To the degree that Bunyan was versed in this tradition, his appreciation of the diverse ways in which events might carry meaning was cultivated.

It may seem curious that the bulk of the specific appearances of occasional meditation in *The Pilgrim's Progress* are to be found in Part Two, but this is quite in keeping with the divergence between the two parts. Christiana learns, by and large, through reflection and meditation, while Christian learns, for the most part, through action. Of course Christian does have his reflective interludes at Interpreter's House and House Beautiful, but the closest approximations to occasional meditation in the first part do not need to be complicated by an explanation in terms of that tradition. This is not true, however, of many of the sights which Christiana enjoys. A good

---

8. "The Sinners Passing-Bell," Works (London, 1629), p. 252.

IN *The Pilgrim's Progress*

example is the episode involving a spider on the wall. After the Interpreter has shown Christiana and her group the Muckraker,

> he has them into the very best Room in the house, (a very brave Room it was) so he bid them look round about, and see if they could find anything profitable there. Then they looked round and round: For there was nothing to be seen but a very great *Spider* on the Wall: and that they overlook't.
>
> *Mer. Then said* Mercie, *Sir, I see nothing; but* Christiana *held her peace.*
>
> *Inter.* But said the *Interpreter*, look again: she therefore lookt again and said, Here is not any thing, but an *ugly Spider*, who hangs by her Hands upon the Wall. Then said he, Is there but one *Spider* in all this spacious Room? Then the water stood in *Christiana's* Eyes, for she was a Woman quick of apprehension: and she said, Yes Lord, there is more here then one. Yea, and *Spiders* whose Venom is far more destructive then that which is in her. The *Interpreter* then looked pleasantly upon her, and said, Thou hast said the Truth. This made *Mercie* blush, and the Boys to cover their Faces. For they all began now to understand the Riddle.
>
> Then said the *Interpreter* again, *The Spider taketh hold with her hands, as you see, and is in Kings Pallaces.* And wherefore is this recorded; but to show you, that how full of the Venome of Sin soever you be, yet you may by the hand of Faith lay hold of, and dwell in the best Room that belongs to the Kings House above?
>
> *Chris.* I thought, said *Christiana*, of something of this; but I could not imagin it all. I thought that we were like *Spiders*, and that we looked like ugly Creatures, in what fine Room soever we were: But that by this *Spider*, this

venomous and ill favoured Creature, we were to learn *how to act Faith*, that came not into my mind. And yet she has taken hold with her hands as I see, and dwells in the best Room in the House. God has made nothing in vain. (pp. 200–01)

Roger Sharrock has searched diligently but without success for some source for this episode in the emblem tradition. This is not surprising since the episode is a dramatization of a simple occasional meditation and as such can be readily traced to its sources in that tradition. In Edmund Calamy's treatise on meditation which appeared in 1680, four years before the second part of *The Pilgrim's Progress*, the spider was referred to, as it often is in the tradition, as confirmation of the claim that even the vilest and humblest creature could provoke holy reflections:

> There is nothing *more easie* than *this ejaculatory meditation to you that are spiritual;* deliberate and solemn meditation is very hard and difficult; but this way of meditation is very easie; and the *reason* is this, because there is no Creature of God but is a teacher of *some good thing;* thou canst not behold a *Spider* but thou maist make some good use of it; the Scripture doth make many rare uses of a *Spider;* a wicked man may be lookt upon in a *Spider*, as in a glass.[9]

If even the spider could be made to yield spiritual meanings, one had good reason to declare, as Bunyan's Christiana does, that "God has made nothing in vain." Similarly, in Edward Bury's collection of occasional meditations, which antedated Calamy's treatise by three years, the author reflects at some length upon the lowly spider:

9. *Art of Divine Meditation*, p. 14.

IN *The Pilgrim's Progress*

> Observing the industry, diligence, and painful labour of the spider, a contemptible creature, how busy she was in weaving her nets, how industriously she plys her work, and though oftentimes she meet with disappointments, had her work spoiled, and her self indangered, yet never a whit discouraged, or disheartned, she begins again; this is one of these *four things that Solomon had observed in the earth, that were little but wise, &c, the spider that taketh hold with her hands, and is in Kings palaces. Pro. 30.24 &c.* she doth her work painfully, and curiously spins (saith one) a finer thred then a woman can do . . . : When I had a while pleased my self with the curiosity of the work, and commended the diligence of the workman, I began to consider what her end might be of all this pains, or what benefit did accrue to her by this her diligenee [sic]? [1]

Bury, like Calamy and Bunyan, is more than casually interested in the spider as a humble spokesman of divine truth. And these parallels indicate that in the related passage in *The Pilgrim's Progress* Bunyan was drawing upon the conventions of an established tradition. The principal meaning which he derives from the "very great spider on the wall" is of special interest, for it is in fact another outcropping of a vein of subtlety which we explored above in discussing Christian's visit to Interpreter's House. The spider's "taking hold by his hand" is to be understood, Interpreter explains, as a figure of faith.

Of the other occasional meditations which are of some interest that appear in the episode at hand, I shall discuss several which are given *seriatim:*

> He had them then into another Room where was a Hen and Chickens, and bid them observe a while. So one of the

1. Bury, p. 229.

Chickens went to the Trough to drink, and every time she drank she lift up her head and her eyes towards Heaven. See, said he, what this little Chick doth, and learn of her to acknowledge whence your Mercies come, by receiving them with looking up. Yet again, said he, observe and look: So they gave heed, and perceived that the Hen did walk in a four-fold Method towards her Chickens. 1. She had a *common call*, and that she hath all day long. 2. She had a *special call*, and that she had but sometimes. 3. She had a *brooding note*. And 4. she had an *out-cry*.

Now, said he, compare this *Hen* to your King, and these Chickens to his Obedient ones. For answerable to her, himself has his Methods, which he walketh in towards his People. By his common call, *he gives nothing*, by his special call, he always *has something to give*, he has also a brooding voice, *for them that are under his Wing*. And he has an out-cry, to give *the Alarm when he seeth the Enemy come*. I chose, my Darlings, to lead you into the Room where such things are, because you are Women, and they are easie for you. (pp. 201–02)

Interpreter's final comment here is important. The scenes which Christian sees in his visit at Interpreter's House are quite complex in their significations: in the scene of the fire mysteriously maintained, for example, the fire is "the work of Grace that is wrought in the heart," and other counters are Christ, the devil, the unction of the Spirit and the concealing wall, which represents the inscrutability of grace. The action is contrived, with the elements selected beforehand to yield the desired scheme of significances. This is the strong meat which Christian can digest, as a man. In contrast with this more sophisticated parabolic form, occasional meditation, such

IN *The Pilgrim's Progress*

as that on the hen and her chicks, begins with natural circumstance just as it presents itself to the attention (it has of course been "planted" by Bunyan). This is the kind of easy moralizing of which Christiana and Mercy, as weaker vessels, are capable.

These scenes are concerned with the primary subject of occasional meditation, the *res creati*, as are the meditations which follow:

> So he had them into the Slaughter-house, where was a *Butcher* a killing of a Sheep: And behold the Sheep was quiet, and took her Death patiently. Then said the *Interpreter:* You must learn of this Sheep, to suffer: And to put up wrongs without murmurings and complaints. Behold how quietly she takes her Death, and without objecting she suffereth her Skin to be pulled over her Ears. Your King doth call you his Sheep.
>
> After this, he led them into his Garden, where was great variety of Flowers: and he said, do you see all these? So *Christiana* said, yes. Then said he again, Behold the Flowers are divers in *Stature*, in *Quality*, and *Colour*, and *Smell*, and *Virtue*, and some are better then some: Also where the Gardiner has set some, there they stand, and quarrel not one with another.
>
> Again he had them into his Field, which he had sowed with Wheat and Corn: but when they beheld, the tops of all was cut off, only the Straw remained. He said again, this Ground was Dunged, and Plowed, and Sowed; but what shall we do with the Crop? Then said *Christiana*, burn some and make muck of the rest. Then said the *Interpreter* again, Fruit you see is that thing you look for, and for want of that you condemn it to the Fire, and to be trodden under foot of men: Beware that in this you condemn not your selves. (p. 202)

In directing the pilgrims to his slaughterhouse, his garden, and his fields, Interpreter has gone quite afield from his Significant Rooms to find spiritual food for his guests, a fact that bears out the obvious point that in these scenes he is availing himself of incidental occasions for meditation which present themselves about his house and grounds. Bunyan is in full agreement with Thomas Taylor's observation that "The whole world is his [God's] booke: so many pages as there are severall creatures; no page is empty, but full of lines; every quality of the creature, is a severall letter of these lines, and no letter without a part of Gods wisdome in it."[2]

After Interpreter has counseled his guests with a number of edifying proverbs,

> he takes them out into his Garden again, and had them to a Tree whose *inside* was all rotten, and gone, and yet it grew and had Leaves. Then said *Mercie*, what means this? This Tree, said he, whose *out-side* is fair, and whose *inside* is rotten; is it to which many may be compared that are in the Garden of God: Who with their mouths speak high in behalf of God, but indeed will do nothing for him: Whose Leaves are fair; but their heart Good for nothing, but to be *Tinder* for the Devils *Tinderbox*. (p. 204)

The topic of the fruitless tree was a favorite one for Puritan homilies, since Christ had sanctified the metaphor, and it finds its way into occasional meditation as well. Edward Bury's meditation "Upon a leavy yet barren tree" offers several parallels to Bunyan's. Bury says,

> me thinks this barren tree resembles many in our times, *that have a form of godliness, but deny the power of it,* 2 *Tim.* 3.5. they have leaves but no fruit, a shadow but no

---

2. Taylor, p. 23.

substance; those hollow professors are like an old tree, tall but pithless, sapless and unsound; these men do as players in a Comedy, in voice and gesture act divine duties, but in heart deny them; formality (as one saith) is like a bull-rush, the colour fresh, the skin smooth, but within nothing but a spungeous substance.[3]

If this is not an example of direct influence, it at least provides evidence that Bury and Bunyan were tapping a tradition in which a number of topics had become commonplace, with more or less standardized interpretations.

There is a certain propriety in Bunyan's relegation of occasional meditation as an element in the "action" of *The Pilgrim's Progress* to the second part. Occasional meditation, as Calamy described it, came within the "Parenthesis" of leisure that the individual enjoyed in his daily affairs. It presupposed moments when the person could step outside the stream of compulsive routines and reflect upon the creatures that constituted a part of those routines. Christian's pilgrimage, however, is impelled by a dread urgency, and it has, for the most part, the tempo of flight and the race. He flees from the wrath to come and runs for the prize of the high calling. Not until he reaches the Land of Beulah does his pilgrimage make conspicuous room for rest. (Rest earlier had brought on him severe judgment when he slept in the arbor and lost his roll.) In light of these facts, it is not surprising that Bunyan does not have Interpreter train Christian in the skills of occasional meditation, as he does Christiana and her company. Christian's pilgrimage offers little opportunity for reflection upon the creatures. Christiana, in contrast, spends a month at House Beautiful alone and has abundant opportunity on her pilgrimage to tour field and garden, using the skills learned from Interpreter.

3. Bury, p. 385.

9

MEDITATION ON EXPERIENCE AND *THE PILGRIM'S PROGRESS*

The Rationale of Meditation on Experience

When Bunyan's Christian comes to House Beautiful, he is advised by Watchful, the porter: "I will call out one of the Virgins of this place, who will, if she likes your talk, bring you in to the rest of the Family, according to the Rules of the House" (p. 46). Christian passes the first screening, administered by Discretion, and soon he is invited in:

> So when he was come in, and set down, they gave him something to drink; and consented together, that until supper was ready, some one or two of them should have some particular discourse with *Christian*, for the best improvement of time; and they appointed *Piety* and *Prudence* and *Charity* to discourse with him; and thus they began:
> Piety. *Come good* Christian, *since we have been so loving to you, to receive you in to our House this night; let us, if perhaps we may better our selves thereby, talk with you of all things that have happened to you in your Pilgrimage.*

> *Chr.* With a very good will, and I am glad that you are so well disposed. (p. 47)

We do not wonder that the ladies of the household are interested in Christian's story, but we may well be curious about their pointed concern to make it serve the ends of edification. At any rate, the discourse that follows extracts from Christian's pilgrimage its full didactic content, and Piety is not discouraged in her efforts to "better" herself by Christian's experiences. Christian, we may assume, has profited too.

This episode is one among many in *The Pilgrim's Progress* in which the action halts while a lengthy recapitulation and reflection upon past events is provided, and such episodes represent the implementation in Bunyan's allegory of one of the most common of Puritan devotional practices: formal meditation upon the individual's past. Scholars have repeatedly drawn attention to Puritan spiritual autobiography, noting its role in the development of such modern genres as biography and the novel, but it was only one of a variety of manifestations of Puritanism's extraordinary interest in the personal past. Another manifestation was a discipline of meditation, which by the time of Bunyan had become formalized and which from all indications was coextensive with Puritanism. We shall examine its rationale and methodology, and then explore in detail its influence upon Bunyan's narrative.

One can without difficulty isolate the reasons for this Puritan emphasis. The primary one was the concern to find in the events of one's life the assurance of election, to search one's past for evidences of "sincerity." Richard Baxter urges:

> Remember what *discoveries* of thy *state* thou hast made formerly in the walk of *self-examination;* how oft God hath convinced thee of the *sincerity* of thy *heart:* Remember all the former Testimonies of the *Spirit;* and all the *sweet feelings* of the Favour of God; and all the

prayers that he hath heard and granted; and all the rare *preservations* and *deliverances;* and all the progress of his *Spirit* in his workings on thy Soul; and the disposals of *Providence*, conducing to thy good: . . . And though one of these considered alone, may be no sure evidence of his special love, (which I expect thou shouldst try by more infallible signs) yet lay them altogether, and then think with thy self, Whether all these do not testifie the good-will of the *Lord* concerning thy *Salvation*, and may not well be pleaded against thine unbelief? (*SER*, Pt. 4, p. 190)

One's certainty of election was at best precarious, since "sincerity" was a quality of heart subject to no verification through reasoning from externals. Furthermore, since any species of subjective verification was open to disqualification by even a suspicion of selfish or demonic origin, the only escape from the dilemma was a resolute act of faith wholly discontinuous with the morass of verification.[1] Unfortunately, reflection upon this act of faith which had lifted the question of certitude off the plane of reasoned proof and settled it by a claim which brought its own kind of certainty tended to broach the question again on the original level. If the act of faith was not then dismissed altogether by the anxious seeker after election, it was apt at least to be questioned on the grounds that it had been vitiated by elements of doubt, had not been "saving faith." Against these disturbing questions the reflective convert could arrange all those occasions of God's stirring within him which he had taken the precaution

1. Bunyan has perhaps allegorized the ontological anxiety which gnawed at the roots of Puritan certainty, and the saving *non sequitur* of faith, in his episode of Doubting Castle, wherein Christian and Faithful are saved from the self-perpetuating cycle of doubt and defeat by faith in and use of the key of Promise. The turn from the agonizing circularities of reasoned verification in an impulsive act of faith is a typical feature of Puritan spiritual autobiography.

of memorializing in writing. The tendency to treasure spiritual experience was widespread in Puritanism, showing itself in many private notations that were never organized into the form now referred to as the spiritual autobiography. The Puritan often had occasion to refer to "all the former testimonies of the Spirit," and if they were secured in writing, so much the better. Significantly, Baxter in addressing a general Puritan audience in his *Saints Everlasting Rest* could urge them to prove to their cold hearts the truth of the Scripture in the words, "Study all confirming *Providences;* call forth thy own recorded *experience*,"[2] and probably many in his audience could carry out the latter instruction. This treasuring of experience as a battery of evidence to be arranged against one's doubts of election underlies both meditation upon experience and the spiritual autobiography, a fact which is insufficiently appreciated by the critic L. D. Lerner when he suggests that the latter literary form stems largely from "Puritan egoism" and the "assurance that one's own experiences *matter*" with a "consequent stress on one's own importance."[3] This assuredly enters into the picture; yet much of the material for these autobiographies was accumulated not because it mattered to another but because it mattered so much to the writer. The individual was not so interested in proving his importance to another as he was in proving to himself that he was important to God. The charge of egoism should, perhaps, be kept for those autobiographies which were too consciously designed for an audience.

Retrospection for evidences of election is, however, only one among several readily discernible sources for the Puritan interest in personal experience. Another was his passionate concern to orient and stabilize himself in the historical flux.

2. *SER*, Pt. 4, p. 189.
3. L. D. Lerner, "Puritanism and the Spiritual Autobiography," *Hibbert Journal*, 55 (1956–57), 381.

Rootless for the most part, vigorously dissenting against a young Establishment which was itself searching for roots, and deprived of the opportunity of extending his historical identity along the axis of a corporate tradition, he elaborated for himself a private tradition in which the individual past became a kind of outrigger for stabilizing the individual present.

This stratagem was of course no more than a particular application of Reformation teaching on vocation. The emphasis of the Reformers upon the divine calling of every Christian nourished the conviction that every life was unified in such a way that retrospection could find encouragement and composure in discerning the shape of the emerging whole. Henri Talon touches on this point with respect to Bunyan's *Grace Abounding* when he says: "Bunyan was haunted by the desire to survey his whole life in one glance, to hold his soul in his hands, the better to possess himself. He never named this need; he neither perceived it nor singled it out in his moral life, but he nevertheless succumbed to it." [4] The fact is that the desire which Talon ascribes to Bunyan was clearly felt in Puritanism at large. It had been consciously elaborated in precise disciplines of meditation, among other expressions, and Bunyan was one with his movement in wishing to see his life in this way. The passing of time found the Puritan Christian engaged in the awesome process of constructing a unity toward which the whole *telos* of his life was directed. Bunyan certainly hit upon the best figure possible when he represented such a temporal structure as a pilgrimage of which the end is the influence that determines all which goes before. *End*, that ambiguous term which can mean both terminus and informing purpose, points to the way in which teleological unity and pilgrimage cohere.

In reviewing his past experience, then, the Puritan was discerning the shape of the divinely ordered whole which his life

4. Talon, p. 132.

was becoming. It must be noted that his pose was not at all that of Bunyan's waterman, always "looking one way and rowing another": to read the past, he kept a careful eye on the future as well. Of that time when the end was attained, the very title of Baxter's masterwork, *The Saints Everlasting Rest*, perhaps suggests something of importance. There was heavy emphasis in Puritan eschatology upon the heavenly consummation as an everlasting cessation of labor: death marked a triumph, the abundant and ambiguous energies of the individual life wrought by God into a perfect whole which might be regarded as a monument to the accomplished divine purpose.

A basic element in the expressions of the Puritan's interest in past experience was the profound belief that experience formed the kind of rational whole in which God's activity could be descried as an explication and confirmation of biblical statement. In his private experience, as much as in the Word, the Puritan discerned God's voice speaking instruction and doctrine. Indeed, insofar as he made edifying use of his past, he tended to read it as *logos*, as an elaborate allegory of intelligible statement. He made of his past a surrogate for ecclesiastical tradition, and the surrogate was evaluated as a private tradition in which God had disclosed His mind by the way in which He carried out promises and threatenings, in his providences and judgments. Life was a second scripture by which to understand the written Word, and it was read largely in terms of those same simple categories which the Puritan used in understanding the Bible: precepts, examples, promises, threatenings. Perhaps the most conspicuous feature of Puritan meditation on experience is the naïve certainty that the life, as a rational whole, could be analyzed into its rational parts, which might then be accurately "catalogued."

Experience read as *logos* was the final authority of the Puritan. This is understandable, for his problems could not be settled merely by assuming the inerrancy and perfect clarity of

Scripture. The gulf fixed between the principles of the Word and their relevant application in seventeenth-century England was not to be gainsaid, and occasionally a Puritan displays honest candor on the matter. Admitting the breach between Word and experience, for example, Richard Baxter says:

> It is no easie matter to rejoyce at that which we never saw, nor never knew the man that did see it; and this upon a meer promise which is written in the Bible; and that when we have nothing else to rejoyce in, but all our sensible comforts do fail us: But to rejoyce in that which we see and feel, in that which we have hold of, and possession already, this is not difficult. (*SER*, Pt. 4, p. 217)

The reference to a "meer promise" is striking, since Puritanism on the whole laid enormous emphasis on the value of the binding obligations imposed by God upon Himself; but any comfort of the Word, any admonition, was vacuous until it could be appreciated as an encouraging or indicting reality in experience. This natural need to interpret the Word in terms of experience entailed the some simplistic attitude toward experience which characterized Puritan attitudes toward experience recorded in Scripture. Hence Thomas Adams could say, "The Lord, when he sends raine or drought, respects our sinne or obedience: he considers not in what position heaven is, but in what disposition we are."[5] The possibility of ambiguity in historical existence was all but ignored: any joy was interpreted in terms of scriptural promise (that is, as outright providence), and every affliction was interpreted as a judgment fulfilling a particular admonition, or as the "trial of faith," with some special promise applicable to this particular testing. So experience became the proving ground of the Word and in effect the final authority for the Puritan. True, one might distinguish, as Isaac Ambrose does, between "natural"

5. Adams, *Meditations Upon the Creed, Works*, p. 1154.

and "spiritual" experience—the latter being the species relevant to the understanding of the Word—but his distinction was of little weight, since any natural experience had only to be subjected to a spiritual construction to become in fact spiritual. Ambrose observes:

> *Experience* (say some) *is a knowledge and discovery of something by sense not evident in it self, but manifested by some event or effect.* This description containes both Natural and Spiritual *Experience;* but my purpose is to speak only of the latter, and in that respect I look strictly at *Experiences,* as *Real proofes* of *Scripture truths.* When I mark how true every part of Gods Word is, how all the Doctrines, Threatnings and Promises contained therein, are daily verified in others, and in my own self, and so improve or make use of them to my own Spiritual advantage, this I call *Experience.* (PMU, 2, 164)

It may strike the reader as odd to talk about "proof" of the Scriptures, to set about proving one's final authority, but Ambrose, like a host of other Puritans, apprehended the disjunction between the *de jure* authority of the Word and the *de facto* authority of experience. If in the Church with which the Reformers broke the authority of the Word was mediated to the immediate exigencies of the private life through the accumulated experience of a corporate tradition, in Puritanism the circumscribed tradition of one's personal past provided the mouthpiece through which the Word spoke.[6] Thus Richard Sibbes remarked:

---

6. I do not mean to imply that this position was solipsistic. The Puritan strove to benefit from the experience of others, of course. It too glossed the Scripture. As Thomas Adams says, "The lives of holy men is a kind of Commentary or interpretation of the holy writ." We should "not onely lay them before us, and looke on them, but write after them" (*The Happinesse of the Church, Works,* p. 596).

> In reading of the Scriptures, let us compare experiments [i.e., experiences] with rules: Neh. i. 8, 9, "If you sin you shall be scattered; and if you return again, I will be merciful." We should practise this in our lives, to see how God hath made good his threatenings in our corrections, and his promises in our comforts.[7]

Yet what superficially seems a process of verification was indeed a dialogue between experience and Scripture in which the Puritan settled for himself the critical problems of how, for example, promises and threatenings were actually to be understood. Obviously, if, as Sibbes urged, a Christian looked to experience for examples of divinely initiated corrections, the particular "corrections" he happened to have experienced would be those he construed as the fulfillment of divine threatenings. Puritanism did not of course completely skirt the pitfall of those who centuries earlier had asked, "Master, who did sin, this man, or his parents, that he was born blind?" Afflictions, interpreted as corrections, were immediately linked with divine purpose, at the same time that benefits were construed as special providences. If the individual's afflictions were heavy—as was surely the case for many persecuted dissenters —he was apt to take a jaundiced view of his own merits and to practice a sober resignation to a chastising deity. This Puritan understanding of providence and correction was undoubtedly an important prop to the Calvinist emphasis on depravity; it is suggestive at least that as Puritanism passed into Whiggery and persecution declined, the emphasis upon human depravity also waned.

The relation, then, between Word and experience was one of reciprocal illumination. Just as the Puritan read experience in the light of the unambiguous divine purpose he found in the Scripture, so he read Scripture in light of the peculiar contours

---

7. *Divine Meditations, Works,* 7, 208.

of his own experience, looking for—and finding—special promises which corresponded to his comforts and special threatenings which corresponded to his corrections. This was the inevitable outgrowth of that emphasis, well summarized by Thomas Gouge in his *Christian Directions* of 1661: "In reading the Promises and Threatnings, the Exhortations and Admonitions, and other parts of the Scripture: So apply them to thy self, as if God by name had delivered the same unto thee." [8] The individual who saw the Bible as personally addressed to him had to use his past experience as the inevitable touchstone by which he saw how the Word had explained itself in his special case. In a sense, no other experience was relevant to the special meanings God's Word was to have for him. This was not to make the Word of "private interpretation," for it was understood that such general utterances as promises and exhortations would have particular relevance for each reader.

The Methodology of Meditation on Experience

The Puritan, we have observed, stressed personal experience for several reasons: he treasured it for its evidences of election, he appreciated it as a disclosure of the kind of rational whole his life was elaborating, and he valued it as the private tradition in which the authority of the Word was interpreted and translated into relevant imperatives. The last two values, in particular, evidence the Puritan's treatment of experience as *logos*. Now we must consider how this emphasis upon experience was implemented in formal meditation, and Isaac Ambrose is a convenient figure with which to begin.

In his *Prima Media & Ultima*, Ambrose gives a full chapter to the subject of the use a Christian is to make of experience, and the devotional discipline he outlines is essentially that of meditation. He begins by suggesting "That our *Experiences*

---

8. This is taken from his *Works* (London, 1706), p. 199.

may further us in the way to Heaven, we must learne, 1. To gather them: 2. To improve them" (*PMU*, 2, 165) and then explains the first duty:

> For the gathering of them, the only way is, —
> 1. To mark things which fall out; To observe the beginnings and events of matters, to eye them every way, on every side, that they may stand us in stead for the future: This observation and pondering of events, with the causes that went before, is the ripener of wit; . . . .
> 2. To treasure up, and lay in these observations, to have in remembrance such works of God as we have known and observed . . . . *I remember the dayes of old,* saith *David;* I remember how thou didst rebuke *Abimelech,* and overthrow *Nimrod,* and *Pharaoh,* and *Ahitophel:* and thus, would we treasure up *Experiments,* the former part of our life would come in to help the latter, and the longer we live, the richer in Faith we should be; even as in Victories, every former overthrow of an Enemy, helps to obtain a succeeding Victory. This is the use of a sanctified memory, it will lose nothing that may help in time of need, or in the evil day; it records all the breathings, movings, stirrings, workings of a soul towards Christ, or of Christ towards a soul.

It may be noted that Ambrose is recalling experiences not so much for the sake of re-creating them "in tranquillity," and so enjoying again their affective content, as for the purpose of exploiting their evidential value. With this the use of remembered experience in Catholic meditation may be briefly contrasted. St. Anselm, for example, in addressing a novice in his *Book of Meditations and Prayers,* says:

> How often, as you were singing or reading, did He not enlighten with His light the senses of your soul! How often, when you prayed, did He not ravish you with

ineffable longings for Himself! How often, your mind being withdrawn from earthly things, did He not transport you into the midst of heavenly delights and the joys of paradise! Think of all these things, and turn them over in your mind, that all your heart's love may be turned over to him.[9]

The stress here is less upon the evidential value of such experience and more upon the rekindling of the original emotion, less upon the instruction or assurance to be derived and more upon the experience as an unreduced whole. The Catholic and the Puritan, by and large, had different ends in view when they turned to experience as a subject for meditation.

In the procedure that Ambrose outlines for the second duty he recommends, that of "improving" experiences, he shows the characteristic interest of the Puritan in an orderly and logical implementation of his devotions and in a reading of experience as a detailed confirmation of the Word and the divine purpose:

For the improving of *Experiences,*—

1. We must consider what Scripture truth is verified thereby.

        Others.

in

        Ourselves.

1. In *others,* as, if we consider how God blesseth and cheareth the religious, wherein that Text is verified, *Blessed are the righteous, for it shall be well with them, for they shall eat the fruit of their doings:* or if we observe how God punisheth the carnal and hypocritical, wherein that text is verified, *Wo unto the wicked, it shall be ill with them, for the reward of their hands shall be given them.*

---

9. St. Anselm, *Book of Meditations and Prayers,* pp. 226–27.

2. In *our selves*, as, if by a spiritual *Experience* we *taste God to be good;* wherein that text is *verified, If so be ye have tasted that the Lord is gracious:* If we finde *the things given us of God* to be *good;* as that his Spirit is good, according to that Text, *Thy Spirit is good* . . . .

2. We must endeavour to produce that fruit, that frame of heart, which the Lord requires, directs, and looks for in such and such cases. Thus the Sanctification of *Experiences* is evidenced by the *Dispositions* answering Gods minde, which are left upon the heart, and brought forth in the life afterwards; namely, when Divine discoveries are the more strongly believed; the hearts by threats more kindly awed; adherence to the Promises more strongly confirmed. (*PMU*, 2, 167–68)

Ambrose illustrates this discipline of meditation in eight pages of examples, two of which are particularly interesting:

Experiences. 1643	Texts.	Dispositions required in this case, and to be prayed for.
Feb. 9. Preston was taken by Parliaments forces, severall Papists slain in it, some naturally of a good disposition; and therefore many mourned for their untimely death, but rejoyced in the accomplishment of the Promise.	Rev. 16.6,7. *They have shed the blood of Saints, and thou hast given them blood to drink.—* *Even so Lord God Almighty, true and righteous are thy judgements.* Rev. 19.2. *He hath judged the great whore, which did corrupt the earth with her fornications, &c.*	Rev. 18.4. *Come out of her my people that ye not be partakers of her sins, and that ye receive not of her plagues.* Rev. 18.20. *Rejoyce over her thou Heaven, and ye holy Apostles and Prophets, for God hath avenged you on her.*

(*PMU*, 2, 182)

Ambrose's ingenuous delight in the juggernaut of the divine purpose driving on to fulfillment may seem to the modern reader to have divested him of more natural sympathies, but his announced intent in cataloguing the occurrence is to make it a spur to spiritual improvement through meditation. He had prefaced his illustrations with these words: "Let us pray with fervency (whenever we set a time apart to view over our *Experiences*) that those *Dispositions* answering Gods mind in every particular *Experience* may be written in our hearts, and brought forth in our life afterwards. This will be the chief use and choice comfort of the soul in this duty" (*PMU*, 2, 181). In another experience, Ambrose expands upon a visitation akin to that which Bunyan describes in his episode of the Valley of Humiliation. The experience is presumably Ambrose's own, though he relates it in the third person:

Experiences. 1648	Texts.	*Dispositions required in this case, and to be prayed for.*
April 4. and 17. A poor creature in the night was fearfully troubled in his dreams with devils and torments and Satans power over his soul; he apprehended strongly that Satan was with him, and very busie to ensnare him, which at his very first awaking struck him with trembling and horror of heart.	2 Cor. 2.11. *We are not ignorant of his devices.* Ephes. 6.11.—*Of the wiles of the devil:*— Revel. 2.24. *Of the depths of Satan.*— 1 Thes. 3.5. *By some means the tempter hath tempted you.* 1 Pet. 5.8. *Your adversary the devil as a roaring lyon, walketh about, seeking whom to devour.*	*Eph.* 6.11. Put on the whole armor of God, that ye may be able to stand against the wiles of the devil. *Jam.* 4.7. Resist the devil, and he will flee from you.— 1 *Pet.* 5.9. Whom resist stedfast in the faith. 2 *Pet.* 2.9. The Lord knoweth how to deliver the godly out of temptations.

(*PMU*, 2, 185)

With some idea of Ambrose's methodology, we may turn to a special side of Puritan meditation upon experience upon which he touches. The Puritan's interpretation of experience as a secondary Scripture—as a private tradition which was indeed a *de facto* final authority disclosing the voice of God as it echoed the biblical revelation in the process of speaking in all the circumstances of one's life—meant that the God who was thus bringing his Word to fulfillment was necessarily immanent within human history in an extraordinary way. The Puritan unquestionably assumed that his life was a tightly knit fabric of providences (with the consequence, noted above, that he saw his life as a divinely ordered and rational whole), and the divine providences which the individual discerned in his past constituted the most important single topic for meditation in this tradition. Ambrose, it is true, is more astute than some in recognizing the problems of such an approach to experience, as when he cautions:

> In gathering *Experiences, Beware of misprision of Gods Providences*. There are many mistakes now a days, and therefore it is our best and onely course, for our security, to interpret all Gods works out of his Word: We must make the Scriptures . . . a construing book to the book of Gods Providences: Judge neither better of prosperity, nor worse of adversity, then Gods Word warrants us. This was the Psalmists cure, his *Experience* put a *Probatum est* to this prescription, *When I thought to know this, it was too painful for me, until I went into the Sanctuary of God, then understood I their end:* God may prosper a wicked man, and he may construe this as an argument, and note it as an *Experience* of Gods gracious dealing with him, and dear love unto him: O take heed! (*PMU*, 2, 176–77)

Yet while Ambrose is aware of the abuses of the systematic search for providences, he does not seem to discern the difficulty that lies at the heart of his own cautious position. Even when the Scriptures are made the "construing book to the book of Gods Providences," the problem of whether any particular event in the life of the Christian is to be construed as a providence remains unresolved.

The reading of experience as a record of providences was

of course a natural development of the individual's search for evidences of election. The seeker was encouraged to discern nuances of eternal import in the casual events of his life. Every providence represented a special favor, an intervention in the system by its Maker for the purpose of meeting the creature's need. Before the individual attained to assurance, he sought —and found—providences as proof of God's special interest in him and consequently as grounds for hope; and after he was assured of election, he expected to discern providences in his experience as the outworking of God's special attention to a favorite. Not surprisingly, the austere Calvinistic understanding of the deity as arbitrary sovereign who had voluntarily bound himself by covenant led to a concern to find further evidence of God's beneficent will in acts which confirmed His promises.

The work of the principal Puritan exponents of meditation upon one's providences reveals immediately how clearly such meditation depended upon a reading of experience as *logos*. Past events were reduced to simple statements of fulfilled promise or threat; in effect, they showed God "speaking" to the individual. John Owen, who touches repeatedly upon the importance of meditation in his treatise *The Grace and Duty of Being Spiritually Minded*, first published in 1681, gives careful attention to meditation upon providences, and, though he limits his discussion to those providences which are divine chastisements, his remarks give especially clear witness to the way in which the Puritan reduced experience to doctrinal statement:

> Observe *the especiall calls of providence*, and apply your minds unto thoughts of the duties required in them and by them. There is a voice in all signal dispensations of providence: "The LORD'S voice crieth unto the city, and the man of wisdom shall see thy name: hear ye the rod, and who hath appointed it," Micah vi. 9. There is a

call, a cry in every rod of God, in every *chastising providence*, and therein [he] makes a declaration of his name, his holiness, his power, his greatness. This every *wise, substantial man* will labour to discern, and so comply with the call. God is greatly provoked when it is otherwise: "LORD, when thy hand is lifted up, they will not see: but they shall see, and be ashamed," Isa. xxvi.11. If, therefore, we would apply ourselves unto our present duty, we are wisely to consider what is the voice of God in his present providential dispensations in the world. Hearken not unto any who would give another interpretation of them but that they are plain declarations of his displeasure and indignation against the sins of men .... The fingers that appeared writing on the wall the doom of Belshazzar did it in characters that none could read, and words that none could understand, but Daniel; but the present call of God in these things is made plain upon tables, that he may run who readeth it. If the heavens gather blackness with clouds, and it thunder over us, if any that are on their journey will not believe that there is a storm coming, they must bear the severity of it.[1]

This necessary duty of meditating upon providence Owen then examines under two heads, the first of which is "A diligent *search into ourselves,* and a holy watch over ourselves, with respect unto those ways and sins which the displeasure of God is declared against. That present providences are indications of God's anger and displeasure, we take for granted." Owen's unequalified reading of affliction as divine judgment is a sterner approach to the matter than that taken by most Puritans, but it witnesses to the widespread inclination within Puritanism to adopt an overly simple equation between historical event and divine purpose. The second duty which Owen recommends is the

1. *Works*, 7, 308 ff.

diligent endeavour to *live in a holy resignation of our persons, our lives, our families, all our enjoyments, unto the sovereign will and wisdom of God,* so as that we may be in readiness to part with all things upon his call without repining. This, also, is plainly declared in the voice of present providences. God is making wings for men's riches, he is shaking their habitations, taking away the visible defences of their lives, proclaiming the instability and uncertainty of all things here below; and if we are not minded to contend with him, we have nothing left to give us rest and peace for a moment but a holy resignation of all unto his sovereign pleasure.

It is true that the attitude toward "misfortune" expressed here does not wholly accord with that voiced in the previous duty, since Owen appears to make allowance for misfortune, not as the indication of divine displeasure, but as God's method for turning man's thoughts heavenward. The basic position underlying the two is the same, however: divine purpose is to be discerned immediately behind events, and man is to cooperate with it.

John Bartlet, in the discussion of meditation upon experience in his *Practical Christian*, devotes his whole attention to meditation upon providences, but he gives that term its more common meaning. In his treatment, as in Owen's, we perceive the Puritan conviction that any memorable benefit was not simply the upward turn of the wheel of fortune, or the fructification of value inherent in the creation, but a special intervention by the Creator:

Meditate on the Experience you have had of God's faithfulness, and goodness you have had in all his Providences: and this will not only enlarge your hearts in thankfulness for the present, but quicken, and strengthen you to an holy dependence, and confident expectance of the like for the future, as it did the Apostle, 2 *Cor.* 1, 9, 10. To help you herein, you shall do well to make a Catalogue, and keep a Diary of God's special providences; to take a Book, and write down the most remarkablest Providences of God, over you, and yours: often read them over, and ponder them well in your minds; and that, *first*, because you may find this to have been the practise of the Saints, To observe, and register God's dealings with them, and theirs, to speak of them, and erect Monuments in memorial of them . . . . *Secondly*, Because there is an equity in it, Shall God take notice of us, and we not take notice of Him? . . . *Thirdly*, There's a kind of necessity of writing down these special Providences, in regard of the weakness of our memories . . . . *Fourthly*, Great will be the profit of it, the sight of such a Catalogue of gracious Providences, will so much the more affect our hearts with love to so good a God, and quicken us to a holy dependence on Him.[2]

It would seem that, though Bartlet stresses the value of "cataloguing" one's providences, he approaches the individual providence more as an actual experience than as a datum on a tally sheet. He is certainly interested in the affective weight of such experience, yet scrutiny of his list of arguments shows that his position is essentially that of the *logos*-oriented Puritan. The providences were assumed to be eminently reducible

2. *The Practical Christian*, pp. 69–70. Cf. similar remarks by Thomas Adams: "Let the eye of our mind be alwayes fixed on this Divine Providence; that considering the unspeakable goodnesse it hath continually done us, in all necessities wee may hope that it will help us. Through all the passages of our life, let us gather observations of it: how it kept us in the wombe, brought us into the world, watched our cradles, guarded our infancy, tutor'd our youth, preserved us from dangers, supplied us with blessings; that thus finding it always hitherto graciously present, we may assure our selves it will never be absent" (*Meditations upon the Creed, Works*, p. 1165).

to a notation in a diary, and in meditation one reflected not so much upon the conflation of image and verbal construct, evoked immediately from the memory, as upon the verbalized record of one's private register. Moreover, the emotion which Bartlet expects to be evoked by such meditation does not represent a partial recovery of the original emotion attending the enjoyment of the providence but, rather, the simple derivative emotions of "thankfulness for the present," a sense of dependence, and "confident expectance." This kind of affective use of meditation is of course characteristic of the wide sweep of Puritan meditation which was summed up in the line of Hall, but such a procedure should not be confused with the imaginative reconstruction of the past found in Catholic meditation and the Puritan tradition of heavenly mindedness.

Finally, Richard Baxter's approach to experience shows the same divergence from common Puritan practice as his handling of Scripture, but the elements of that divergence illuminate this discussion, as do the number of points on which he conforms to general practice. His emphasis upon "recorded" experience and the ready discernibility of providence in one's past reveals a sympathy with Puritanism's orientation toward *logos*—truth is memorialized in verbal statement, and the past forms a divinely ordered pattern which recommends itself to analysis by the reason—but his imaginative reconstruction of past providence for meditation shows the distinctive emphasis of heavenly meditation. Shortly after he has presented his defense of employing the senses and imagination in meditation, Baxter suggests, "Compare also the Mercies which thou shalt have above, with those particular Providences which thou hast enjoyed thy self, and those observable Mercies which thou hast recorded through thy life" (*SER*, Pt. 4, p. 229). He then outlines a procedure wherein the past is relived in imagination:

> If thou be a Christian indeed, I know thou hast, if not in thy Book, yet certainly in thy Heart, a great many pre-

cious favours upon record. The very remembrance and rehearsal of them is sweet: How much more sweet was the actual enjoyment? But all these are nothing to the Mercies which are above. Look over the excellent Mercies of thy youth and Education; the mercies of thy riper years or age; the mercies of thy prosperity, and of thy adversity: the mercies of thy several places and relations; are they not excellent, and innumerable? Canst not thou think on the several places thou hast lived in, and remember that they have each had their several mercies? the mercies of such a place, and such a place; and all of them very rich and engaging mercies? O how sweet was it to thee, when God resolved thy last doubts? when he overcame and silenced thy fears and unbelief? when he prevented the inconveniences of thy life, which thy own counsel would have cast thee into? when he eased thy pains? when he healed thy sickness, and raised thee up as from the very grave and death? . . . If I have had so much in this strange Country at such a distance from him; what shall I have in Heaven in his immediate presence, where I shall ever stand about his Throne? (*SER*, Pt. 4, pp. 229–30)

It is not difficult to appreciate the new dimension in meditation upon experience which characterized Baxter's examples, with his "remembrance" and "rehearsal" of the original emotions involved. That dimension emphasizes by contrast the distinctive qualities of the more conventional meditations, which will constitute the principal focus of our attention as we turn now from the historical context to *The Pilgrim's Progress* itself.

Meditation on Experience in *The Pilgrim's Progress*

The discussion in which Christian participates at House Beautiful, which was used in introducing this chapter, may now be examined more closely. When Piety, Prudence, and

Charity, in the interest of the "best improvement of time," undertake to examine Christian regarding his past experiences, the conversation proceeds as follows:

> Piety. *Come good* Christian, *since we have been so loving to you, to receive you in to our House this night; let us, if perhaps we may better our selves thereby, talk with you of all things that have happened to you in your Pilgrimage.*
>
> Chr. With a very good will, and I am glad that you are so well disposed.
>
> Piety. *What moved you at first to betake yourself to a Pilgrim's life?*
>
> Chr. I was driven out of my Native Countrey, by a dreadful sound that was in mine ears, to wit, That unavoidable destruction did attend me, if I abode in that place where I was.
>
> Piety. *But how did it happen that you came out of your Countrey this way?*
>
> Chr. It was as God would have it; for when I was under the fears of destruction, I did not know whither to go; but by chance there came a man, even to me, (as I was trembling and weeping) whose name is *Evangelist*, and he directed me to the Wicket-gate, which else I should never have found; and so set me into the way that hath led me directly to this House.
>
> Piety. *But did you not come by the House of the Interpreter?*
>
> Chr. Yes, and did see such things there, the remembrance of which will stick by me as long as I live; specially three things; *to wit*, How Christ, in despite of Satan, maintains his work of Grace in the heart; how the Man had sinned himself quite out of hopes of Gods mercy; and also the Dream of him that thought in his sleep the day of Judgement was come. (pp. 47-48)

They further discuss Christian's visit at the House of Interpreter, and then Piety asks:

> *And what saw you else in the way?*
>
> Chr. Saw! Why, I went but a little further, and I saw one, as I thought in my mind, hang bleeding upon the Tree; and the very sight of him made my burden fall off my back (for I groaned under a weary burden) but then it fell down from off me. 'Twas a strange thing to me, for I never saw such a thing before: Yea, and while I stood looking up, (for then I could not forbear looking) three shining ones came to me: one of them testified that my sins were forgiven me: another stript me of my rags, and gave me this Broidred Coat which you see; and the third set the mark which you see in my forehead, and gave me this sealed Roll (and with that he plucked it out of his bosom).

So the probing continues. Soon Prudence takes up:

> *Do you not think sometimes of the Countrey from whence you came?*
>
> Chr. Yes, but with much shame and detestation; *Truly, if I had been mindful of that Countrey from whence I came out, I might have had opportunity to* have returned; but now I desire a better Countrey; that is, an Heavenly.
>
> Pru. *Do you not yet bear away with you some of the things that then you were conversant withal?*
>
> Chr. Yes but greatly against my will; especially my inward and carnal cogitations; with which all my Countreymen, as well as my self, were delighted; but now all those things are my grief: and might I but chuse mine own things, I would chuse never to think of these things more; but when I would be doing of that which is best, that which is worst is with me.

> Pru. *Do you not find sometimes, as if those things were vanquished, which at other times are your perplexity?*
>
> Chr. Yes, but that is but seldom; but they are to me Golden hours, in which such things happens to me.
>
> Pru. *Can you remember by what means you find your annoyances at times, as if they were vanquished?*
>
> Chr. Yes, when I think what I saw at the Cross, that will do it; and when I look upon my Broidered Coat, that will do it; also when I look into the Roll that I carry in my bosom, that will do it; and when my thoughts wax warm about whither I am going, that will do it.
>
> (pp. 49–50)

The first observation to be made about this conversation concerns its confessed end. Piety's initial request, "Let us, if perhaps we may better our selves thereby, talk with you," indicates that the review of Christian's experience is made not for pleasure but for edification, and the brief pointed questions of Piety and Prudence simulate those of a catechism. Christian too, is expected to benefit from his questioning, for the sisters are bringing his experience back before his eyes so that he will remember the lessons he has learned and keep in mind the goals he honored in setting out. The modern reader probably finds the protracted recapitulation tedious, and it certainly is unnecessary in terms of demands of the narrative, for no reader is apt to have forgotten the events which so shortly before befell Christian. Moreover, it is impossible to dismiss the recapitulation as the natural conversation which would result when a pilgrim stops for lodging where the residents are eager to hear of his adventures: the interrogators do not prime Christian to hear of his adventures but are interested in what he has learned, in his visit at Interpreter's House and in his conversion; nor does Christian say anything about his mishaps in the Slough or at the foot of Sinai, the two experiences he has already undergone which might be supposed to be of most interest as story. Thus the recapitulation as Bunyan presents it is not an integral element in the narrative but serves as a pause in the action while Christian's experiences, in true Puritan fashion, are reviewed and reflected upon.

The conversation which follows Prudence's question, "Do you not yet bear away with you some of the things that then you were conversant withal?" represents a brief reflection upon Christian's besetting sins. And the means by which Christian has been able on occasion to overcome his annoyances are for the most part varieties of Puritan meditation upon experience. As he describes them, "When I think what I saw at the Cross, that will do it; and when I look upon my Broidered Coat, that will do it; also when I look into the Roll that I carry in my bosom, that will do it; and when my thoughts wax warm about whither I am going, that will do it" (p. 50). Reflection upon his experience at the cross refers to meditation upon the crowning providence of his life, which was, of course, part of every Puritan's meditation upon the "observable mercies" of his past. His broidered coat and his roll represent special providences, meditation upon which is able to warm his spirit and free his mind from the oppression of besetting guilt. His last example does not exemplify meditation upon experience, of course, but that focus of the Puritan's attention which was discussed in Chapter 7.

Immediately after his departure from the House Beautiful, Christian undergoes two of the most severe tests of his pilgrimage—his adventures in the Valley of Humiliation and in the Valley of the Shadow of Death—and the second of these furnishes further illustration of Bunyan's handling of meditation upon experience. Christian's night in the Valley of the Shadow is Bunyan's dream become unmitigated nightmare. But the night eventually ends.

> Then said *Christian, He hath turned the shadow of death into the morning.*
>
> Now morning being come, he looked back, not out of desire to return, but to see, by the light of the day, what hazards he had gone through in the dark. So he saw more perfectly the Ditch that was on the one hand, and the Quag that was on the other; also how narrow the way was which lay betwixt them both; also now he saw the Hobgoblins, and Satyrs, and Dragons of the Pit, but all afar off; for after break of day, they came not nigh; yet they were discovered to him according to that which is written, *He discovereth deep things out of darkness, and bringeth out to light the shadow of death.*
>
> Now was *Christian* much affected with his deliverance from all the dangers of his solitary way, which dangers, though he feared them more before, yet he saw them more clearly now, because the light of the day made them conspicuous to him; and about this time the Sun was rising, and this was another mercy to *Christian:* for you must note, that tho the first part of the Valley of the Shadow of Death was dangerous, yet this second part, which he was yet to go, was, if possible far more dangerous. (pp. 64–65)

When Bunyan allegorizes reflection upon experience as an actual backward look, as in this passage, he encounters difficulties, one of which is apparent in the hasty qualifications he adds to the statement, "he looked back." It was not, Bunyan explains, "out of desire to return," a distinction that might seem a grim jest if it did not suggest the admonition of Jesus regarding that man who puts his hand to the plow. About the further problem presented by Christian's actually turning his gaze behind him—the curious fact that, even though the way yet before him is "if possible far more dangerous" than the way he has traversed in the night, he can still find a breathing space when he can take his attention from immediate perils and look back—Bunyan does not concern himself. Christian's wish *is* wholly natural, revealing both the urge to glimpse the horrors of the Valley when he can appreciate them more objectively and the Puritan compulsion to take note of his providences. As Bunyan observes, he is "much affected with his deliverance from all the dangers of his solitary way," and his brief backward look gives him strength to face the hazards yet before him.

When Christian leaves the Valley, he breaks into a spontaneous song which rehearses the whole preceding episode and plainly catalogues providences:

> O world of wonders! (I can say no less),
> That I should be preserv'd in that distress
> That I have met with here! Oh, blessed bee
> That hand that from it hath delivered me!
> Dangers in darkness, Devils, Hell, and Sin
> Did compass me, while I this Vale was in;
> Yea, Snares, and Pits, and Traps, and Nets did lie
> My path about, that worthless silly I
> Might have been catch't intangled, and cast down:
> But since I live, let JESUS wear the Crown. (p. 66)

His motivation here is the characteristically Puritan one of meditating upon past experience for edifying ends, and we may note, *en passant*, that he makes use of such recapitulatory and memorial songs after most of the important episodes in his pilgrimage. Roger Sharrock suggests that one reason for this was Bunyan's interest in presenting his side to a controversy in the Bedford congregation about the place of hymns in the life of the church, which may well be the case. In occasion and substance, however, the songs witness to motivations Bunyan would have shared with both sides of that

IN *The Pilgrim's Progress*   223

particular controversy. The bulk of Christian's songs are not only simple meditations upon the edifying truth of the episode immediately past but also the kind of versified memorialization which would make recall at later times easy (hinting at the stratagems of oral tradition). The songs that best illustrate these points are those which follow Christian's experiences at Interpreter's House (p. 37), the Cross (p. 38), the Valley of Humiliation (p. 60), the Valley of the Shadow of Death (p. 66), Vanity Fair (p. 97), Hill Lucre (p. 108), Doubting Castle (p. 119), and the Delectable Mountains (p. 123).

Shortly after he leaves the Valley of the Shadow, Christian overtakes Faithful, and Bunyan observes that "they went very lovingly on together; and had sweet discourse of all things that had happened to them in their Pilgrimage" (p. 66). The lengthy discourse that follows, in which the two pilgrims share their edifying experiences, suggests instructions which Sibbes and others give in their programs for devotional use of experience, and which reflect a preoccupation of Puritanism. Sibbes, for example, declares:

> It were a course much tending to the quickning of the faith of Christians, if they would communicate one to another their mutuall experiences, this hath formerly been the custome of Gods people. *Come and heare all ye that feare God, and I will declare what he hath done for my soul.* (SC, p. 392)

And Isaac Ambrose urges the same:

> Let us communicate our own Experiences to the good of others. *David* in his deliverances invites others to have recourse unto him. *Bring my soul out of prison, that I may praise thy Name, then shall the righteous compasse me about when thou shalt deal bountifully with me.* Conceal not within our bosomes those things, the communicating whereof may tend to publike profit; surely it were

> a course more tending to the quick'ning of the faith of all, if we would impart to one another our mutual *Experiences.*
>
> ... Let us trade others *Experiences* to our own particular profit. Thus *David* in desertion hath recourse to Gods gracious dealings with his fore-fathers, *Our fathers trusted in thee; they trusted, and thou didst deliver them; they cryed unto thee, and were delivered; they trusted in thee, and were not confounded.* What favour God shewed to any one, he will vouchsafe to every one that seeketh him dilligently, if it may be for his good. Thus we finde in Scripture that sometimes a personal *Experience* was improved to an universal advantage. *James* 5.11. *Hebr.* 13. 5,6. (*PMU, 2,* 180–81)

Ambrose's last observation has, of course, special relevance to the use Bunyan was making of his own experiences, since perhaps more than any other Puritan, Bunyan succeeded in improving personal experience to "an universal advantage."

Among the variety of experiences that Christian and Faithful "trade" for the other's good, one merits special attention. Christian urges Faithful:

> *Tell me now, what you have met with in the way as you came; for I know you have met with some things, or else it may be writ for a wonder.*
>
> *Faith.* I escaped the Slough that I perceive you fell into, and got up to the Gate without that danger; only I met with one whose name was *Wanton,* that had like to have done me a mischief.
>
> *Chr. 'Twas well you escaped her Net;* Joseph *was hard put to it by her, and he escaped her as you did, but it had like to have cost him his life. But what did she do to you?*
>
> *Faith.* You cannot think (but that you know som-

> thing) what a flattering tongue she had, she lay at me hard to turn aside with her, promising me all manner of content.
>
> Chr. *Nay, she did not promise you the content of a good conscience.*
>
> Faith. You know what I mean, all carnal and fleshly content.
>
> Chr. *Thank God you have escaped her: The abhorred of the Lord shall fall into her Ditch.*
>
> Faith. Nay, I know not whether I did wholly escape her, or no.
>
> Chr. *Why, I tro you did not consent to her desires?*
>
> Faith. No, not to defile my self; for I remembred an old writing that I had seen, which saith, *Her steps take hold of Hell.* So I shut mine eyes, because I would not be bewitched with her looks: then she railed on me, and I went my way. (pp. 68–69)

The passage is perhaps the finest bit of realistic dialogue in the whole of *The Pilgrim's Progress.* Bunyan's disclosure of Faithful's story by fragments, with titillating *double entendre,* represents dialogue used for the end of entertainment. Diverting as the conversation is, however, it clothes the framework of a meditation upon experience, for Christian and Faithful are both concerned with construing the experience as a confirmation and commentary upon scriptural truth. The equating of Madam Wanton with the wife of Potiphar, which gives the episode historical depth, entails that Faithful's experience with her has a special relationship with biblical experience. In this and a number of other passages, such as the description of the ditch in the Valley of the Shadow as the "*Quagg King* David *once did fall*" into, Bunyan gives the props of his allegory—his landscape and those figures who, like Wanton, are not pilgrims but more or less fixed aspects of the landscape—a historicity *sui generis* which makes of them a backdrop against which biblical and contemporary experience can be seen as a continuity. In fact, Bunyan's bold stroke allowed his characters to regard their experiences as something more than confirmation of biblical truths. As Christian and Faithful traveled the way to the Celestial City they were themselves inditing a Scripture—a fact quite in keeping with Bunyan's conception of his creative process as a revelatory dream and the widely held Puritan evaluation of experience as *logos*. In their discussion of Madam Wanton, then, Christian and Faithful have every justification for recapitulating personal experience as a normative guide, since their experience is homologous with the normative experience of biblical history.

After Faithful's death at Vanity Fair, Christian is joined by his new companion, Hopeful. After a variety of adventures, these two reach the Delectable Mountains, where they are entertained by four shepherds: Knowledge, Experience, Watchful, and Sincere. (In passing, it is significant that Experience is one of the group, for the four suggest a quadrumvirate of the presiding elements which entered into Puritan piety.) After Christian and Hopeful learn the nature of their whereabouts from the shepherds, they in turn are questioned, and Bunyan says:

> I saw also in my Dream, that when the *Shepherds* perceived that they were way-fairing men, they also put questions to them, (to which they made answer as in other places) as, Whence came you? and, How got you into the way? and, By what means have you so persevered therein? For but few of them that begin to come hither do show their faces on these mountains. But when the shepherds heard their answers, being pleased therewith, they looked very lovingly upon them; and said, *Welcome to the delectable Mountains.* (pp. 119–20)

The shepherds, like Piety and Prudence, are interested, not in the pilgrims' adventures, but in the special providences which their experiences have disclosed, and the questions they raise are noteworthy. The kind of reflection upon their pilgrimages which Christian and Hopeful are invited into by the question, "By what means have you so persevered therein?" is precisely the kind in which every Puritan engaged when he turned his gaze on that part of his pilgrimage that lay behind him. The "means" of perseverance, interpreted as mercies and providences, were carefully catalogued against the day when one had occasion to doubt God's faithfulness. In the words of Sibbes:

> For our better incouragement in these sad times, and to help our *trust* in God the more, wee should often call to minde the former *experiences*, which either our *selves* or *others* have had of Gods goodnesse, & make use of the same for our spirituall good; *Our Fathers trusted in thee*, (saith the head of the Church) *and were not confounded* [Ps. ix. 10]; Gods *truth* and *goodnesse* is unchangeable, *hee never leaves those that trust in him;* so likewise in our owne experiences, wee should take notice of Gods dealings with us in sundry kindes, how many wayes hee hath refreshed us, and how good wee have found him in our worst times. After wee have once tryed *him* and *his truth*, wee may safely trust him; God will stand upon his credit, hee never failed any yet, and hee will not beginne to breake with us; . . . . It is good therefore to observe and lay up Gods dealings; Experience is nothing else, but a multiplyed remembrance of former blessings, which will help to multiply our faith. (*SC*, pp. 390–92)

Later on in their shared pilgrimage, Christian and Hopeful enter a "certain country, whose air naturally tended to make one drowsy," and they fall into a discourse which is more transparently meditation upon experience than anything yet considered. Bunyan, moreover, holds up the discourse as a model when he has Christian sing as preface:

> When Saints do sleepy grow, let them come hither,
> And hear how these two Pilgrims talk together;
> Yea, let them learn of them, in any wise,
> Thus to keep ope their drowsie slumbring eyes.
> Saints fellowship, if it be manag'd well,
> Keeps them awake, and that in spite of hell. (p. 137)

When Christian then launches into a careful cross-examination of Hopeful concerning his conversion, the discourse is *Grace Abounding* in miniature. Bunyan, evangelical preacher that he is, makes sure that he provides his readers a complete and simple guide to conversion. But it is introduced on the ruse of serving to keep the pilgrims awake and actually represents a protracted meditation upon experience, the kind of reflection upon one's conversion that occupied an important place in the devotional life of every Puritan. Even the modern reader will not find the meditation wholly tedious when he encounters such statements as Hopeful's reply to Christian's question, "What was it that brought your sins to mind again?"

> *Hope.* Many things, As,
> 1. If I did but meet a good man in the Streets; or,
> 2. If I have heard any read in the Bible; or,
> 3. If mine head did begin to Ake; or,
> 4. If I were told that some of my Neighbours were sick; or,
> 5. If I heard the Bell Toll for some that were dead; or,
> 6. If I thought of dying my self; or,
> 7. If I heard that sudden death happened to others;
> 8. But especially, when I thought of my self, that I must quickly come to Judgement. (pp. 138–39)

IN *The Pilgrim's Progress* 229

At Christian's urging, Hopeful proceeds to relate the whole story of his conversion: his conviction of sins, his trifling momentarily with a religion of works, and his closing with Christ. The description of the last stage, the high point of the recapitulation, occurs when Christian asks "And how was he revealed unto you?"

> I did *not* see him with my bodily eyes, but with the eyes of mine understanding; and thus it was. One day I was very sad, I think sader then at any one time in my life; and this sadness was through a fresh sight of the greatness and vileness of my sins: And as I was then looking for nothing but *Hell*, and the everlasting damnation of my Soul, suddenly, as I thought, I saw the Lord Jesus look down from Heaven upon me, and saying, *Believe on the Lord Jesus Christ, and thou shalt be saved.*
>
> But I replyed, Lord, I am a great, a very great sinner; and he answered, *My grace is sufficient for thee.* Then I said But Lord, what is believing? And then I saw from that saying, [*He that cometh to me shall never hunger, and he that believeth on me shall never thirst*] That believing and coming was all one, and that he that came, that is, run out in his heart and affections after Salvation by Christ, he indeed believed in Christ. Then the water stood in mine eyes, and I asked further, But Lord, may such a great sinner as I am, be indeed accepted of thee, and be saved by thee? And I heard him say, *And him that cometh to me, I will in no wise cast out.* . . . And now was my heart full of joy, mine eyes full of tears, and mine affections running over with love, to the Name, People, and Ways of Jesus Christ.
>
> Chr. *This was a Revelation of Christ to your soul indeed.* (pp. 142–43)

Christian and Faithful, it is certain, were using "sanctified" memory in the manner that Isaac Ambrose[3] urged on the Christian: "This is the use of a sanctified memory, it will lose nothing that may help in time of need, or in the evil day; it records all the breathings, movings, stirrings, workings of a soul towards Christ, or of Christ towards a soul" (*PMU, 2,* 165). The "time of need" for the two pilgrims happens to be their passage over Enchanted Ground, and Bunyan has shown considerable ingenuity in furnishing justification within the allegory for including a meditation upon experience which is at the same time an outline of the way of salvation. Since it is too long to be included as a simple interruption of the action, Bunyan allows the discourse to function as an accessory to the unfolding plot.

Meditation upon experience does not have the prominence in Part Two of *The Pilgrim's Progress* that it has in Part One, but it is nonetheless evident.[4] The most conspicuous example is Christiana's catalogue of providences when she and Mercy are being questioned by Interpreter concerning the causes of their making a pilgrimage. She describes, for instance, two special dispensations: "I had a Dream of the well-being of my Husband, and a Letter sent me by the King of that Country where my Husband dwells, to come to him. The Dream and the Letter together so wrought upon my mind, that they forced me to this way" (p. 205). After she describes several

---

3. To the remarks of Ambrose one might compare those of Richard Sibbes: "We should therefore register God's favours, which is the best use we can put our memories to, and make them so many arguments to build upon him for time to come, as David, 'The Lord that delivered,' saith he, 'out of the paw of the lion, and out of the paw of the bear, will deliver me out of the hand of this Philistine,' 1 Sam. xvii.37." *The Saint's Safety* (London, 1633), *Works, 1,* 320.

4. Consider, e.g., Great-Heart's detailed recapitulation of Fearing's adventures (pp. 249–55). Christiana, Mercy, Mathew, and James all testify to their spiritual benefit from the narrative.

further experiences, Interpreter says, "Thy beginning is good, thy latter end shall greatly increase. So he addressed himself to *Mercie:* and said unto her, *And what moved thee to come hither sweet-heart?*" But Mercy blushes and is silent; finally, at Interpreter's urging, she answers, revealing the peculiar plight of the Puritan Christian who has no catalogue of providences to point to as a sign of election: "Truly sir, my want of Experience, is that that makes me covet to be in silence, and that also that fills me with fears of coming short at last. I cannot tell of Visions and Dreams as my friend *Christiana* can" (p. 206). But after Interpreter hears the rest of her story, he reassures her: "Thy setting out is good, for thou hast given credit to the truth, Thou art a Ruth." And Bunyan makes certain that the remainder of her pilgrimage supplies her providences enough under the intrepid guardianship of Great-Heart to set her mind at rest concerning the outcome of her venture in faith.

In summary, it seems reasonable to assume that Bunyan had to be familiar with a tradition so widespread and so organic to Puritanism as meditation upon experience. An earmark of his narrative procedure is the arresting of the forward thrust of the action while experience is reviewed not for the entertainment but for the edification of the listener. This insatiate interest of his pilgrims in the road behind as well as the road before is a characteristic of the Puritan's orientation in time and gave rise to a discipline which is, as a formal program of meditation at least, virtually unique to Puritanism and which undoubtedly was a shaping influence upon Bunyan's artistry.

10

THE INTERIOR VOICE IN MEDITATION AND AURAL FEATURES OF *THE PILGRIM'S PROGRESS*

When Christiana and her group arrive at the Land of Beulah, they avail themselves of the security of the place to rest for a time:

> But a little while soon refreshed them here, for the Bells did so ring, and the Trumpets continually sound so Melodiously, that they could not sleep, and yet they received as much refreshing, as if they had slept their Sleep never so soundly. Here also all the noise of them that walked the Streets, was, *More Pilgrims are come to Town*. And an other would answer, saying, And so many went over the Water, and were let in at the Golden Gates to Day. They would cry again, There is now a Legion of Shining Ones, just come to Town; by which we know that there are more Pilgrims upon the Road, for here they come to wait for them and to comfort them after all their Sorrow. (p. 303)

The sharp aural images which carry the burden of this passage's evocative power mark one of Bunyon's particular talents, which is in evidence from the opening sentences of the allegory. The most telling details in his realistic episodes are often those presented to the reader's auditory sensibility.

For several reasons, which this chapter will explore, Puritanism gave priority to the sense of hearing, and the fact is not without its significance for *The Pilgrim's Progress* and the creative process behind it. It is interesting, for example, that the passage cited above continues, "Then the Pilgrims got up and walked to and fro: But how were their Ears now filled with heavenly Noises, and their Eyes delighted with Celestial Visions?" The priority of the ear is hinted again in the following: "In this Land, they *heard* nothing, *saw* nothing, *felt* nothing, *smelt* nothing, *tasted* nothing, that was offensive to their Stomach or Mind."

In the memorable opening scene of the story, we recall, the aural image confirms and seals the animate reality of the character first confronted as a statuesque figure in a tableau. Bunyan says:

> I dreamed, and behold *I saw a Man cloathed with Raggs, standing in a certain place, with his face from his own House, a Book in his hand, and a great burden upon his Back.* I looked, and saw him open the Book, and Read therein; and as he read, he wept and trembled: and not being able longer to contain, he brake out with a lamentable cry; saying, *what shall I do?* (p. 8)

Bunyan asterisks the italicized phrase and identifies it as "His Out-Cry" in the margin, indicating that this cry is the real point of departure for the pilgrimage.[1] True, after uttering it,

---

1. It is probable that in this detail Bunyan embodies a convention of Puritan spiritual autobiography. The outcry against sin was the beginning of pilgrimage and the first evidence of the effectual working of grace, hence election. Mrs. Elizabeth Moore, whose *Evidences for Heaven* were bound with the Yale copy of the second edition of Edmund Calamy's *The Godly Mans Ark* (London, 1658), cites for an "evidence" the following: "The Lord brought me to a spiritual aston-

the ragged man returns home, and his family is introduced, but soon he is back in the fields meditating: "Now, I saw upon a time, when he was walking in the Fields, that he was (as he was wont) reading in his Book, and greatly distressed in his mind; and as he read, he burst out, as he had done before, crying, *What shall I do to be saved?*" After this full circle back to the opening, Evangelist hears the cry, and the progress of the convicted pilgrim commences.

If the point of departure for the pilgrimage is a cry of sore conviction, the terminus is a resounding hosannah. Christian and Hopeful are met at the gates of the city by Shining Ones who give them harps and crowns:

> Then I heard in my Dream, that all the Bells in the City Rang again for joy; and that it was said unto them, *Enter ye into the joy of your Lord.* I also heard the men themselves, that they sang with a loud voice, saying, *Blessing, Honour, Glory, and Power be to him that sitteth upon the Throne and to the Lamb for ever and ever.* (p. 162)

Throughout the pilgrimage between these termini the reliance upon the power of aural imagery is as heavy as the prominence of such imagery at beginning and close might suggest. Christian's way is one of cry and song, groaning and sighing, the roar of demon and giant, angelic remonstrances and encouragements. Bunyan's dream vision was by no means dumb spectacle.

Roger Sharrock, in the introduction to his edition of *Grace Abounding*, calls attention to Bunyan's handling of scriptural metaphor in that spiritual autobiography and cites "the manner in which the biblical texts speak to him as voices, like the

ishment, that I cried out, *What shall I do to be saved!* and said with Paul, *Lord! what wouldest thou have mee to do?*" (p. 238). Here was the first crisis-moment in the protracted process of Puritan conversion, marked in later stages by wrestling with uncertainties, inconclusive decisions, and the slow maturing in confidence.

Word of God descending upon the Old Testament prophets." [2] This judgment is readily documented by the work. In noting how scriptural texts forced themselves upon the consciousness of Bunyan, we shall be outlining a characteristic Puritan trait which can be understood fully only in the light of meditative techniques. These techniques, in turn, illuminate Bunyan's handling of aural imagery in *The Pilgrim's Progress*, in addition to glossing several of the incidents.

Though Sharrock suggests that Bunyan's description of the way Scripture came to him audibly illustrates "his tendency to turn metaphor into myth," with the implication that in his retelling he has perhaps embroidered the fact, it is difficult to escape the impression that Bunyan records genuine psychological phenomena which nowadays might be regarded as automatisms. The inner voices seem real in such passages as the following description of an encouragement and a severe temptation:

> Then I began to give place to the Word, which with power, did over and over make this joyful sound within my Soul, *Thou art my love, thou art my Love; and nothing shall separate thee from my love;* . . . Now about a week or fortnight after this, I was much followed by this Scripture, *Simon, Simon, behold, Satan hath desired to have you,* Luk. 22.31. And sometimes it would sound so loud within me, yea, and as it were call so strongly after me, that once above all the rest, I turned my head over my shoulder, thinking verily that some man had behind me called to me, being at a great distance, methought he called so loud, it came as I have thought since to have stirred me up to prayer and to watchfulness . . . . Also as I remember, that time as it called to me so loud, it was the last time that it sounded in mine ears,

2. *Grace Abounding*, p. xxvi.

> but methinks I hear still with what a loud voice these words, *Simon, Simon,* sounded in my ears.[3]

In retrospect, Bunyan determines that the sound was a heavenly warning preparing him for an especially grueling temptation in the offing. But at the time he could only wonder "what should be the reason that this Scripture, and that at this rate, so often and so loud, should still be sounding and ratling in mine ears." On another occasion, he is struck down by the statement of Hebrews asserting that Esau could find no place of repentance, though he sought it with tears:

> Now was I as one bound, I felt myself shut up unto the Judgment to come; nothing now for two years together would abide with me, but damnation, and an expectation of damnation: ... These words were to my Soul like Fetters of Brass to my Legs, in the continual sound of which I went for several months together.[4]

This apprehension of the Word as an insistent inner voice may be traced in part, of course, to Bunyan's individual psychic constitution. The voices he describes in *Grace Abounding* are not always the oracles of Scripture, for his active imagination and sensitive conscience collaborate to make a sure audience for all manner of fancied admonitory voices. But we are perhaps entitled to see the relevance of widespread techniques for meditative approach to the Word as voice to the whole of Bunyan's extraordinary aural sensitivity, since they plainly encouraged the monitoring of an inner voice as part of devotion. It takes little imagination to see why the Puritan orientation toward the Word as *logos* encouraged an aural sensitivity. The ear was quite naturally exalted at the

3. Ibid., pp. 29–30.
4. Ibid., pp. 43–44.

expense of the eye. Richard Alleine asks pointedly, in his *The World Conquered:*

> How came Sin and death into this world, and all the Plagues and miseries we are labouring under, or lyable to? which way came they in? *By the eye* they came in: when the Woman [saw] the fatal Apple, then she lusted and tasted, *Gen.* 3.
>
> How came Life and Immortality, Grace and peace, and all our glorious Hopes in again? *By the ear,* they came in: By this the Promise entred, by this *Faith* entred, *Rom.* 10.17. *Faith cometh by hearing.*[5]

If divine revelation spoke to human reason without trammeling up the dumb images of the visual imagination, the verbal and rational message might still display those quickening features which marked it as *spoken* revelation. Throughout Puritanism, significantly, the ordinance of attendance upon the sermon was denominated "Hearing the Word."[6] The Scripture itself spoke through the medium of the minister and, addressed to the ear, wrought effectually. Nicholas Byfield lists ten benefits of hearing the word, giving as the tenth: "What shall I say, but as the Evangelicall Prophet saith? If you can doe nothing else, yet *heare and your soules shall live* . . . for *Salvation is brought unto us by hearing, Act.* 28. 18. and 4.16."[7] But even more important, the Bible appropriated in reading and meditation in the privacy of one's house was regarded as the "speaking" Word. One can without difficulty find the impetus toward this attitude in Calvin's insistence that the Bible was truly an intimate address to the individual in his

---

5. Richard Alleine, *The World Conquered* (London, 1668), pp. 293–94.

6. See, for example, Ambrose, *PMU*, 2, 377 ff. and Jeremiah Burroughs, *The Rare Jewel of Christian Contentment* (London, 1652), Pt. 2, 161 ff.

7. Byfield, *Commentary*, p. 50.

private needs; it was natural to regard the Word as speaking, its written text quickened by the indwelling Spirit meeting the reader in vital rendezvous. Calvin declares:

> Although oracles are not now brought down from heaven, let us know that continual meditation on the word is not ineffectual; for as new difficulties perpetually arise before us, so God, by one and another promise, establishes our faith, so that our strength being renewed, we may at length arrive at the goal. Our duty, indeed, is attentively to hear God speaking to us.[8]

Isaac Ambrose explicitly states the implicit ramifications of such a conception of a Spirit-filled, speaking revelation in his discussion of *"Reading the holy Scriptures,"* which, he explains, "is nothing else but *a kind of holy conference with God, wherein we enquire after, and he reveals unto us himself and his will*" (*PMU*, 2, 477). When we read the Bible, he says:

> We cannot otherwise conceive of our selves then as standing in Gods presence, to hear what he will say unto us: So much the Prophet seems to imply, when he expresseth his consulting with Gods Word, by that phrase *of going into the sanctuary of God . . . in going in unto God; as going into the Sanctuary* is termed, 2. Sam. 7.18. so by *reading the Word we come in unto God, we stand in the presence of God, to enquire at his mouth.* (*PMU*, 2, 477)

---

8. Calvin, *Commentaries on . . . Genesis*, *1*, 265. Cf. Lukin, pp. 175–76. "So that in reading any command or prohibition in Scripture we must make particular application of it to our selves, as if God had directed it to us in particular or had spoken to us by name; or sent a special message from heaven to us." Also cf. Perkins, *Arte of Prophecying*, *Works*, 3, 734: "The manner of perswading is on this wise: The Elect having the Spirit of God doe first discerne the voyce of Christ speaking in the Scriptures. Moreover, that voyce, which they doe discerne, they do approove: and that which they doe approove, they doe beleeve."

Such a frame of mind, brought to meditation upon the Word must necessarily have stimulated the sort of inward hearing found so pronouncedly in Bunyan and given powerful immediacy to a number of passages in *The Pilgrim's Progress.* As discussed earlier, for example, Bunyan's description of Mt. Sinai is enhanced by the scriptural words which issue with fire from the mountain. Similarly, in the dream of the damned soul who constitutes one of the examples in Interpreter's House, the dramatic voices represent the Scripture speaking and are part of a vivid scene which is in its entirety a meditative reconstruction, bringing together congruent scriptural images:

> So I looked up in my Dream, and saw the Clouds rack at an unusual rate, upon which I heard a great sound of a Trumpet, and saw also a Man sit upon a Cloud, attended with the thousands of Heaven; they were all in flaming fire, also the Heavens was on a burning flame. I heard then a voice saying, *Arise ye Dead, and come to Judgement;* and with that the Rocks rent, the Graves opened, & the Dead that were therein came forth . . . . I heard it also proclaimed to them that attended on the Man that sat on the Cloud, *Gather together the Tares, the Chaff, and Stubble and cast them into the burning Lake;* and with that the Bottomless pit opened, just whereabout I stood; out of the mouth of which there came in an abundant manner Smoak, and Coals of fire, with hideous noises. It was also said to the same persons *Gather my Wheat into my Garner.* (p. 36)

Since Bunyan draws upon no less than seventeen passages of Scripture in constructing the scene, the fact that the result reads as gripping narrative rather than concordance is testimony both to his genius and to those meditative practices which allowed the Word to commend itself to memory in the form of agglutinative images. With respect to the immediate discussion, it is clear that images deriving from an aural approach to a "speaking" Word can function to gird narrative with the imperious authority of revelation. Even the skeptic must share something of the dreamer's abject terror.

If the point were simply that Bunyan's familiarity with meditative approaches to the Bible as speaking Word influenced his handling of text as aural image in *The Pilgrim's Progress*, we might proceed with a consideration of such episodes as Christian at the Cross, Christiana's group at the River of Death, and Christian and the Flatterer, and of such details as Evangelist's language, which is a pastiche of Scripture. But Bunyan's aural sensitivity to Scripture—which has undoubtedly been sensed by every reader who has related the Bunyan of *Grace Abounding* to the Bunyan of *The Pilgrim's Progress*, even if he did not associate it with Puritan meditative practice—is scarcely novel, nor is it the most important influence derived from the material. The fact is that the aural orientation toward the Word, with the Scripture a voice for the inner ear, proved remarkably congenial to a conception of meditation as inner oratory, in which the voice was not necessarily that of Scripture but might be that of the spiritual or rational self expostulating with the sensuous nature. This emphasis in meditation had strong roots in Catholic tradition, as Louis Martz has demonstrated,[9] and in the rich soil of Puritanism's exaltation of the aural and rational route to truth the emphasis thrived.

In their persuasion that the stirring of affections meant ministering to the auditory faculty, Hall, Ambrose, and Baxter are in perfect agreement, whatever their differences regarding the utility of the imagination. The modern reader may wonder at that obtuseness which prevented Hall, for example, from seeing that an aural percept, like a visual percept, implied the

9. See his *The Poetry of Meditation*, pp. 32ff., esp. pp. 38–39.

mediation of sense and the reproductive imagination, just as he may find strange the general Puritan unwillingness to admit that rhetorical manipulation of such images might work results on the emotions traceable neither to the Holy Spirit nor to the rousing of spiritual reason, with its quickening judgments. But such problems latent in the procedure apparently did not significantly curtail its popularity. It is suggestive, in this connection, that Bunyan makes such meditative procedure a vital adjunct of Christiana's conversion, a matter to be explored more fully later.

The illustrative passages of meditation cited here are obviously best read aloud, since their design is to present the novice with examples of affective soliloquy. The first is from Hall's regimen:

> Let the heart . . . first conceive and feele in it self the *Sweetnesse* or *bitternesse* of the matter meditated; which is never done without some passion, nor expressed without some hearty exclamation.
>
> Oh blessed estate of the Saints: O glorie not to bee expressed, even by those which are glorified! O incomprehensible salvation! What savour hath this earth to thee? Who can regarde the worlde, that beleeveth thee? Who can thinke of thee, and not be ravished with woonder and desire? Who can hope for thee, and not rejoyce? Who can knowe thee, and not be swallowed up with admiration at the mercie of him that bestowes thee? O blessednesse, worthy of Christs blood to purchase thee! worthie of the continuall songs of Saints and Angels to celebrate thee! Howe should I magnifie thee! Howe should I long for thee! how should I hate all this world for thee![1]

One can readily see how such use of anaphora and erotema might implement a stirring of the affections. The devices are

1. *The Art of Divine Meditation*, pp. 152–54.

of well-proven mettle, and their testing is part of long use in the more public forms of oratory and debate. Yet it was not for a moment to be conceded that the magic of rhetoric was not in fact the miracle of grace. Isaac Ambrose, in introducing a volume which treats of Bible reading, meditation, and other duties, insists:

> And yet by way of caution I desire the Reader to remember, that if at *anytime* in the exercise of *any of the* Duties within written, he also feels his heart warmed or savingly affected (which is the very Spirit, Power, Grace, Comfort, Presence and sweetness of Christ) that he consider, it is not the *duty*, it is not the bare Ordinance that elicites such divine and noble acts in the heart and affection, but it is the Blood of Christ, the Intercession, of Christ, sprinkling those *duties*, that makes them work such Graces in the Soul.[2]

Ambrose's presentation of actual meditations, however, makes it plain that his naïve confidence obscures certain more immediate sources for the efficacy of his procedure. A theological defense of rhetoric in meditation, when all concessions were made, was of course perfectly possible, but no such rationale was attempted. Presumably it would have had to confront the implied divine sanction of sensory excitement of the affections, and the fiction of the severance of word from the taints of the sensory was not to be so easily discarded.

Here is Ambrose with a sample meditation:

> Oh give me this image, give me *righteousness and holinesse*, for that is the image of God; give me thy presence, give me *the visions of God, and fruitions of God;* such things are in heaven; and as the earnest of my inheritance give

2. This is quoted from the recto of fol. 5 of the unpaginated "To the Reader," prefacing *Media*, the second of the three volumes bound in *PMU*.

> me the first-fruits, give me some acquaintance of thy blessed self in every ordinance, let there be a stronger union betwixt God and my soul: let me enjoy God in the creature, and God in the ordinances, and God in all things; yea let me enjoy God in my self, and my self in God. (*PMU*, 2, 269)

The elaborate prolyptoton, with exploitation of words for their sound, is the very trademark of Ambrose's method. Unquestionably the method is effective. Even while he is engaged in the self-conscious enterprise of constructing a meditation to illustrate his argument, he is stirred. Shortly after writing the words quoted above, he says:

> Let me taste of *Eternity* by these real experiments in my own soul. And now Lord, that thou hast in some sweet measure assured me, in that thou beginnest to warm my heart, and to persuade my soul that I have a right and interest to this Eternity, what else means this.

In Richard Baxter, whose work in this vein was known to Ambrose, the appeal to the ear through devices like incremental repetition and the manipulation of stress is implemented in most systematic fashion. He, like Ambrose, does not attempt a rationale of the efficacy of his rhetoric, but he is able to find scriptural precedent for such procedure, declaring:

> Thou hast all Christs personal Excellencies to study; thou hast all this [sic] particular mercies to thyself, both special and common; thou hast all his sweet and near relations to thee, and thou hast the happiness of thy perpetual abode with him hereafter; all these do offer themselves to thy *Meditation*, with all their several branches and adjuncts. Only follow them close to thy heart; ply the work, and let it not cool: Deal with thy heart, as Christ did with *Peter,* when he asked him thrice over, *Lovest thou me?*

till he was grieved, and answers, *Lord, thou knowest that I love thee.* So say to thy Heart, Lovest thou thy Lord? and ask it the second time, and urge it the third time, Lovest thou thy Lord? till thou grieve it, and shame it out of its stupidity, and it can truly say, Thou knowest that I love him. (*SER*, Pt. 4, p. 196)

At the close of his dissertation upon procedures in meditation, Baxter appends a full-length illustration of "this Heavenly Contemplation." The note struck in the opening sentences is an interesting confirmation of those lines of thought we have been developing:

> Rest! How sweet a word is this to mine ears! Methinks the sound doth turn to substance, and having entred at the ear, doth possess my brain, and thence descendeth down to my very *heart;* methinks I feel it stir and work, and that through all my parts and powers; but with a various work upon my various parts; to my wearied *senses* and languid *spirits*, it seems a quieting powerful *Opiate;* to my dulled powers it is spirit and life: to my dark eyes it is both eye-salve, and a prospective; to my Taste it is sweetness; to mine ears it is melody; to my hands and feet it is strength and nimbleness: Me-thinks I feel it digest as it proceeds, and increase my native heat and moisture, and lying as a reviving cordial at my *heart;* from thence doth send forth lively *spirits*, which beat through all the pulses of my Soul. (*SER*, Pt. 4, p. 254)

This is a remarkable series of effects to be attributed to a mere sound, but the emphasis is consonant with the whole orientation of the Puritan movement. "Sound" was continually being changed into "substance" as the divine Word, through preaching, hearing, and reading, was transmuted into the flesh and bone of the Christian life. As word becoming flesh it was, to be sure, an analogue to the Incarnation.

The two most significant appearances of meditation as interior oratory in *The Pilgrim's Progress* are associated with Christian's return to the arbor where he had left his scroll and with Christiana's conversion at the Cross. The first of these demonstrates Bunyan's familiarity with a very popular topic of Puritan meditation (Christian's self-flagellating soliloquy is in fact a specimen of meditation upon sin) and its method is a refined rhetorical assault upon the inner ear such as might be expected in the Puritan context:

> Thus therefore he now went on, bewailing his sinful sleep, saying, *O wretched Man that I am,* that I should sleep in the day time! that I should sleep in the midst of difficulty! that I should so indulge the flesh, as to use that rest for ease to my flesh, which the Lord of the Hill hath erected only for the relief of the spirits of Pilgrims! How many steps have I took in vain! (Thus it happened to *Israel* for their sin, they were sent back again by the way of the Red-Sea) and I am made to tread those steps with sorrow, which I might have trod with delight, had it not been for this sinful sleep. How far might I have been on my way by this time! I am made to tread those steps thrice over, which I needed not to have trod but once: Yea now also I am like to be benighted, for the day is almost spent. O that I had not slept! (p. 44)

Not surprisingly, in Calvinist Puritanism the subject of sin was a favorite for meditation, regardless of one's tenure on the way of grace.[3] The seasoned Christian meditated long and

---

3. The topic, for example, that Edmund Calamy uses in *The Art of Divine Meditation* in illustrating the use of argument in meditation is the *"sinfulness of sin"* (pp. 177 ff.). Bishop Ussher in his *A Method for Meditation* (London, 1657) lists in the table of contents six duties of the Christian as foci for his discussion in the work. The fifth of these is "seriously to meditate on the nature and heinousnesse of sin. First by considering the greatnesse of God, against whom we sinne; secondly the

carefully upon his missteps to remind himself of his utter reliance upon the divine sufficiency, just as the seeking novice meditated upon his sins to make his repentance a saving one. A chance blunder like Christian's at the arbor was not to be slighted, for much profit might be gained from a stern address to the stumbling flesh. Thomas Hooker put it concisely: "Meditation is as it were the register and remembrancer, that looks over the records of our daily corruptions, and keeps them upon file, and brings them into court and fresh consideration *Job*. 13.26."[4] The judicial images here are quite congruous with the kind of inner litigation which was actually practiced, and since one hoped not only to convict but to persuade the untoward nature, all the devices and techniques of oratory were employed. So Christian's return to the arbor is improved by meditative soliloquy calculated to burn his misdeed deep in his conscience, and to save him from repeating the blunder.

By means of a skillful narrative use of the device of meditation as interior oratory Bunyan solves a difficult problem which confronted him in describing Christiana's conversion. In Christian's pilgrimage a significant interval elapses between his reception onto the Way through the Wicket Gate and the jettisoning of his burden at the Cross. His entrance through the gate technically marks his conversion, but, as the case was for his maker, Bunyan, the onus of sin continues to plague for some time afterwards. Well after Bunyan had begun to preach, the burden of guilt was a problem for him. In *Grace Abounding*, he says, "I went my self in chains to preach to them in chains, and carried that fire in my own conscience that I persuaded them to beware of. I can truly say, and that without dissembling, that when I have been to preach, I have gone full

---

little cause or reason we have to sinne; thirdly, the means that God hath used to keep us from sinne; fourthly, the multitude of our sinnes; fifthly, the dangerous fruits of sinne, which are these." The duty is elaborated in pp. 53–148 of the text.

4. Hooker, *Of Redemption*, p. 212.

of guilt and terrour even to the Pulpit-Door."[5] The place of the Cross thus takes on signal importance for Christian; it is in fact a meeting with Christ in confirming grace. The Cross seems barren to the outer eye, but Christian speaks of it this way in House Beautiful, in answer to Piety's question, "And what saw you else in the way?"

> Saw! Why, I went but a little further, and I saw one, as I thought in my mind, hang bleeding upon the Tree; and the very sight of him made my burden fall off my back (for I groaned under a weary burden) but then it fell down from off me. 'Twas a strange thing to me, for I never saw such a thing before. (p. 49)

Though Christiana carries no such burden, it is certain that the place of the Cross cannot be ignored in her pilgrimage, and Bunyan now faces the problem of stressing properly her meeting with the central symbol of Christian faith. How shall Christ appear to her, if at all? Part One leaves the issue of Christ's appearance ambiguous, for Christian sees Him, as he thought, in his mind. The problems in Part Two are complicated by the fact that the Keeper of the Wicket Gate is clearly presented as Christ (whereas in Part One it is Good Will, rather than the Keeper, who tends the gate). After bringing Mercie in with the words, "I pray for all them that believe on me, by what means soever they come unto me," he grants pardon to the guests, takes them to the top of the Gate, and shows them by what deed they were saved. They look to the distant cross, and the margin explains, "Christ Crucified seen afar off." The gatekeeper has already told them "that that sight they would have again as they went along in the way, to their comfort," so Christ must be somehow present at the cross, with confirming grace, however and wherever He is present elsewhere.

5. *Grace Abounding*, pp. 85–86.

Bunyan neatly handles the problems by having Christ draw nigh as spiritual Presence to Christiana at the cross, as she addresses him in meditation. Great-Heart lays the groundwork by a sophisticated exposition of the manner in which Christ's death made salvatory virtue available. He then goes on to praise the value of "Consideration," or meditation seen as an adjunct of preaching:

> There is not only comfort, and the ease of Burden brought to us, by the sight and Consideration of these; but an indeared Affection begot in us by it: For who can, if he doth once think that Pardon comes, not only by promise, but thus [i.e., by the crucifixion]; but be affected with the way and means of his Redemption, and so with the man that hath wrought it for him? (p. 212)

Christiana rejoins with meditation:

> True, methinks it makes my Heart bleed to think that he should bleed for me. Oh! thou loving one, Oh! thou Blessed one. Thou deservest to have me, thou hast bought me: Thou deservest to have me all, thou hast paid for me ten thousand times more than I am worth. No marvel that this made the Water stand in my Husbands Eyes, and that it made him trudg so nimbly on, I am perswaded he wishes me with him; but vile wretch, that I was, I let him come all alone.

Thus she confronts Christ, His presence being implied by her address. The reader is led to infer that it is to the inner eye of faith that He shows Himself, and that the sight is validated by the warming of her affections. Great-Heart makes plain that the warming of the heart witnesses to a gift of grace akin to that which loosed Christian from his burden:

> So that all you have, my Daughters, you have by a peculiar impression made by a Divine contemplation upon what I

have spoken to you. Remember that 'twas told you, that the *Hen* by her common call, gives no meat to her *Chickens*. This you have therefore by a special Grace. (p. 213)

The place, then, is fittingly commemorated for Christiana, as it was for Christian. In each case a special dispensation of grace means the profound quickening of the heart. In Christiana's "Divine contemplation," we note also, there is evidence of Bunyan's acquaintance with and narrative use of meditation as inner oratory. Indeed, a specific source for this is known to have been familiar to Bunyan: in the *Practice of Piety* Bishop Bayly, describing "The Soules Soliloquy ravished in contemplation of the Passion of our Lord," asks:

> What hast thou done, O my sweet Saviour, and aye blessed Redeemer, that thou wast thus betrayed of *Judas*, sold of the *Jewes*, apprehended as a Malefactor, and led bound as a Lambe to the slaughter? . . . What was thine offence? Or to whom didst thou ever *wrong?* that thou shouldst bee thus pittifully *scourged* with whips, *crowned* with thornes, *scoffed* with flowtes, *reviled* with words, *buffeted* with fists, and *beaten* with staves? O Lord, what diddest thou deserve, to have thy blessed face *spit* upon, and *covered* as it were with shame?[6]

Puritanism's orientation toward the aural is an integral part of the total picture we have been elaborating, and basic to the composition is the conviction that God speaks. Revelation in word rather than spectacle or event enjoyed the determinacy and rationality as well as the intimacy of personal address so desired by the Puritan. True, it was perfectly biblical to speak of revelation in terms of *light*, but the publicity and muteness implied were suspect, and in Quakerism and other leftist sects the universalistic and solipsist heresies to which the image lent itself were painfully apparent. That light which lighted every

---

6. Bayly, pp. 802–03.

man who came into the world was assuredly to be judged by the Word. The possible inadequacy of both emphases, taken in isolation, which is hinted by the felicity of their union in the opening paeon of Hebrews,[7] was not allowed. This Word, become flesh in Christ and doctrine in Scripture, was at the center of Puritan devotion. In the public assembly, the sermon was the Word addressed to the ear and the reason. After all, as Richard Baxter said, "Man is a Rational *Creature*, and apt to be moved in a Reasoning Way" (*SER*, Pt. 4, p. 180). In private devotion, as we have seen, contradictory emphases existed side by side. But, whatever else it was, the Bible was first of all a speaking word addressed to each reader; meditation that amplified upon the text or moved to other subjects ordinarily preserved the nexus of voice and ear, with devotee both speaker and audience.

The signs of disequilibrium in this synthesis are inescapable. A biblical rationalism would eventually go on to criticize its own purview, a development in fact shadowed in Baxter's work by mid-century. The predisposition toward *logos*, the Aristotelian category, would take fuller account of the *logos* enfleshed of John 1 and the *logos spermatique* of natural revelation. The imagination, harnessed in devotion, would gain in stature, though new prejudices—Hobbesian, Lockian, Shaftesburian—would come to bear.

As the whole movement lost its raging millennial fervor, the speaking Scripture with its uncompromising personal address as well as those devotional practices for the full application of

---

7. Cf. 1.1–3. "God, who at sundry times and in divers manners spake in time past unto the fathers by the prophets, Hath in these last days spoken unto us by his Son, whom he hath appointed heir of all things, by whom also he made the worlds; Who being the brightness of his glory, and the express image of his person, and upholding all things by the word of his power, when he had by himself purged our sins, sat down on the right hand of the Majesty on high." The imagery of light and word are inseparable here.

word to heart were to give place to less coercive authority. Common sense and the golden mean were guides with which one dared to relax. Soldier Christian gives way to Christiana, and Christiana gives way to her children and her children's children who, *mirabile dictu,* form a church on the very banks of the River of Death, with the way of pilgrimage behind them, its persecutions and terrors as far from their thoughts as that ominous City of Destruction from which the ragged Graceless once fled in despair. "And since I came away," Bunyan confides to his reader, "I heard one say, that they were yet alive, and so would be for the Increase of the Church in that Place where they were for a time."

It is clear that not every era is one demanding arduous pilgrimage.

BIBLIOGRAPHY

For works published prior to 1700, I have included Short-Title Catalogue numbers, using the abbreviation *STC* for A. W. Pollard and G. R. Redgrave's compilation, and the abbreviation Wing for Donald G. Wing's continuation of the work. In the listing of both primary and secondary sources, I have mentioned only works cited in the text.

Primary Sources

Adams, Thomas, *A Commentary or, Exposition upon the Divine Second Epistle Generall, written by the Blessed Apostle St. Peter*, London, 1633. *STC*, 108.

———, *The Workes*, London, 1629. *STC*, 104.

Alleine, Richard, *The World Conquered*, London, 1668. Wing, A1009.

Ambrose, Isaac, *Prima, Media, & Ultima*, London, 1654. Wing, A2962. Wing lists as A2961 an earlier issuing in one volume of the three sections of the work, all of which had seen independent publication.

Ames, William, *The Marrow of Sacred Divinity*, London, 1642. Wing, A3000.

Anselm, St., *Book of Meditations and Prayers*, trans. from the Latin by M. R. London, London, Burn and Oates, 1872.

Augustine, St., *Pious Breathings. Being the Meditations of St.*

Augustine, *His Treatises of the Love of God, Soliloquies and Manual,* trans. George Stanhope, 6th ed. London, 1728.

Barrow, Isaac, *The Theological Works,* ed. Alexander Napier, 9 vols. London, Cambridge University Press, 1859.

Bartlet, John, *The Practical Christian,* London, 1670. Wing, B983.

Baxter, Richard, *The Practical Works,* ed. William Orme, 23 vols. London, James Duncan, 1830.

———, *The Saints Everlasting Rest,* 4th ed. London, 1653. Wing, B1386.

Bayly, Lewis, *The Practice of Pietie,* London, 1628. This is an unnumbered edition not listed in *STC.*

Baynes, Paul, *An Entire Commentary upon the Whole Epistle of St. Paul to the Ephesians,* Edinburgh, James Nichol, 1866.

Bernard, St., *Cantica Canticorum: Eighty-six Sermons on the Song of Solomon,* trans. and ed. Samuel Eales, London, Elliot Stock, 1895.

Bolton, Robert, *Some Generall Directions for a Comfortable Walking with God,* London, 1625. *STC,* 3250.

Bunyan, John, *Grace Abounding,* ed. Roger Sharrock, London, Oxford University Press, 1962.

———, *The Pilgrim's Progress,* ed. James Blanton Wharey, 2nd ed., rev. Roger Sharrock, Oxford, Clarendon Press, 1960.

———, *The Works,* ed. George Offor, 3 vols. London, Blackie and Son, 1856.

Burroughs, Jeremiah, *The Rare Jewel of Christian Contentment,* London, 1652. Wing, B6106.

Bury, Edward, *The Husbandmans Companion,* London, 1677. Wing, B6207.

Byfield, Nicholas, *An Exposition upon the Epistle to the Colossians,* London, 1615. *STC,* 4216.

Calamy, Edmund, *The Art of Divine Meditation,* London, 1680. Wing, C227.

Calvin, John, *Commentaries on the First Book of Moses Called*

Genesis, trans. from the Latin by Rev. John King, 2 vols. Edinburgh, Calvin Translation Society, 1847.

———, *Commentary on the Book of Psalms,* trans. from the Latin by Rev. James Anderson, 5 vols. Edinburgh, Calvin Translation Society, 1845.

———, *Institutes of the Christian Religion,* trans. Henry Beveridge, 2 vols. London, James Clarke and Co., 1949.

Case, Thomas, *Mount Pisgah: or, a Prospect of Heaven,* London, 1670. Wing, C837.

François de Sales, St., *An Introduction to a Devoute Life,* trans. John Yakesley, 3rd ed. Rouen, 1614.

Goodwin, Thomas, *The Vanity of Thoughts Discovered,* London, 1638. *STC,* 12044.

———, *The Works,* 12 vols. Edinburgh, James Nichol, 1861–66.

Gouge, Thomas, *The Works,* London, 1706.

Greenham, Richard, *The Workes,* London, 1599–1600. *STC,* 12313.

Hall, Joseph, *The Art of Divine Meditation,* London, 1607. *STC,* 12643.

———, *Occasionall Meditations,* 3rd ed. London, 1633. *STC,* 12689.

———, *A Recollection of such Treatises as have been heretofore severally published and are nowe revised, corrected augmented,* London, 1621. STC, 12708. This is an unnumbered edition. The first appeared in 1614.

———, *The Works,* ed. Philip Wynter, 8 vols. London, Oxford University Press, 1863.

Hildersham, Arthur, *CLII Lectures Upon Psalme LI,* London, 1635. *STC,* 13463.

Hooker, Thomas, *The Application of Redemption. The Ninth and Tenth Books,* London, 1657. Wing, H2640.

Jewel, John, *The Works,* ed. for the Parker Society by Rev. John Ayre, London, Cambridge University Press, 1847.

Luis de Granada, *Of Prayer, and Meditation*, Rouen, 1584.
———, *The Sinner's Guide*, trans. from the French by Francis Meres, London, 1614. This is not listed in *STC*. The work was first translated into English in 1598.
Lukin, Henry, *An Introduction to the Holy Scriptures*, London, 1669. Wing, L3476.
Moore, Elizabeth, *Evidences for Heaven*. This work, bound with Edmund Calamy's *The Godly Mans Ark* (London, 1658), is not mentioned in Wing. Wing's number for Calamy's book is C248.
Owen, John, *Of the Divine Originall, Authority, self-evidencing Light, and Power of the Scriptures*, Oxford, 1659. Wing, o784.
———, *The Works*, ed. Rev. William H. Goold and Rev. Charles W. Quick, 17 vols. Philadelphia, Leighton Publications, 1850.
Pemble, William, *Vindiciae Gratiae; a Plea for Grace*, London, 1627. *STC*, 19591.
Perkins, William, *The Workes*, 3 vols. London, 1612. *STC*, 19650.
Preston, John, *Life Eternall*, 2nd ed. London, 1631. *STC*, 20232.
Rogers, Nehemiah, *A Strange Vineyard in Palaestina: in an Exposition of Isaiahs Parabolical Song of the Beloved, discovered: To which Gods Vineyard in this our Land is Paralleld*, London, 1623. *STC*, 21199.
Rogers, Richard, *A Commentary upon the Whole Booke of Judges*, London, 1615. *STC*, 21204.
———, *Seaven Treatises Containing Such Direction As Is Gathered Out of The Holy Scriptures*, 3rd ed. London, 1610. *STC*, 21217.
Sibbes, Richard, *A Glance of Heaven*, London, 1638. *STC*, 22497.
———, *Light from Heaven*, London, 1638. *STC*, 22498.
———, *The Soules Conflict*, London, 1635. *STC*, 22508.

———, *The Works*, ed. Rev. Alexander Grosart, 7 vols. Edinburgh, James Nichol, 1862.

Smith, Samuel, *David's Blessed Man: or, a Short Exposition on the first Psalme*, bound in the volume *Samuel Smith on Psalm I., Thomas Pierson on Psalms XXVII. LXXXIV. LXXXVII. and William Gouge on Psalm CXVI*, Edinburgh, James Nichol, 1858.

Spurstow, William, *The Spiritual Chymist: or, Six Decads of Divine Meditations on several Subjects*, London, 1666. Wing, S5097.

Taylor, Thomas, *Meditations from the Creatures*, 2nd ed. London, 1629. *STC*, 23833.

Teate, Faithful, *A Scripture-Map of the Wildernesse of Sin, and Way to Canaan*, London, 1655. Wing, T615.

Ussher, James, *A Method for Meditation*, London, 1657. Wing, U192.

Ward, Samuel, *A Collection of Such Sermons as have been written by S. Ward*, London, 1627–28. *STC*, 25031.

Whitaker, William, *Disputation on Holy Scriptures against the Papists, especially Bellarmine and Stapleton*, trans. for the Parker Society by Rev. William Fitzgerald, London, Cambridge University Press, 1849.

Wilson, Thomas, *The Rule of Reason*, London, 1553. *STC*, 25811.

Secondary Sources

Coleridge, Samuel Taylor, *Coleridge's Miscellaneous Criticism*, ed. T. M. Raysor, London, Constable and Co., 1936.

———, *Notes on English Divines*, ed. Rev. Derwent Coleridge, 2 vols. London, Edward Moxon, 1853.

Golder, Harold, "Bunyan's Valley of the Shadow," *Modern Philology*, 27 (1929), 55–72.

Good, H. G., "Puritanism," *Encyclopedia of Religion and*

Ethics, ed. James Hastings (13 vols. Edinburgh, T. and T. Clark, 1908–27), *10*, 507–15.

Greene, Herbert, "The Allegory as employed by Spenser, Bunyan, and Swift," *PMLA*, *4* (1888–89), 145–93.

Joseph, Sr. Miriam, *Shakespeare's Use of the Arts of Language*, New York, Columbia University Press, 1947.

Lerner, L. D., "Puritanism and the Spiritual Autobiography," *Hibbert Journal*, *55* (1956–57), 373–86.

Lynch, William F., *Christ and Apollo*, New York, New American Library, 1960.

Martz, Louis, *The Poetry of Meditation*, New Haven, Yale University Press, 1954.

Miller, Perry, Introduction to Jonathan Edwards' *Images or Shadows of Divine Things*, New Haven, Yale University Press, 1948.

Mitchell, W. Fraser, *English Pulpit Oratory*, London, SPCK, 1932.

Patrick, J. G., "The Realism of 'The Pilgrim's Progress,'" *Baptist Quarterly*, *13* (1949–50), 18–24.

Rupp, Gordon, *Six Makers of English Religion, 1500–1700*, London, Hodder and Stoughton, 1957.

Sharrock, Roger, *John Bunyan*, London, Hutchinson's University Library, 1954.

——, "Personal Vision and Puritan Tradition in Bunyan," *Hibbert Journal*, *56* (1957–58), 47–60.

Talon, Henri, *John Bunyan: The Man and his Works*, trans. from the French by Barbara Wall, Cambridge, Harvard University Press, 1951.

Tavard, George, *Holy Writ or Holy Church*, New York, Harper and Brothers, 1959.

Wallace, Ronald S., *Calvin's Doctrine of the Word and Sacrament*, London, Oliver and Boyd, 1953.

Wellek, René, and Austin Warren. *Theory of Literature*, New York, Harcourt, Brace and Co., 1956.

INDEX

Adams, Thomas, 56, 63, 111, 137, 188, 202, 203 n.
Allegory: biblical, 37–38, 52 ff., 72, 81–82; *The Pilgrim's Progress* as, vi–viii, 5–7, 17–19, 22–23. *See also* Character, Example, Imagery, Metaphor, Puritanism
Alleine, Richard, 57, 237
Ambrose, Isaac, 121, 130, 134, 159–60 n., 183, 202–03, 205–10, 223–24, 230, 237–38, 242–43
Ames, William, 40, 48
Analogy of Faith, 27, 108–17 passim; Perkins' definition of, 108
Anselm, St., 127, 207
Aquinas, St. Thomas, 29, 43
Aristotle, 9 f.
Augustine, St., 125
Aural orientation of Puritans. *See* Baxter, Bunyan, Hall, Puritanism

Barrow, Isaac, 18
Bartlet, John, 69, 213–14
Baxter, Richard, 66, 70–71; aural features of his meditations, 243–44; *The Life of Faith*, 69, 114; meditation on experience, 197 ff., 202, 215–16; rationalism, 59 n., 179, 250; *Saints' Everlasting Rest*, 59, 66, 118 n., 130, 201; significance for heavenly meditation, 23, 135, 138, 141–42, 145 ff., 156 ff., 171–72
Bayly, Lewis, 137, 159 n., 249
Baynes, Paul, 110
Bellarmine, Robert, 28–29, 33
Bernard, St., 32–33, 41–42
Beulah, 162–65, 195, 232–33
Bolton, Robert, 179
Bunyan, John, "The Apology," 1–2, 7–14 passim, 20, 153 ff.; aural sensitivity, 232–36, 239–40; *The Barren Fig-Tree*, 54–55; *Grace Abounding*, 18, 169, 234 ff., 246–47; *Mr. Badman*, 152; presense as narrator in *The Pilgrim's Progress*, 8, 164–65; realism as characteristic of his narrative technique, *see* Realism; *Solomon's Temple Spiritualized*, 133; tension in his aesthetic, 3–24; truth, his conception of, 11, 14, 112
Bury, Edward, 182, 186–87, 190–91, 194–95

INDEX

Byfield, Nicholas, 26, 51 n., 91–92, 237

Calamy, Edmund, 119, 121, 131 ff., 190, 245

Calvin, John, 9, 20, 31–34 passim, 47, 51–54 passim, 66 n., 237–38

Case, Thomas, 26

Character: allegorical, 89–90; biblical wayside, 94, 100–01; character-as-example, 89–105 passim; insincere wayfarer, 94, 97–100; sincere wayfarer, 94 f.; wayside memorial, 94, 101–05. See also Evangelist, Honest, Ignorance, Interpreter, Mercy, Talkative, Worldly Wiseman

Chesterton, G. K., 97

Coleridge, S. T., 6 f., 81–84 passim, 97–98, 113

Collection, 36

Divine Comedy, The, 105, 107

Edification, 12, 20, 71

Evangelist, 8, 16–20 passim, 64–68 passim, 91, 106, 113, 234

Example, 68–79; Baxter's views on, 70; definition of, 68; exemplary history, 80–83; Perkins' views on, 71; rationale of, 80; Sibbes' views on, 70. See also Allegory, Character, Parabolic drama

Faerie Queene, The, 107

Faith, 62–67

Forster, E. M., 45

Francis de Sales, St., 178

Freeman, Rosemary, 81

Gansfort, Johan Wessel, 121

Golder, Harold, 162

Good, H. G., 60

Goodwin, Thomas, 53–54, 59, 180–81, 184

Gouge, Thomas, 45, 205

Greene, Herbert, 7

Greenham, Richard, 42–43, 127

Hall, Joseph, 120–33 passim, 167–68; aural features of his meditation, 241; line of, 130–33, 136, 185

Heavenly meditation, 133–50; episode of Beulah Land as illustration of, 162–64; life as pilgrimage and, 133–35; qualification of Puritan view of Scripture as *logos* within the tradition of, 139–50, 156–58; world as means and, 136. See also Baxter, Imagination, Sibbes

Heavenly-mindedness. See Heavenly meditation

Hermeneutics, 21–60 passim; Anglican, 28–32; Catholic, 23, 32 f., 66; Christian's training in, 61–67; definition of, 25; Puritan, see Puritan hermeneutics; Quaker, 44. See also Collection, Holy Spirit, Interpreter, *Logos*, *Mythos*, Notation, Resolution, Scripture

Hildersham, Arthur, 47–48

Holy Spirit, role in interpretation, 62–67 passim, 78–79

Honest, 90

Hooker, Thomas, 126, 246

House Beautiful, 175, 188, 195 ff., 216–20

Ignorance, 77, 113

Imagery: Anglican use of contrasted with Puritan, 151–53; Bunyan's use of, 152–56, 165–71

Imagination, 56–58, 250; Catholic use of in meditation, 124–125, 127; Puritan distrust of, 8–9, 125–28; Puritan reclamation of within the tradition of heavenly meditation, 143–50; relevance to exegesis, 40–41

Interpreter, 61–79 passim, 188–95 passim
Jewel, John, 31–32, 40
Joseph, Sister Miriam, 122–23
Joyce, James, 160
Keach, Benjamin, 22

Leavis, F. R., vii
Lewis, C. S., 89
Literalism, 8, 11, 27, 32, 37–38, 40, 152–53; literal-didactic mode in *The Pilgrim's Progress*, 5 ff., 19–20. See also *Logos*, Scripture
Logos, 9 ff., 15, 19–20, 120, 124, 126, 133, 250; example and, 68; heavenly meditation and qualification of Puritan view of Scripture as, 139–50, 156–57; Scripture as, 23–24, 28, 33 ff., 43, 45, 49–55
Luis de Granada, 124–25
Luis de la Puente, 128–29
Lukin, Henry, 49, 69–70, 83 n., 97, 149–50
Lynch, William F., 33 n.

McCall, John P., 32
Martz, Louis, 115, 121, 135–36, 139–40, 145
Mauburnus, Joannes, 121–22, 129
Meditation: biblical prototypes for, 118; on experience, *see* Meditation on experience; on heaven, *see* Heavenly meditation; on hell, 159–60; Ignatian, 121, 128 ff., 147; imagination, role of in, *see* Imagination; as inner oratory, 24, 240–49; on life of Christ, 139–42; memory, role of in, 139, 153–55, 239–40; on occasions of immediate experience, *see* Occasional meditation; Puritan rationale for, 118–20; on sin, 220, 245–46; understanding, role of in, 128–30. *See also* Baxter, Hall, Sibbes

Meditation on experience, 24, 196–231; definition of, 197; discernment of providences, 209–16; examples of in *The Pilgrim's Progress*, 216–31; glossing of Scripture, 201–05; search for assurance, 197–99; search for vocation, 199–201; sharing of experience, 223–24; songs in *The Pilgrim's Progress* as, 222–23
Memory, role of in meditation. *See* Meditation
Mercy, 95–97, 230–31
Metaphor, 8–11 passim, 12 f., 154; Puritan interpretation of, 35–36, 51, 149, 156 f., 162; Bunyan's imaginative use of scriptural, 160–65
Miller, Perry, 8–9, 39, 151–53, 167–68
Mitchell, W. Fraser, 40 n.
Moore, Elizabeth, 233 n.
Mystery: event as, 66, 141; doctrine as, 66, 111, 129
Mythos, 9 ff., 15, 17, 20; Scripture as, 28, 36–37, 40, 43, 147, 153; mythic mode in *The Pilgrim's Progress*, 5 ff., 16–17, 20–22, 151–74 passim

Narrator. *See* Bunyan
Notation, 36

Occasional meditation, 175–95; and aural orientation of Puritanism, 184; definition of, 175; examples of in *The Pilgrim's Progress*, 175–76, 188–94; Puritan motivations for practicing, 179–87; sources of the tradition of, 177–78
Owen, John, 37–39, 42, 44, 46, 65–66, 92–93, 108–10 passim, 127–28, 180–82, 184, 211–13

Parabolic drama, 83–89
Patrick, J. G., 166–67
Pemble, William, 63–64
Perception, Puritan understanding of, 56–58
Perkins, William, 35 f., 49, 63, 71, 81, 108, 153–54, 238 n.
Preston, John, 65
Promise, 68, 73–79, 201–02
Proportion of faith, 44. See also Analogy of Faith
Puritan hermeneutics: issue of authority in, 41–45; issue of determinateness in, 37–39; issue of guidance in, 44–49; role of faith in, 62–67; union of exegesis and homiletics in, 23–27 passim; use of dialectic in, 39. See also Hermeneutics
Puritanism: allegorical temper of, 151–53, 167; emphasis upon hearing in, 236–38; general rationale for meditation in, 118–20. See also Imagination, Literalism, Logos, Metaphor, Puritan hermeneutics, Rationalism, Scholasticism

Ramus, Petrus, 39
Rationalism, 18, 39, 58 f., 179, 250
Realism, viii, 17, 23 f., 112, 165–74, 168–69
Resolution, 36–37
Revelation: Calvin's doctrine of, 34 ff., 55–56; Puritan conception of, 55–60. See also Hermeneutics, Holy Spirit, Logos, Mythos, Scripture
Robinson Crusoe, 24
Rogers, Nehemiah, 49–50
Rogers, Richard, 26, 81–82, 118 n., 119
Romance, 21, 162
Rupp, Gordon, 6 f.

Scholasticism, Puritan, 47
Scripture: exemplary history in, 80–83; genres of, 48–49, 167; as logos, see Logos; metaphors of, 35–36, 51, 149, 156 f., 160–65; as mythos, see Mythos; one sense of, 27–30 passim, 35, 37–40 passim. See also Evangelist, Example, Hermeneutics, Literalism, Revelation
Sharrock, Roger, 4 n., 6–7, 12–13, 81, 98 n., 140, 190, 222, 234–35
Sibbes, Richard, 23, 46, 56, 58, 118 n.; *Bowels Opened*, 142; *The Bruised Reed*, 142; *The Christian Work*, 70, 93–94; contemporary reputation, 142; *Divine Meditations*, 94, 136; *A Glance of Heaven*, 134, 138; *Light from Heaven*, 134, 140–41; meditation on experience, 203–04, 223, 227, 230 n.; significance for heavenly meditation, 142–46; *The Soules Conflict*, 56, 58, 118 n., 142–46, 156
Sinai, 16–20, 239
Smith, Samuel, 50 ff.
Song of Songs, 38–39 n., 163
Spurstow, William, 177, 185–86
Swift, Jonathan, 89–90 n.

Talkative, 77
Talon, Henri, 154–55, 200
Tavard, George, 110 n.
Taylor, Jeremy, 28
Taylor, Thomas, 179, 194
Teate, Faithful, 38–39 n.
Teresa, St., 125
Threatening. See Promise
Tindall, William York, 22
Typology, 30, 37–38, 134

Understanding, use of in meditation. See Meditation
Ussher, James, 119, 245–46 n.

Valley of the shadow of death, 78, 159–62, 164, 169–70, 220–23

Wallace, Ronald S., 34
Ward, Samuel, 184
Warren, Austin, 10
Wellek, René, 10
Whiggery, 24
Whitaker, William, 28–30, 31, 40
Willard, Samuel, 111
Wilson, Thomas, 123–24
Worldly Wiseman, 16, 18, 64

10-3-69
BG

OHIO UNIVERSITY LIBRARY

Please return this book as soon as you have finished with it. In order to avoid a fine it must be returned by the latest date stamped below.

APR 0 3 2000

MAR 1 5 2000

CF

Principles and Applications of
HOMOGENEOUS CATALYSIS